MEDIEVAL ROMANCE

English Literature

Editor

JOHN LAWLOR

Professor of English Language and Literature
in the University of Keele

To Richard, my knight.

On his birthday. June 10th. 1974

With love from his "Ladye Fayre".

x x x

MEDIEVAL ROMANCE

THEMES AND APPROACHES

John Stevens

Fellow of Magdalene College, Cambridge
and University Lecturer in English

HUTCHINSON UNIVERSITY LIBRARY

LONDON

HUTCHINSON & CO (*Publishers*) LTD
3 Fitzroy Square, London W1

London Melbourne Sydney Auckland
Wellington Johannesburg Cape Town
and agencies throughout the world

First published 1973

*This book has been set in Bembo type, printed in Great Britain
on smooth wove paper by Anchor Press, and
bound by Wm. Brendon, both of Tiptree, Essex*

ISBN 0 09 114000 5 (cased)
0 09 114001 3 (paper)

FOR ARTHUR

CONTENTS

PREFACE

Medieval romance, like other branches of medieval writing, has too often been regarded as the property of specialists. The barrier of unfamiliar language has led some to the illogical conclusion that there must be something equally unfamiliar and estranging about the poems (and prose tales) themselves. It still needs to be said, and repeated, that the concerns of medieval romance are the concerns of all narrative fiction: man loving; man fighting; man with his lover, his leader or his friends; man alone; man facing mystery, or death; man seeking for God. Nor is there anything special about the way the romance writer conducts his narrative and achieves his effects. A generation or two ago it might have been necessary to apologize for the absence of a sustained and continuous naturalism, and to defend the romances against the accusation of being mere fairy-tales by claiming for them some of the qualities admired in the nineteenth-century novel. In the meantime the wide popularity of works as different from one another as Kafka's novels, Beckett's plays and Tolkien's epic-fantasy, *The Lord of the Rings*, has made such a defence supererogatory. Even those works formerly most admired for holding the mirror up to life, 'life as it really is', are now praised also for symbolic complexity and formal patterning.

I do not attempt, needless to say, a full coverage of the subject nor refer to all the surviving romances, even in English. Least of all do I pretend to note or assess the huge corpus of secondary material which scholars have amassed over the years. What I have tried to do is to provide an approach which will enable others to take their own bearings and find their own sense of direction. This book, therefore, is about the traditions of romance and the concerns of romancers and not primarily about specific romances. It refers principally to romances in medieval English and medieval French and only occasionally to German, Provençal, Latin or other literatures. The choice of French is not arbitrary. By the thirteenth century, at latest, French was the language of an international court-culture. As an Italian writer described it, *'La parleur française est plus delitable et plus commune a toutes gens'*. What is more, it was the principal literary language of England in the two centuries before Chaucer. To try to understand the surviving English poems without taking the French into consideration is rather like trying to put a jigsaw puzzle together with half the pieces missing.

However, I ought to make it clear that I do not attempt to assemble the cultural jigsaw, an extremely complex and wide-ranging task. I do not even, for present purposes, find it necessary to distinguish between Anglo–French and Continental French romances, different as they are. My account is as resolutely ungeographical as it is unchronological. To have complicated an introductory book, such as this is, with historical speculations about the development of romance would have clouded its main purpose, which is to give a general view rather than a conducted tour of each and every locality. The needful thing in the beginning is, I believe, to see what the romances have in common, before being confronted with all their inexhaustible variety. Nevertheless, the chronological connections between romances are interesting and sometimes revealing. For that reason a brief Historical Note is included (pp. 238–41) so that readers can easily discover when the principal romances were composed.

My debt to the specialists will be evident enough, and in particular to the editors of texts; I hope I have always acknowledged their help. It remains to thank the friends, colleagues and pupils who have helped me, sometimes without knowing it in conversation and argument, sometimes at the sacrifice of their own time and interests. Amongst them I should like to mention particularly Ian Ousby, John Winter, Gary Waller and Jane Tipping. Robert Smith earned my gratitude by allowing himself to be used to represent the ideal novice for whom the book is principally intended; Karl Reichl kindly read the greater part of the typescript when he could have been taking a well-earned holiday. In particular, I must express my gratitude to John Lawlor, the general editor of the series, who offered me not only encouragement but numerous comments, suggestions and corrections; and to Richard

Axton, who read the whole book in draft and whose perceptive criticisms caused me to re-write two substantial sections. Mrs Vanessa Solway typed the greater part of it with an elegance that deserved to be perpetuated.

In the final stages I have been specially helped by two friends; Derek Brewer, generously emerging from sabbatical retreat, detected errors and suggested improvements, in particular to the glosses; Arthur Sale, in the midst of a busy teaching term, found time to read the proofs and to leave the imprint of his vigilance on almost every page. I should also like to thank Ann Douglas of Hutchinson University Library for her exemplary patience and for a kindliness which expressed itself in the most practical ways.

Magdalene College   JOHN STEVENS
Cambridge

AUTHOR'S NOTE

Books, editions and articles are referred to in the notes by author's name, with short title if necessary. Full bibliographical details will be found in the Booklist (pp. 242–6).

French texts are translated in full; the translations are my own unless otherwise stated. My translations are fairly literal since their principal aim is to enable the reader to follow the original text; but when, for example, the French text has the kaleidoscopic changes of tense which are characteristic of the style, I have sometimes regularized them. The symbols ⟨ ⟩ enclosing word or phrase indicate that I have made an alteration in the translation which I am quoting.

English words are glossed, only occasionally translated in full. Word by word glossing can never be more than a rough-and-ready procedure. I have aimed to give the reader sufficient help to avoid a wild misreading of any passage; the crudity of some of the 'equivalences' will be readily apparent.

All medieval English and French texts (which form the great bulk of the material used) have been quoted in the original, the orthography alone being modernized as in standard editions of Chaucer. The intention is not to give an air of scholarship, but to provide those who are new to the subject with some sense of the elegance and refinement of, say, Chrétien de Troyes's verse, some sense of the rude vigour of *Gamelyn* and *Horn*. In this matter a large ignorance is even more dangerous than a 'little learning'.

From the Booklist it will be clear which editions of the texts I have used. For permission to quote from translations, and from other copyright material, I am grateful to the following: Columbia University Press: J. J. Parry's trans. of *The Art of Courtly Love* by Andreas; J. M. Dent & Sons Ltd: W. W. Comfort's trans. of *Cligés, Lancelot* and *Yvain* by Chrétien de Troyes and Lucy A. Paton's trans. of *Morte Arthure*; J. M. Dent & Sons Ltd and the Trustees of the Joseph Conrad Estate: *Lord Jim* and *The Shadow-Line* by Joseph Conrad; Faber and Faber Ltd: 'The Man with the Blue Guitar' by Wallace Stevens; Oxford University Press: Frank Davison's trans. of *The Lost Domain* by Alain-Fournier; Oxford University Press and the Society of Jesus: 'As kingfishers catch fire' and 'The Wreck of the Deutschland' by Gerard Manley Hopkins; Oxford University Press (New York): C. W. Kennedy's trans. of *The Battle of Maldon*; Penguin Books Ltd: Michael Alexander's trans. of *The Dream of the Rood*, A. S. Fedrick's trans. of *Tristran* by Beroul, A. T. Hatto's trans. of *Tristan and Isolt* by Gottfried von Strassburg, P. Matarasso's trans. of *Aucassin and Nicolette*, Lewis Thorpe's trans. *History of the Kings of Britain* by Geoffrey of Monmouth; Random House Inc.: R. S. and L. H. Loomis's trans. of *Perceval* by Chrétien de Troyes; Search Press Ltd: M. B. Salu's trans. of the *Ancrene Riwle*; M. B. Yeats and the Macmillan Companies of London and Canada: 'Sailing to Byzantium' by W. B. Yeats.

I

INTRODUCTION:

THE PERMANENCE OF ROMANCE

'Why study romance?', one may properly ask. One answer is paramount. The romance stands to medieval literature as the novel stands to the literature of the nineteenth and twentieth centuries. It is the major secular genre from the time of Chrétien de Troyes (c. 1180) to Chaucer (d. 1400) and beyond. Many of the major achievements of Elizabethan literature either are in the widest sense romances (Spenser's *Faerie Queene*, Sir Philip Sidney's *Arcadia*) or are deeply indebted to romance tradition (Elizabethan courtly comedy, such as *A Midsummer Night's Dream*). What is more, hardly had the fairy-monster 'romance' been knocked on the head by the champions of neo-classical virtues—unity of action, *vraisemblance* and so forth—than it obstinately began to revive. In the eighteenth century Hurd's *Essays on Chivalry and Romance*, Bishop Percy's *Reliques of English Poesy*, Warton's *History of English Literature*, to name no others, restated the claims of 'the Gothick'. The results were far-reaching—for Coleridge in 'Christabel', for Keats in 'The Eve of St Agnes', for Scott in a host of novels . . . and for Miss Catherine Morland in Jane Austen's *Northanger Abbey*. There Henry Tilney, picturing to that credulous young lady the midnight adventures she may expect, parodies the fashionable Gothic novel of the period:

. . . you must be aware that when a young lady is . . . introduced into a dwelling of this kind, she is always lodged apart from the rest of the family. While they snugly repair to their own end of the house, she is formally conducted by Dorothy, the ancient housekeeper, up a different staircase, and along many gloomy passages, into an apartment never used since some cousin of kin died in it about twenty years before. . . . she gives you reason to suppose that the part of the Abbey you inhabit is undoubtedly haunted, and informs you that you will not have a single domestic within call. . . . on the second, or at furthest the *third* night . . . you will probably have a violent storm . . . there is a secret subterraneous communication between your apartment and the chapel of St Anthony, scarcely two miles off. Could you shrink from so simple an adventure? No, no; you will proceed into this small vaulted room, and through this into several others, without perceiving anything very remarkable in either. In one, perhaps, there may be a dagger, in another a few drops of blood, and in a third the remains of some instrument of torture; but there being nothing in all this out of the common way . . . you will return towards your own apartment.

Quite evidently, 'romance', in the broadest sense of the word, can never die, even if it fades from time to time, for it is a special experience (or, rather, a set of experiences) of fundamental and continuing importance to Western man. In terms of literature, romance is a genre the conventions of which express these special experiences. We must, in fact, distinguish these two uses of the word—to describe experiences and to denote a genre.

(1) The romantic *experiences*, love, honour, terror, adoration. In *Northanger Abbey* the experience parodied is the *frisson* of the unexpected, of the hidden terror. In the advertisement tag, 'I found romance in a box of dates', the experience recommended is the particular thrill of the exotic and of the 'perfumed East'.

(2) The romantic *genres* (this must also be a plural)—various types of medieval romance; the Italianate Elizabethan romance; the heroic play of the Restoration period; the Gothic novel; the horror film; science fiction. One could add a large number of other supremely interesting works of prose fiction for which the title 'novel' seems only partly appropriate: such works as Hawthorne's *The Marble Faun*, Conrad's *Youth*, *The Shadow-Line* and other tales; Melville's *Moby Dick*; Alain-Fournier's *Le Grand Meaulnes*; and Henry James's *The American*.

Romance as a genre, a series of related genres, is characterized by conventions, motifs, archetypes, which have been created in order to express the experiences in their essential nature. Amongst these motifs are, for instance: the mysterious challenge or call; the first sight of the beloved; the lonely journey through a hostile land; the fight with the enemy, often a monstrous creature. It is the experience which *creates* these conventions, because it cannot be described so well in any other way. The same experience *re*-creates the same conventions.

It is merely naïve, therefore, to speak of romance as an 'artificial' mode in the normal modern derogatory sense of the word—or, even worse, as a 'conventional genre', as if this simply disposed of it. Conventions are not arbitrary; they are the creations of human minds seeking forms of expression. The same acts and facts, if treated in a different way in a different spirit, become something different. The romantic experience of Tristan and Isolde as it might have appeared in an interchange of correspondence between the solicitors acting for the injured party, King Mark, and the defendant, has been amusingly reconstructed for us by C. S. Lewis and Owen Barfield.[1] In Chaucer's *Canterbury Tales* the rivalry between two young men for the love of a lady appears quite differently in the Miller's and in the Knight's account of it. At the risk of labouring the obvious I shall try to show in this chapter not merely that the concerns of medieval romance are fundamental and permanent but also that these concerns create and re-create the conventions—of plot, image and character—essential to their expression.

Amongst the works of prose fiction which are inadequately described as novels I included Henry James's *The American* (1877). This would be justified if only because James himself later made it the occasion for a fascinating discussion of the nature of romance as distinct from novel. In his preface to the New York edition he wrote:

The only *general* attribute of projected romance that I can see, the only one that fits all its cases, is the fact of the kind of experience with which it deals— experience liberated, so to speak; experience disengaged, disembroiled, disencumbered, exempt from the conditions that we normally know to attach to it and, if we wish so to put the matter, drag upon it, and operating in a medium which relieves it, in a particular interest, of the inconvenience of a *related*, a measurable state, a state subject to all our vulgar communities.

James wrote against the background of the nineteenth-century novel and his definition makes sense first as a means of distinguishing the romantic novel from the thorough-going realistic novel, the novel 'embroiled' and 'encumbered' with this preposterous, pragmatical pig of a world. The notion of 'experience liberated . . . exempt from the conditions that we normally know to attach to it' is a perceptive one. Medieval romance deals indeed with 'experience liberated' in this way. However, in the Middle Ages there are many kinds of fiction which meet this demand. In fact, one is tempted to say that there are none which do not. The *fabliau*, for instance, often regarded as a 'slice of life', realistic fiction in the making, is no closer to what we like to call 'real life'—even if it does deal with the appetites of sex and greed—than, say, a West End farce.

The anonymous *La Borgoise d'Orleans* is typical *fabliau* and may stand for all:[2]

A citizen's wife is having an affair with a *clerc* (a student). The husband gets wind of it and sets a trap for them: he pretends to go away on business but comes back to meet his wife at the rendezvous she has fixed with her lover. It is dark at the orchard-gate and she greets him warmly; but as they walk across the orchard to the house she sees through the disguise—and his trick. Cunningly, she keeps up the pretence that she is meeting her lover and tells her husband that she must shut him upstairs until the household has gone to bed. This she does, locking him up securely. Then she goes back to the orchard-gate, meets her real lover and takes him to her boudoir. After dinner she tells her servants that there's a man locked upstairs who's been a nuisance to her. It will be doing her—and their absent master—a good turn if they go and beat him. This they do with zest; they end up by throwing him on the dung-hill. Hours later, when the student and the wife have had their night of fun, the husband crawls back home, badly bruised and pretends that he has been waylaid on the road. He is now convinced that his wife is a model of fidelity and chastity.

This is the kind of tale from which Chaucer's infinitely superior but even more implausible *Miller's Tale* derives. It is a non-realistic fiction, like romance, but with a commercial—or spiritually commercial— basis. Life is to the go-getter, the grafter, the quick-witted, cunning and unscrupulous. The *fabliau* is full of the hard common objects, full of *things* and of four-letter words. But this does not make it to any significant degree 'real'. On the simplest level, for example—how can we believe that the household servants would not recognize their own master when beating him up? There is, apparently, no trace of irony here. The *fabliaux* are fantasies of one-upmanship. Here is 'experience liberated' indeed—liberated by laughter. There are no moral realities, no good and bad characters, only the Have-Nots (repressed wives, penurious students) and the Haves (prosperous clerics, complacent business-men and jealous, middle-aged husbands).

It is scarcely necessary to demonstrate how James's definition, which fits *fabliau* as well as romance, is equally applicable to other forms. In the saint's life the stereotyped holiness is 'liberated' from everything which is not heroic, from all the grinding and degrading pettinesses of the common lot; and in the medieval chronicle history is 'liberated' from economic realities and social change. Rather let us return to *The American* and see what the book itself can tell us.

Henry James had written a novel in which a rich American, Christopher Newman, having 'made his pile' early in life, comes to Europe, feeling 'as simple as a little child':

A vague sense that more answers were possible than his philosophy had hitherto dreamt of had already taken possession of him, and it seemed softly and agreeably to deepen as he lounged in this brilliant corner of Paris with his friend. . . . It struck him that if he had never done anything very ugly, he had never, on the other hand, done anything particularly beautiful.

The principal 'beautiful thing' which he does is to fall in love with a young widow, the daughter of the proud and ancient family of Bellegarde. This haughty family first accept Newman as Claire's suitor with a cool, negative acceptance and then, at the point of marriage, draw back from so gross and plebeian an alliance. What is more, they draw their daughter back. Newman gets possession of a family secret of the Bellegardes and plans to publish it abroad, to their scandal. But when he has them in his power, he sacrifices his revenge in disgust, obeying in so doing 'one of the large and easy impulses *generally* characteristic of his type'. It is not an act of forgiveness but rather of magnanimity.

In the Preface to the novel, written forty years later, Henry James felt that his 'conception unfurled . . . the emblazoned flag of romance'. The experience of Christopher Newman was 'liberated . . . exempt from the conditions that we normally know to attach to it' in the sense that:

They would positively have jumped . . . the Bellegardes, at my rich and easy American, and not have 'minded' in the least any drawback. . . . Such accommodation of the theory of a noble indifference to the practice of a deep avidity is the real note of policy in forlorn aristocracies.

The book, he argues, does not depict a sequence of events that would have occurred in 'real' life. James's definition, it will be noted, is a definition by *mode* ('the disconnected and uncontrolled experience') and not by *theme* (the experience is not in itself defined). Of the ends which such a 'disconnection' may serve he says no more than is implied in the phrase 'in a particular interest', i.e. with a particular purpose in mind. But the curious and interesting thing is that his novel contains many of the recurrent motifs of the romantic experience in its essential idealism. For in romance the nature of the 'experience liberated' is idealistic.

The idealisms of romance are various and I shall describe in subsequent chapters the idealisms favoured by the Middle Ages. For the moment it is enough to note that Henry James is presenting an idealized attitude on Newman's part towards Claire Bellegarde and to suggest that his presentation is characterized by certain traditional features or 'recurrent motifs'. Among these motifs is, first, *the sense of a vocation.* 'I want extremely to marry . . . I want to do the thing in handsome style. I not only want to make no mistakes, but I want to be a great hit. I want to take my pick. My wife must be a magnificent woman.' The subtleties of the dialogue soften the blatancies of this with social irony.* But he means it—and we are to accept it.

The second motif is *the presentation of the heroine* (we may call her this for short) as distant, mysterious, desirable, inaccessible and beautiful. There is more than a touch of Jaufré Rudel's *amor de lonh* (love from afar) in Newman's aspiration to 'the loveliest woman in the world, the promised perfection'.[3] Claire, Madame de Cintré, is *la princesse lointaine.*

The men only looked at Madame de Cintré. This was inevitable; for whether one called her beautiful or not, she entirely occupied and filled one's vision, just as an agreeable sound fills one's ear. Newman had but twenty distinct words with her, but he carried away an impression to which solemn promises could not have given a higher value. . . . It was the mystery—it was what she was off the stage, as it were—that interested Newman. He could not have told you what warrant he had for talking about mysteries; if it had been his habit to express himself in poetic figures he might have said that in observing Madame de Cintré he seemed to see the vague circle that sometimes accompanies the partly-filled disc of the moon . . . (i.113)

The third motif is *the essential isolation of the hero and his experience.* The natural exclusiveness of romantic love is given fuller force in that Newman is an American in a strange city; he is isolated from complications. Furthermore, as James himself comments, 'He was to be the lighted figure, the others—even [Claire]—were to be obscured. . . . Here then is the romantic *tout caché*—the fine flowers of Newman's

---

* Mrs Tristram counters him, 'You remind me of the heroes of the French romantic poets, Rolla and Fortunio and all those other insatiable gentlemen for whom nothing in this world was handsome enough. But I see you are in earnest, and I should like to help you.' (i.40)

experience blooming in a medium "cut off" and shut up to itself.'*
One might add that this isolation is modified by the presence of two
traditional characters of love-romance—the confidant (Claire's
brother, Valentin) and the 'go-between' (Mrs Tristram).

We note next *the sense of baffled involvement in a mystery*—'the very
effect most to be invoked, that of a generous nature engaged with
forces, with difficulties and dangers, that it but half understands'. The
ancient mansion of the Bellegardes is, indeed, for all the world like
mysterious fortress, the castle which the knight assaults to rescue the
maiden. 'That dark old house over there looks as if wicked things had
been done in it'—more archetypal perhaps than even James suspected.

The motifs I have enumerated serve, in *The American* and elsewhere,
'a particular interest' and, indeed, to a large extent define it. What are
the 'particular interests' of romance, the 'interests' that will distinguish
it from other non-realistic fictions—the *fabliau*, the fairy-tale, the
animal fable, the parable, the saint's life? The 'particular interests',
as I have already hinted, are idealistic—but idealistic in special ways.
Shelley's telling phrase 'beautiful idealisms of moral excellence',
though coined in quite another context, goes a long way to suggest
the combination of aesthetic and spiritual qualities realized in the
greatest romances, of the Middle Ages and of later times.

The idealisms of medieval romance are not archaic oddities fished
out of musty cupboards but fundamental human concerns. The idealized sexual relationship which we call romantic love ('Thou art so
truth, that thoughts of thee suffice/To make dreams truth and fables
histories') is as much the subject of Chaucer's greatest complete poem,
Troilus and Criseyde, as it is of James's *The American*. The idealized
integrity which we call honour ('To thine own self be true;/Thou
canst not then be false to any man') is as deeply the subject of *Sir
Gawain and the Green Knight* as it is of Conrad's *Lord Jim*.†

So-called medieval motifs recur, even if unconsciously, in later
'romance' literature. I have tried to show how in *The American* an
idealization of love created such motifs—the isolated hero, the distant

---

* The man-centredness of the whole experience is a recurrent feature in love-
literature from Chrétien's *Lancelot* to Constant's *Adolphe*. We are centred in
Newman: 'he . . . supremely matters; all the rest matters only as he feels it,
treats it, meets it'.

† I do not wish to imply that all these works merely assert idealisms. The problem
whether a medieval romancer can question his inherited idealisms and still write
romance will have to be discussed later.

lady, the sombre fortress. They are not, in fact, medieval; they are timeless and permanent. The same thing is true of the idealism of the self, in romances of integrity and honour, and of the motifs it creates. Of the many novels preoccupied with this theme, such as Hemingway's *The Old Man and the Sea*, Conrad's *The Shadow-Line*, Patrick White's *Voss*, let us take *The Shadow-Line*.

The unnamed teller of the story is also the central actor in it. He is a young officer who decides, in an Eastern port, to give up his berth ('One day I was perfectly right and the next everything was gone— glamour, flavour, interest, contentment—everything'). After an interlude in a club ashore he is quite unexpectedly singled out for a command. It is an unusual command that others are afraid to take; but he is elated. He joins his ship. The former captain had gone mad and sick and died on board, to be buried at sea. In the pestilential river of the port of Bangkok they lie becalmed waiting for a wind. The first mate, Mr Burns, who had battled desperately for control of the ship with the previous captain, is one of the first to succumb to tropical fever. In his hysteria he prophesies that, even though they are out of the river into the gulf, they will never get past 'the late captain, the old man buried in latitude 8° 20′ . . . ambushed at the entrance of the gulf', on the shadow-line.

The store of quinine on which they were relying to keep the tropical fever at bay turns out to be a store of empty bottles. No one on the ship is free from fever except the young captain (the nameless narrator, the 'I' of the story) and the steward Ransome ('With his serious, clear, grey eyes, his serene temperament, he was a priceless man altogether'). After days of drifting and despair, the crisis comes one night:

I moved forward, too, outside the circle of light, into the darkness that stood in front of me like a wall. In one stride I had penetrated it. Such must have been the darkness before creation. It had closed behind me. I knew I was invisible to the man at the helm. Neither could I see anything. He was alone, I was alone, every man was alone where he stood. And every form was gone, too, spar, sail, fittings, rails; everything was blotted out in the dreadful smoothness of that absolute night. . . . Perfect silence, joined to perfect immobility, proclaimed the yet unbroken spell of our helplessness, poised on the edge of some violent issue, lurking in the dark. (pp. 112ff.)

The captain falls over 'something big and alive' crawling on the deck ('It was an added and fantastic horror which I could not resist. The hair of my head stirred even as I picked myself up, awfully scared . . .

completely, boundlessly, and as it were innocently scared—like a little child.') The Thing attempts to stand up—it is the mad, sick first mate, Mr Burns.

'Skulking's no good, sir,' he attacked me directly. 'You can't slink past the old murderous ruffian. It isn't the way. You must go for him boldly, as I did. Boldness is what you want.' (p. 116)

Meanwhile the breeze which had sprung up abated.

The spell of the deadly stillness had caught us up again. There seemed to be no escape.
    'Hallo!' exclaimed Mr Burns in a startled voice. 'Calm again!'
    I addressed him as though he had been sane.
    'This is the sort of thing we've been having for seventeen days, Mr Burns,' I said with intense bitterness.
    'A puff, then a calm, and in a moment, you'll see, she'll be swinging on her heel with her head away from her course to the devil somewhere.' He caught at the word. 'The old dodging Devil,' he screamed piercingly, and burst into such a loud laugh as I had never heard before. It was a provoking, mocking peal, with a hair-raising, screeching over-note of defiance. I stepped back utterly confounded. (p. 119)

The fever-stricken ship's company stagger up on deck, appalled. And Burns cuts his 'derisive screeching' short to exhort them to laugh:

'Laugh—I tell you. Now then—all together. One, two, three—laugh!'
A moment of silence ensued, of silence so profound that you could have heard a pin drop on the deck. (p. 120)

Mr Burns faints, normality is restored, the crisis is over and the 'shadow-line' is crossed.
    Conrad in the Author's Note to the book writes that, 'primarily the aim of this piece of writing was the presentation of certain facts which certainly were associated with the change from youth, carefree and fervent, to the more self-conscious and more poignant period of maturer life'. And the opening of the tale contains a beautiful evocation of romantic experience in traditional imagery. But, person-ally, I can only think that to concentrate on this blurs the main issue of the tale. The significance of the 'obscure experience' which Conrad relates to the 'supreme trial of [a] whole generation' in the First World War was *associated*, certainly, for him with the change from youth to maturity. But the experience itself seems to go deeper into the nature of mature man than he implies.
    The qualities idealized are the expected Conradian ones of courage,

endurance, selflessness; the experience which embodies them is one in which not just physical danger but evil must be faced—the evil of despair, perhaps, the living death of the personality? Instead of the usual single hero, there are in effect three, the young captain (expecting 'that special intensity of existence which is the quintessence of youthful aspiration' but finding himself 'bound hand and foot' under an 'evil spell' with an 'awful, death-haunted command'); Ransome (the steward with the weak heart, but imperturbable, constant, utterly reliable, despite his 'mortal fear of starting into sudden anger our common enemy it was his hard fate to carry consciously within his faithful breast'); and, strangely enough, Mr Burns himself (whose 'boldness' drags him up on deck to utter peals of defiant laughter against the 'old dodging Devil' lying at the entrance to the gulf). But, despite the three persons, the heroism is a single experience. The heroism of a high calling is embodied in the young captain ('A ship! My Ship! She was mine, more absolutely mine for possession and care than anything else in the world'); the ship is his 'spell-bound enchanted princess' whom he is bound to serve. But this heroism is supplemented, certainly not contrasted, with the heroism of Ransome—heroism of the conscious will, calculated, deliberate and open-eyed; and also with the more purely instinctive survival-heroism, if that is the word, of Mr Burns, whose heroic defiance of death is, incidentally, the turning-point in his own illness. In a sense one could say that the ship's company is Mankind ('a wildly rushing ship full of dying men'), a ship inert, drifting, tossed hither and thither on the ocean, trying to keep its integrity and to succeed in the great adventure.

I have already mentioned, without singling out, the various basic romance-motifs in this romance of integrity, of the idealized Self: the call, youthful aspiration engaged by a sudden vocation of a challenging kind; the quest, culminating in the great *adventure* (here, the crossing of the dead man's latitude); the sense of an evil to be conquered, a death to be encountered, a plague to be dispersed. The disengagement of these experiences from 'ordinary life', the traditional domain of the novel, is achieved first, and obviously, by its being set at sea—the sea replaces the more common symbolic landscape, the forest or 'wilderness'. But there is also the powerful unreality of the narrative climax itself. There is no reason in the logic of ordinary experience why the three events should coincide—the dispersal of the dead plague-ridden calm by a lively breeze; Mr Burns's defiant exhortation to laughter, followed by the health-giving sleep that recovers him from his sickness; and the crossing of the latitude where the 'evil brute', the dead captain lies. However, it is essential to the *imaginative* logic of the tale that they do and that we should experience the climax as in some sense a 'supernatural' event.★

The American and *The Shadow-Line* both unfurl in their different ways 'the emblazoned flag of romance'. Both deal with 'experience liberated', and in both the 'particular interest' is, in Shelley's phrase, 'a beautiful idealism'. 'Ideal' is, of course, almost as difficult a word to use precisely as 'real'. There are perhaps three senses in which the word 'ideal' could be applied to a work of art. It could be argued, and has been from the Greeks onward, that all art idealizes. This, it seems, is one side of what Wallace Stevens is saying in his poem, *The Man with the Blue Guitar*: an art, a poem, which simply transcribes everyday reality is no art, no poem:

> The man bent over his guitar,
> A shearsman of sorts. The day was green.
>
> They said, 'You have a blue guitar,
> You do not play things as they are.'
>
> The man replied, 'Things as they are
> Are changed upon the blue guitar.'
>
> And they said then, 'But play, you must,
> A tune beyond us, yet ourselves,
>
> A tune upon the blue guitar
> Of things exactly as they are.'. . .
>
> I sing a hero's head, large eye
> And bearded bronze, but not a man,
>
> Although I patch him as I can
> And reach through him almost to man.
>
> If to serenade almost to man
> Is to miss, by that, things as they are,
>
> Say that it is the serenade
> Of a man that plays a blue guitar.

★ Conrad, it is interesting to note, goes to great pains in his preface to *deny* that *The Shadow-Line* is an attempt on his part 'to give the fullest scope to my imagination by taking it beyond the confines of the world of the living, suffering humanity'. But, in fact, his objection is to 'the mere supernatural, which . . . is but a manufactured article'; and his remarks constitute a subtle and persuasive defence of the inexplicable and mysterious in human experience.

It is in different senses from this that the medieval romance writer would have said that he was 'idealizing', though his senses reinforce this one. He sings 'a hero's head, large eye/And bearded bronze', first, because he treats the claim of the ideal—the ideal love, the ideal self, the ideal society—and, secondly, because he inhabits a world in which ideals, 'universals', are the ultimate, unquestioned, metaphysical realities. The first, the 'beautiful idealisms of moral excellence', will be the main subject of the following chapters. The second, metaphysical idealism, requires some consideration here.

Ian Watt, in his book, *The Rise of the Novel*, discusses interestingly the very general correspondence which he finds between the new philosophies of scientific objectivity and the 'dispassionate and scientific scrutiny of life which underlies the aesthetic of the novel':

The general temper of philosophical realism [from Descartes and Locke] has been critical, anti-traditional and innovating; its method has been the study of the particulars of experience by the individual investigator, who, ideally at least, is free from the body of past assumptions and traditional beliefs; and it has given a peculiar importance to semantics, to the problem of the nature of the correspondence between words and reality. All of these features of philosophical realism have analogies to distinctive features of the novel form, analogies which draw attention to the characteristic kind of correspondence between life and literature which has obtained in prose fiction since the novels of Defoe and Richardson.[4]

The principal analogies which Professor Watt finds are: the 'unprecedented value' set on originality; the emphasis on 'particular people in particular circumstances'; 'the problem of defining the individual person'*; circumstantiality of time and space; 'the adaptation of prose style to give an air of complete authenticity'. Things were otherwise in the Middle Ages. As Dr Raby has written:

The spiritual and moral universe, like the world of Plato's ideas, was the real and intelligible universe, of which the world of phenomena was only a shadow. Hence the world of things was worth understanding only as a step towards the understanding of the world of reality. . . . The whole visible universe in its smallest details appeared to them as fraught with hidden meaning.[5]

---

* Moll Flanders, Robinson Crusoe, Pamela Andrews, are novelistic names, individualizing their owners; Allworthy, Heartfree, Thwackum belong to the old world of type-characters—Una, Perdita, Volpone, Christian. In this connection, the names in James's 'romance' are worth pondering for their associations: Christopher Newman, Claire Bellegarde, Tristram, Valentin.

Amongst the many medieval texts that one could cite in evidence is this from Alan of Lille, the twelfth-century theologian:

> Omnis mundi creatura
> quasi liber et pictura
>   nobis est in speculum,
> nostrae vitae, nostrae sortis,
> nostri status, nostrae mortis
>   fidele signaculum.

(Every created thing serves us for a mirror, as a book or a picture does; it is a true indication of our life, our destiny, our state of being, our death.)[6]

This way of looking at the world is, in the widest sense, symbolic. It is explicit in thousands of texts, and implicit in painting, architecture, musical composition, every branch of mental activity. It is this, for instance, which makes sense of the curious and striking dictum coined by a medieval theorist of music: 'Sounds pass quickly away but numbers remain'. That is to say, the music we make and hear is transient, like all earthly things, but the music of heaven, the rhythms ('numbers') of the God-created Universe, are permanent and ever-lasting.

This attitude to the world of things has important implications for the way we read medieval romance, as I shall attempt to show later (Chapter 7). For the moment it is only necessary to see that the attitude strongly reinforces—indeed, forms the metaphysical basis for—the deep idealizing tendencies of the genre as a whole.

> I sing a hero's head, large eye
> And bearded bronze, but not a man

One might think at first that a literature full of heroes' heads rather than men was bound to be somewhat dull. But, as Charles Muscatine has pointed out in his stimulating book on Chaucer's poetry:

> the experience of the idealizing imagination is no less varied than that of realistic observation and no less true. If the themes of most of Chaucer's conventional poems seem to converge toward the single point of recognizing supernal values in human affairs, the nature of the pointing differs with each poem. We do not read Chaucer, after all, for his philosophical conclusions, but for his workings-out, his poetry.[7]

The truth of this is abundantly clear if we think of three tales such as the Prioress's (with its presentation of idealized innocence in the little 'clergeon' singing the praises of the Blessed Virgin), the Clerk's (with its presentation of idealized obedience in 'patient Griselda', who shadows forth a spiritual 'marriage' also), and the Knight's (with its idealization of the ordered courtly way of life, its aspirations and frustrations). That the same is true of romance as a whole will, I hope, become clear in the course of this book.

To sum up, the essential romance experiences are idealistic. The quality which is 'liberated' or 'disengaged' from 'all our vulgar communities' is expressive of a supreme claim (in a medieval world where realities are spiritual *and transcendental*), or of a supreme aspiration (in a modern world where man's own feelings are the final 'realities'). This is not the place to state in general terms the claims of moral idealism. In a world of deadening affluence and materialism, the statement seems unnecessary. We can deal with the question squarely, simply on literary grounds. The old saying, *Homo sum; nihil humanum a me alienum puto* (I am a human being and reckon nothing human as irrelevant to me), is as true of literary as of other experience. We do not go to literature merely to find the forcefully iterated confirmation of our own petty and limited selfhood, but to know, in some sense, the whole range, the gamut of human feelings. We wish sometimes, need sometimes, to explore the 'foule and pestilent congregation of vapours', but at others to see, as in romance, 'this brave o'erhanging firmament, this Majesticall Roofe, fretted with golden fire'.

1. *Mark vs. Tristram*, Ed. W. Hooper (1967).
2. Johnston and Owen, no. 6, p. 21.
3. *Amor de lonh;* the phrase is from the best known poem of the troubadour Jaufré Rudel of Blaye (*fl.* 1125–50?). See below, p. 37.
4. Watt, p. 12.
5. Raby, *Christian-Latin Poetry*, p. 355.
6. The Latin text is quoted by Raby, loc. cit.
7. Muscatine, p. 175.

2

MAN AND WOMAN:

IDEALISMS OF LOVE

The central and most frequently recurring idealism of the huge body of literature which we call Romance is that of love. Every schoolboy knows, or thinks he knows, that in the twelfth century the poets of the south of France 'invented' the idea of romantic love—that is, of the sexual attraction of Man and Woman seen as a powerful imaginative experience—and 'codified' it as 'courtly love'. Fortunately it is now widely realized that 'courtly love,' *amour courtois*, is not a medieval term but one invented by nineteenth-century scholars as a convenient way of referring to a type of experience which seemed to them peculiar to the Middle Ages. Nevertheless the term still causes difficulty.[1]

Firstly, it has given rise to the idea that there was only one imaginative experience of love between the sexes, uniformly acceptable and unquestioned (except by severe moralists) from the twelfth to the fifteenth century. Secondly, the innocent or unthinking have fallen too easily into believing that this 'courtly love' was different in kind from other experiences of love which they may have read about or lived through themselves. These two erroneous notions—of the simple singleness and of the archaic remoteness—of 'courtly love' have made possible the most extraordinary idea of all. 'Courtly love' is often spoken of as if it had been a system with a fixed 'code' of 'rules' which every lover (at least in fiction) was expected to obey.

As in all our dealings with the Middle Ages—or, for that matter, with any period remote from our own—we find that the most important question to ask is *not*, straightaway, 'What is this worth to me?' but 'What was this worth to *them*?' Systems of thought, patterns of feeling, codes of behaviour, styles in literature and art—in a word, conventions—are not invented for their own sake and do not maintain their life on those terms. They come into being because they are needed. They are needed, primarily, for explanation; they are needed to order experience, to impose meaning on life. The system, pattern, code, convention of courtly love was a live and necessary thing at least up to the time of Chaucer. It developed as a psychology of sexual experience viewed as an imaginative happening; as a terminology, a language, a way of talking about the experience; as a social ideal, a set of motifs round which aristocratic companies could play their endless, leisurely variations, in conversation, 'game' and act; an iconography, with a set of images, borrowed or invented—Cupid's bow, the Garden of Love, etc.; even a hagiography—Dido and Aeneas, Troilus and Criseyde, are the saints of love's religion, the Ideal People.

One work more than all others has helped to give currency to the notion of courtly love as a fixed code of rules. For this reason it must claim our attention. It is the *De Arte Honeste Amandi* of Andreas Capellanus. Andreas, who as his name implies must have been a cleric, wrote his 'art of honourable love' in the early thirteenth century. It takes its place in a tradition of works owing their literary inspiration to Ovid's *Ars Amatoria* but making his arguments new for their own purposes. The work envisages, as fiction if not as fact, a connection between Andreas and the court of Marie, Countess of Champagne, patroness of Chrétien de Troyes;[2] both she and her mother, Queen Eleanor of Aquitaine, wife of Henry II, give judgments in the book on points of love. In the first book love is defined:

Love is a certain inborn suffering derived from the sight of and excessive meditation upon the beauty of the opposite sex, which causes each one to wish above all things the embraces of the other and by common desire to carry out all of love's precepts in the other's embrace.[3]

Andreas goes on to ask and to answer such questions as: 'Between what persons may love exist?' (*Ans:* Between two persons who could properly marry but are not married)—'Where does Love get its name?' (*Ans:* From Latin *Hamus*, a hook)—'In what manner may love be acquired, and in how many ways?' (Eight specimen dialogues follow) —'What status has a cleric as a lover?' (*Ans:* It is dependent on the rank and standing of his parents). The courtly and aristocratic nature of the love which Andreas codifies is evident from his remarks about the love of peasants: 'For a farmer hard labour and the uninterrupted

solaces of plough and mattock are sufficient.' It is not expedient that
they should be instructed in love 'lest while they are devoting themselves to conduct which is not natural to them, the kindly farms which
are usually made fruitful by their efforts may through lack of cultiva-
tion prove useless to us'. One should avoid falling in love with peasant
women. If the undesirable happens, one should puff them up with
flattery, await a convenient moment and 'use a little compulsion',
since they are 'naturally inflexible'.[4]

Book II of the *De Arte* is entitled, 'How Love May Be Retained'.
It deals with how love may be kept, how a love once consummated
may be increased, in what ways love may be decreased, and so on.
It contains various decisions in love 'cases':

The Queen (Eleanor) was . . . asked what was preferable: the love of a young
man or of one advanced in years. She answered this question with wonderful
subtlety by saying, 'We distinguish between a good and a better love by the
man's knowledge and his character and his praiseworthy manners, not by his
age.' . . . The Countess of Champagne was also asked what gifts it was proper
for ladies to accept from their lovers. To the man who asked this the Countess
replied, 'A woman who loves may freely accept from her lover the following:
a handkerchief, a fillet for the hair, a wreath of gold ors ilver, a breastpin, a
mirror, a girdle, a purse, a tassel, a comb, sleeves, gloves, a ring, a compact,
a picture, a washbasin, little dishes, trays, a flag as a souvenir . . . and any little
gift which may be useful for the care of the person or pleasing to look at or
which may call the lover to her mind.'[5]

These decisions are followed by a section in which the 'rules' of
love are expounded: the Lover is to avoid avarice and falsehood;
he is to be courteous, obedient, modest and chaste (i.e. sexually
faithful to one Lady); above all he is to be discreet both about his
own and about other affairs of the heart. Jealousy is essential to love;
and marriage is no excuse for not loving.

The third and last book presents us with a complete volte-face:

Now, friend Walter, if you lend attentive ears to those things which after
careful consideration we wrote down for you because you urged us so strongly,
you can lack nothing in the art of love, since in this little book we gave you
the theory of the subject, fully and completely. . . . You should know that we
did not do this because we consider it advisable for you or any other man to
fall in love, but for fear lest you might think us stupid; we believe, though,
that any man who devotes his efforts to love loses his usefulness. Read this
little book, then, not as one seeking to take up the life of a lover, but that,
invigorated by the theory (*doctrina refectus*) and trained to excite the minds of

women to love (*mulierum edoctus ad amandum animos provocare*), you may, by refraining from so doing, win an eternal recompense and thereby deserve a greater reward from God. For God is more pleased with a man who is able to sin and does not, than with a man who has no opportunity to sin.[6]

The moral opportunism of this opening paragraph is hard to beat. It certainly does not encourage us to take the pious recantation of Book III very seriously—indeed, it does not encourage us to take anything seriously that Andreas has written. There may, indeed, be philosophical reasons which account for the dualistic nature of Andreas Capellanus's *De Amore*. The idea of a 'double truth', a truth which belongs to reason and a truth which belongs to revelation, was especially popular at this time. It embodies a traditional paradox of Christianity. But this hardly concerns us at the moment, except that it draws attention to the fact that courtly love as expounded by Andreas in Books I and II is 'a philosophy of natural virtue'; love is 'the beatitude of this life, *natural blessedness*'. 'Just as nature is common to all men, so love is common to all men without exception.' One aspect of this great paradox, the human dilemma it poses, is the subject of Chaucer's *Troilus and Criseyde*; another is cogently discussed by Cardinal Newman in the classic passage of his *Idea of a University* where he distinguishes between theological (revealed Christian) virtues and the qualities of the civilized man, the Gentleman, whose code of behaviour is, like the courtly lover's, the very apotheosis of sweet reasonableness.

At the very least this summary philosophical 'placing' of Andreas's work, together with our knowledge of its technical features—use of question and answer, love of definition and classification—confirms a view that one meaning of the *De Amore* is as 'a scholastic joke' (the phrase is Dr Brewer's). This *ars amoris* is in the tradition of semi-scholastic, semi-legalistic analysis which the Middle Ages loved and in which the thirteenth century particularly abounds. Andreas might well have called his treatise *Summa Amoris* or *Speculum Amoris*, except that these fashionable scholastic title-words promise something bigger than Andreas provides. We are still left, however, with teasing questions. For what purpose was this codification made? To whom was it addressed?

The writer speaks in his text to a certain 'Walter', about whom, if he ever existed, nothing is known. Such evidence as exists in the book points rather to a courtly than to a purely clerical milieu; but the two should not be too sharply distinguished—clerics formed part of the throng and of the administration in every important court. Despite the absence or ambiguity of external, historical documents, the references to the Countess Marie and Queen Eleanor cannot simply be disregarded. The treatise clearly belongs to an imaginative, but not wholly *imagined*, world in which theirs were names to conjure with. By far the most likely explanation, therefore, as it seems to me, is that Andreas's treatise belongs to the casuistry of love; it is an earlier document of that 'luf-talkyng' which made its mark on *The Canterbury Tales* and informs Gower's *Confessio Amantis* and which kept its place as part of the 'game of love' in social life for several centuries. Castiglione's *Il Cortegiano* and Sidney's 'Old' *Arcadia* bear witness to the lasting fascination of the pastime (as does today's journalism: ' "That first move"—should a girl make it?').

To return to our main argument, the existence of Andreas Capellanus's treatise, *De Amore*, does not prove the existence of a 'code of courtly love'. It simply establishes the existence of experiences which could be codified and that there was a fashion for codification. What, then, was the experience which is usually called 'courtly love', and how can we know about it? We know about it in one sense, because, as romantic love, it still exists—the perennial theme of European literature, life, art, and our entertainment. From *Lancelot* to *Anna Karenina*, from *Les Deux Amants* to *Les Enfants du Paradis*, it is often quite literally the same story. In its domesticated, neo-Victorian form romantic love is the substance of the women's magazines and the radio serial. In its now equally admired but undomesticated form it is part of the 'resistance movement' of youth—a spontaneous private unregulatable protest against the mediocrities of a middle-aged materialistic society. In George Orwell's *Nineteen Eighty-Four* it takes an overtly political twist.

We know about the experience of courtly love in the other, historical, sense through our reading of medieval romance. Here, heightened and stylized to a degree, are experiences we all recognize. Romantic love makes common ground between the *Tristan* of Gottfried von Strassburg, the *Lais* of Marie de France, the *Lancelot* of Chrétien, and Chaucer's *Troilus*. In each of these works a young man falls hopelessly in love with a beautiful young woman and for her sake is willing to undergo the most excruciating misery, to pay the last farthing of the costs that she exacts or expects in discipline and 'derrying do'.

The classic instance of total submission to the demands of the experience occurs in Chrétien's *Lancelot*, more properly called *The*

B

Knight of the Cart. Early in the poem Lancelot, as yet *incognito*, is in pursuit of a knight who has abducted Queen Guenevere. He comes up with a dwarf drawing a cart of the kind used in those days to carry convicted criminals. Lancelot asks him if he has seen the Queen; the dwarf, a foul low-born creature, does not reply directly.

> Einz li dist: 'Se tu viax monter
> sor la charrete que je main,
> savoir porras jusqu'a demain
> que la reïne est devenue.'   (356)

(Then he said, 'If you are willing to climb into the cart I'm leading, you'll get to learn by tomorrow what has happened to the queen.')

For a second or two Lancelot hesitates. Reason tells him not to incur the disgrace of being paraded as a criminal in a felon's cart. But instantly Love, who 'dwells in the heart' (*est el cuer anclose*), commands him to climb in, which he does. The amazing thing is that when, much later in his quest, he comes face to face with Guenevere, whom he has delivered from her captor, she receives him with a show of cold ingratitude. It is not until they have both suffered a great deal that Lancelot learns from her own lips that he had failed to meet the absolute demands of love by hesitating even for a moment to mount the cart (*quant vos demorastes deus pas*). Lancelot at once admits his sin, asks God to preserve him from another such, and Guenevere to pardon him. The heightening process could scarcely be taken further than it is in Chrétien's *Lancelot*; but it would be a very naïve and inexperienced reader who did not recognize behind the stylized hyperboles of Chrétien's poem a truth about love.[7]

One could go further and claim that in the greater medieval love-romances are present all the principal motifs which characterize the experience of romantic love in subsequent ages. I single out four. Phrased as statements they are as follows: love derives from sudden illumination; it is essentially private, and must be kept a secret from the world; it is intensified by frustration and difficulty; it lifts the lovers on to a new level of being.

The hero of Alain-Fournier's *Le Grand Meaulnes* (1913)[8] undergoes a sudden moment of illumination when in his truant wanderings over the countryside he suddenly comes across a mysterious domain:

At a corner of the wood he came upon two white posts marking the entrance to an avenue. He turned into it and had not gone far when he was brought to a halt in surprise and stood there, stirred by an emotion he could not have defined. Then he pushed on with the same dragging steps. . . . And yet he was now sustained by an extraordinary sense of well-being, an almost intoxicating serenity, by the certitude that the goal was in sight, that he had nothing but happiness to look forward to. (p. 56)

Meaulnes's meeting with Mademoiselle de Galais, to which this is the prelude, was bound up for him with the discovery of a sort of Earthly Paradise. 'Only in death', he later says, 'can I expect to recapture the beauty of that moment.' It changed his life and gave him his 'one reason for living', his 'only hope in the world'. Such a crisis of experience is symbolized in the *Tristan* stories by the drinking of the love-potion; it changes the lives of Tristan and Isolde, for whom nothing else matters thereafter. The symbolic drink is recalled by Criseyde's murmur to herself on seeing Troilus ride by beneath her window— 'Who yaf me drynke?' For Troilus's sudden illumination various favourite medieval images are used: first, he is struck by an arrow from Cupid's bow ('he hitte hym atte fulle', i.209); secondly, her appearance is printed on his heart ('Of hir his fixe and depe impressioun', i.298); and lastly, love mediated through 'the subtil stremes of hire yen' dries up 'the spirit in his herte' (i.305). The line which follows comes from the narrator:

> Blissed be love, that kan thus folk converte!

It is a telling line. Whether 'converte' has a specifically religious meaning, or whether it simply means 'turn from one course to another', the significance is clear. The sight of Criseyde's beauty suddenly alters his life. The experience of 'falling in love' is analogous to certain experiences of religious conversion: it is mysterious, unexpected, imperfectly comprehended; and yet it makes an absolute claim, it establishes a vocation, a way of life. In Kierkegaard's words, 'the absurdity of amorous inclination reaches a divine understanding with the absurdity of religious feeling'.

The second recurrent motif in tales of romantic love is that of secrecy, privateness. Andreas has a 'rule' about this: *Qui non celat, amare non potest* (The man who cannot keep a secret cannot be a lover). The lovers' obligation, the man's especially, to keep their love a secret is frequently referred to in courtly literature—'Shal no man know her name for me'. But we do not have to accept the 'code's' rational explanation—the preservation of the Lady's good name—as fully sufficient; it clearly is not. Obligation of secrecy is not merely a neat bit of statute-making; it corresponds to a deep psychological need, a permanent need, it seems. As the popular song used to have it, 'I had a secret love . . .'; or, to borrow a quotation from a popular magazine, 'they were bound together in a secret world, a world of love and ecstasy that no one could destroy'.

Secrecy, codified in Andreas, is powerfully present in the symbolism of the romances. The exclusiveness (as well as the beauty and the 'pleasance') of love is represented by the mysterious Garden of Love, hard of access, guarded from intrusion.[9] The Lover in the *Roman de la Rose* longs only to be in the Garden and with the Rose; but it

> . . . every dell
> Enclosed was, and walled well
> With highe walles enbatailled.   (A.137)

Chaucer makes use in several poems of the traditional symbol of the garden; but in *Troilus and Criseyde* the imaginative truth of 'love that oughte ben secree' is brought home in a different way. The spaciously developed central scene of Book III uses a non-traditional image:

> . . . swych a reyn from heven gan avale,
> That every maner womman that was there
> Hadde of that smoky reyn a verray feere.   (iii.626)

Later, the storm increases the feeling of snugness and intimacy and emphasizes the self-sufficiency, the self-containedness, the apartness of their love:

> The sterne wynd so loude gan to route
> That no wight oother noise myghte heere.   (744)

It is finally capped by the cameo of Pandarus withdrawing to the fire:

> And with that word he drow hym to the feere
> And took a light, and fond his contenaunce
> As for to looke upon an old romaunce.   (978)

Whether the scene of love is a garden with 'a hegge as thikke a is a castel wal', or a bed-sitter in a large, impersonal, modern city, or the Capulets' orchard by night, or 'the lost *domaine*', or the island of Conrad's *Victory*, the effect is the same—to isolate and to intensify.

---

every dell completely   *avale* fall   *Hadde . . . a verray feere* was truly afraid
route roar   *heere* hear   *drow hym* withdrew   *feere* fire   *fond his contenaunce . . .*
took up an attitude as if . . .

One last example, from Gottfried's *Tristan*. Tristan and Isolde are on a ship returning from her country to Cornwall (she is King Mark's bride-to-be and Tristan her official escort), when by a fatal accident they drink the love-potion. For the remainder of the voyage they enjoy the privateness, the isolation from mundane cares and social pressures, which a ship especially confers:

> During that voyage they were in ecstasy. Now that their shyness was over they gloried and revelled in their intimacy, and this was wise and sensible. . . . And so they passed the voyage in a life of rapture, yet not altogether freely, for they were haunted by fear of the future. They dreaded beforehand what actually came to pass. . . . (p. 204)

Of the other two recurrent motifs of the romantic experience which I singled out—obstacle and uplift—perhaps only the former needs elaboration. Romantic love thrives on frustration—not merely sexual frustration, though this is often part of it, but more generally on difficulties and obstacles. In medieval romance the jealous husband, *le viel gelus*, usually provides the obstacle: he frustrates the would-be lover by making his wife inaccessible; quite often he shuts her up in a tower. The sexual deprivation is often emphasized by the nature of the guard: in the lai of *Yonec* an old psalm-reciting widow; in *Floris and Blauncheflur*, eunuchs; in *Guigemar*, a white-haired eunuch-priest.[10] But the obstacle is also the social taboo; the love is exciting because it is forbidden fruit. Although by no means all medieval romances idealize adulterous situations, as C. S. Lewis's oft-quoted phrase has seemed to imply,[11] it is easy to see why such situations are common in the literature of romantic love from the *Tristan* stories to *Le Rouge et Le Noir*: they provide the ready-made obstacles, physical, moral and social. Other obstacles are readily devised and serve the same purpose (cf. Andreas's Rule XIV: 'The easy attainment of love makes it of little value; difficulty of attainment makes it prized'): the obstinate, possessive father in *Les Deus Amanz*; the family feud in *Romeo and Juliet*; the forced and sudden separations of war-time love-stories (or their looming possibility, as in *Troilus* which is amongst other things a war-time love-story). *Amor de lonh* (love from afar), whether in Jaufré Rudel's Provençal songs or in a modern romance-by-correspondence, is another fertile soil for the romantic emotions; here the sense of strangeness and inaccessibility replaces moral or social taboos. In many tales the difficulty is objectified in a more or less stylized way through a number of somewhat vaguely characterized 'enemies' of love, whose chief activities are talebearing and slander.[12] Mr Hatto has pithily described their necessary function in love-romance. Gottfried von Strassburg's lovers, Tristan and Isolde, he writes,

can no more do without the Jealous One's doorkeepers, spies, and 'slanderers' (who seem always to tell the truth) than revolutionaries without the police. In an ideal world free of *mésalliance* his lovers would go to pieces for sheer lack of opposition: they are heroes of the Resistance, of the underground army of love. (Introd. p. 18)

The relation of marriage to the conventions of medieval romance is often misunderstood. It is rarely that one feels the author is making a moral point by taking a stand against utilitarian marriage or against popular misunderstandings of the Christian theology of sex. Usually this emerges if at all, as a by-product of his central need—to choose or devise a situation and an action which will carry the experience of love as he and his audience wish to see it. Marriage creates a psychological atmosphere which is highly unfavourable to this: it is celebrated as a public contract which exists to fulfil such public functions in the community as the rearing of a family. It is only when something happens to interrupt or end the tranquil sharing of bed and board—separation, estrangement or death—that the 'romance' of marriage can emerge. When a romance-writer like Chrétien has a married couple as hero and heroine, he is bound to estrange them, as in the central episodes of *Erec et Enide* and *Yvain*.[13] The reconciliation of Erec and Enide after their period of miserable estrangement is truly romantic in feeling; they are renewed with all the freshness of new love:

> Or fu Erec toz forz et sains
> or fu gariz et respassez,
> or fu Enyde liee assez,
> or ot sa joie et son delit.
> Ansanble jurent an un lit,
> et li uns l'autre acole et beise:
> riens nule n'est qui tant lor pleise.
> Tant ont eü mal et enui,
> il por li et ele por lui,
> c'or ont feite lor penitance.   (5196–205)

(Now was Erec quite strong again and healthy [after his battles]; now was he totally cured and recovered; now was Enid happy indeed; now she had her joy and her delight. Together they lay in one bed, and embraced and kissed one another; nothing in the world pleases them so much. They have had such misery and sorrow, he for her and she for him, that now their penance is complete.)

It may seem paradoxical to regard the death of one partner as another possible condition of the full 'romantic' experience—at least, until one reflects that in real life a death often does amazingly intensify and simplify our feelings. Chaucer's *The Book of the Duchess* is a courtly elegy on Blanche, Duchess of Lancaster, first wife of John of Gaunt; the fact that Blanche is dead enables one more easily to accept the Black Knight's hyperboles:[14]

> For certes she was, that swete wif,
> My suffisaunce, my lust, my lyf,
> Myn hap, myn hele, and al my blesse,
> My worldes welfare, and my goddesse.   (1037–40)

This fine courtly elegy in honour and eulogy of one of the great ladies of the land disposes, of course, completely of any lingering notion there might be that 'courtly love' did not provide a thoroughly respectable set of concepts for the poetry of marriage and of public 'worship'. It was a natural mode for the expression of high 'solempnitee'.

Denis de Rougemont has observed that in our comparatively permissive modern society the old moral and social taboos have lost their power and that perhaps only two can be counted on to induce the authentic thrill, dependent as this must be on difficulties to be overcome—love for a minor (Nabokov's *Lolita*) and incestuous love (Robert Musil's *Man without Qualities*).[15] However this may be, there are relationships of a more conventional kind, even permanent ones, even marriage, in which, surely, the sense of strangeness and fragility is not totally absent—there is a stranger in all our friends, all our kin. 'Daunger' and Disdain may disappear but there is still an ultimate mystery to baffle, tease and fascinate us.

If the experiences of romantic love in all centuries have been characterized by these motifs—sudden illumination, the desire for secrecy, the need for obstacles and a heightened sense of life—what, we may ask, makes courtly love a distinct variation of romantic love, for it is clearly distinct?

Principally, its aristocratic connections, its identification with the

---

suffisaunce complete contentment   *lust* pleasure   *hap* good fortune   *hele* well-being   *blesse* bliss way of life of a particular class. This is romantic love for the very best people. Not only that, it is romantic love made sociable, fit for the dinner-table and the drawing-room. It is, indeed, the essential paradox of courtly love, that an intensely private experience is made the ground of social well-being:

> The existence of an upper class whose intellectual and moral notions are enshrined in an *ars amandi* remains a rather exceptional fact in history. In no other epoch did the ideal of civilization amalgamate to such a degree with that of love. Just as scholasticism represents the grand effort of the medieval spirit to unite all philosophic thought in a single centre, so the theory of courtly love . . . tends to embrace all that appertains to the noble life. . . . To formalize love is the supreme realization of the aspiration towards the life beautiful.[16]

Huizinga's penetrating generalization about the court civilization of fifteenth-century Burgundy enshrines a truth which holds also for the civilization of the late twelfth century, for which Chrétien de Troyes was a principal spokesman. Huizinga brings out, above all, the importance, during the whole period of the Middle Ages from Chrétien onwards, of romantic love as a humanizing and refining influence, as a socially improving experience. Even *Troilus and Criseyde*, concerned as it is primarily with other implications of courtly love, implications that require us to be fully aware of the poem as a 'just representation of general nature', contains passages which bring out the medievalness of their 'lovynge'. Towards the end of Book I Chaucer strikingly shows the ennoblement of Troilus, his social improvement (to put it no higher):

> And in the town his manere tho forth ay
> Soo goodly was, and gat hym so in grace,
> That ecch hym loved that loked on his face.

> For he bicom the frendlieste wight,
> The gentilest, and ek the mooste fre,
> The thriftiest, and oon the beste knyght,
> That in his tyme was or mighte be.
> Dede were his japes and his cruelte,
> His heighe port, and manere estraunge;
> And ecch of tho gan for a vertu chaunge   (i.1076)

---

tho forth ay from then on   *gat hym so in grace* so increased the favour he was held in   *fre* open-hearted, generous   *thriftiest* most successful   *heighe port* proud manner   *estraunge* aloof   *tho* those

Troilus's love must be recognized as a source of gentlemanliness, and indeed of true 'gentilesse'. The theme is not forgotten in the poem. Near the end the fine stanza, 'Swich fyn hath, lo, this Troilus for love' (v.1828), with its hammerblows in each line, 'Swich fyn . . . Swich fyn . . .', recalls not only his love but his 'grete worthynesse', his royal position, his 'noblesse'. The poem loses part of its meaning, if we fail to recognize that a lofty *social* ideal is at stake. Chaucer raises fundamental questions about civilized living as well as about the conditions of human happiness.

Very few medieval poets were capable of Chaucer's deep critical assessment of the secular ideal of love which is courtly love. But many were capable of depicting the atmosphere of aristocratic refinement which 'courtly love' demanded and which, as I have said, distinguishes it from other manifestations of romantic love in other centuries and other societies. Its intellectual refinement is evident in the rhetoric and casuistry of Gottfried's *Tristan* and of Chrétien's *Cligés*, to name only two.[17] Its emotional refinement is apparent on every page of the *lais* of Marie de France, is the very stuff of the little 'chante-fable', *Aucassin and Nicolette*, and is far from being a negligible factor even in the English version of *Floris and Blauncheflur*. But to illustrate it I choose a major English example, Gower's *Confessio Amantis*. In this vast poem, extending to some 30,000 lines or more, the Lover is questioned about his amorous behaviour, which is analysed under the headings of the Seven Deadly Sins. He confesses his 'sins' to Genius, the priest of Love, who absolves him and gives him ghostly counsel and advice. The very underlying conception of Gower's poem, developing as it does one of the traditional images of love (as a religion with a God, a temple, a priesthood, a congregation of lovers), shows how the stylized refinements of romantic sentiment could be further extended; and its elegant execution shows how they could still be made imaginatively meaningful. Of course, the poem is also an elaborately devised narrative entertainment, and its framing image of the confessional an admirable excuse for a lot of good stories. But the dramatic interludes between the stories in which *Amans* talks to his *Confessor* are full of interest. In them, as vividly as anywhere in fourteenth-century literature, we catch the social tone of aristocratic society, the atmosphere, however idealized, of delicate, considerate refinement. In the following passage the Lover defends himself against the charge of idleness by describing his 'besinesse' in attending upon his Lady:

Thus mot I nedly to hire drawe,
I serve, I bowe, I loke, I loute,
Min yhe folweth hire aboute,
What so sche wole so wol I,
Whan sche wol sitte, I knele by,
And whan sche stant, than wol I stonde:
Bot whan sche takth hir werk on honde
Of wevinge or enbrouderie,
Than can I noght bot muse and prie
Upon hir fingres longe and smale,
And now I thenke, and now I tale,
And now I singe, and now I sike,
And thus mi contienance I pike . . .
. . . forto feigne som desport
I pleie with hire litel hound
Now on the bedd, now on the ground,
Now with hir briddes in the cage;
For ther is non so litel page,
Ne yit so simple a chamberere,
That I ne make hem alle chere,
Al for thei scholde speke wel:
Thus mow ye sen mi besi whiel,
That goth noght ydeliche aboute. (iv.1168-97)

Gower was, indeed, 'moral Gower', deeply interested in the relationship of love to 'Kinde', natural instinct, and to 'Reson'—the subtle knot that makes us man. But in such a passage as this the distinctive medievalness of courtly love comes out not as a particular moral or philosophical attitude but as a pervasive sense of personal refinement, of the potential grace of the human personality.

Not all medieval versions even of the most famous love-stories breathe idealisms of love that can properly be called 'courtly'; some are scarcely even 'romantic', the wider category. So to correct the balance and to conclude the chapter, I should like to consider some English romances which put a different complexion on the relationship between men and women. To begin with there are a number of romances, *King Horn* and *Sir Beves of Hamtoun* amongst them, in which the traditional love-roles are reversed; the woman becomes the active

---

loute make obeisance   *yhe* eye   *smale* slender   *tale* speak   *sike* sigh   *thus mi contienance* . . . 'I cast a meaningful glance' (Bennett)   *feigne som desport* make pretence of cheerful activity   *chamberere* maidservant   *make* . . . *chere* treat politely

agent, the pursuer, the man becomes the pursued. In the extreme traditional case, such as Chrétien's *Lancelot*, the heroine is a very shadowy figure indeed; it is the man, the adventuring knight, who has the experience and must find the meaning. (It is a fascinating paradox that 'romance reading upon the book', which was arguably designed for female consumption in the first place, should so emphasize what goes on inside the *man's* head. It is not until line 4150 or so of *Lancelot* that Guenevere comes to life at all. Up to that point she is little more than a stage-property.) In *King Horn*, however, it is Rymenhild who feels and declares passionate love for Horn, summons him to her bower and, when she gets him there, leaves him in no doubt of what she wants:

> Rymenhild up gan stonde
> And tok him bi the honde.
> Heo sette him on pelle,
> Of wyn to drinke his fulle.
> Heo makede him faire chere
> And tok him abute the swere.
> Oft heo him custe
> So wel so hire luste.
> 'Horn,' heo sede, 'withute strif
> Thu schalt have me to thi wife.
> Horn, have of me rewthe,
> And plist me thi trewthe.'   (419–40)[18]

There is nothing romantic, let alone courtly, in this forthright approach nor is there in Horn's practical and sensible rejoinder:

> 'Ihc am ibore to lowe
> Such wimman to knowe . . .'   (447–8)

But it would be wrong to give the impression that throughout *Horn* their love was presented in such prosaic terms. Horn's love for Rymenhild, symbolized when he is absent from her by the ring he wears, acts as a sort of talisman. In the midst of his battle with the giant who killed his father,

> He lokede on his rynge,
> And thoghte on Rymenhilde.
> He smot him thuregh the herte,
> That sore him gan to smerte.   (931–4)

---

gan stonde stood   *Heo* she   *pelle* fur-rug   *swere* neck   *custe* kissed   *So wel so* . . . to her entire satisfaction   *withute strif* without demur   *rewthe* pity
Ihc I   *him* (933, 934) i.e. the giant

And Rymenhild's passionate, indeed suicidal, grief is depicted with laconic power in the incident of Horn's home-coming when Horn, disguised, tells her of his own 'death':

> Rymenhild sede at the furste,
> 'Herte, nu thu berste,
> For Horn nastu namore,
> That the hath pined the so sore.'
> Heo feol on hire bedde
> Ther heo knif hudde
> To sle with King lothe,
> And hure selve bothe . . .
> To herte knif he sette;
> Ac Horn anon hire kepte.
> He wipede that blake of his swere
> And sede, 'Quen so swete and dere,
> Ihc am Horn thin owe;
> Ne canstu me noght knowe?
> Ihc am Horn of Westernesse;
> In armes thu me cusse.   (1277–94)

Amongst the English romances which seem to concede most to amorous ideals is *Floris and Blauncheflur.* But the concessions are more to sentiment than to *amour.* One could say that Floris and Blauncheflur represent an opposite pole to Horn and Rymenhild. Whereas the latter are all dark passion when they are not being merely business-like, Floris and Blancheflur are counters in a game of sentiment. The author (or 'arranger', rather) of the aristocratic French romance *Floire et Blancheflor* drastically reduced his original; the English poem is about two-fifths of the length of the surviving French poems.[19] But he managed to keep some of the flavour of this immensely popular 'child-romance'; it has something of the appeal of the Babes in the Wood story. The king, Floris's father, decides that his seven-year-old son must be educated:

> Florys answerd with wepyng
> As he stood byfore the kyng;
> Al wepyng seide he,

---

berste burst   *nastu* you have not [double neg.]   *That the* . . . who has caused you so much misery   *Heo feol* she fell   *Ther heo* . . . where she had hidden a knife with which to slay the King she hated [i.e. a rival wooer]   *he* (1287) she   *that blake of* . . . the black off his neck [part of his disguise]   *Ihc* I *cusse* kiss

'Ne schal not Blancheflour lerne with me?
Ne can Y noght to scole goone
Without Blanchefloure,' he seide thane.
'Ne can Y in no scole syng ne rede
Without Blancheflour,' he seide.
The king seide to his soone,
'She shal lerne for thy love.' (15–24)

When this is compared with the sickly sentiment of passages from the
French romance we see that the English author has managed to retain
the innocent charm of their attachment whilst divesting it of the
precocious sexuality which makes it distasteful:

Ensamle lisent et aprendent,
a la joie d'amor entendent.
Quant il repairent de l'escole
li uns baise l'autre et acole.[20] (239–42)

(Together they read and learn and give their attention to the joy of love.
When they come out of school, they kiss and cuddle one another.)

The English author had a splendid opportunity in this poem to
present the quintessence of romantic feeling between two young
people, as Marie de France does in her *lai* of *Les Deuz Amanz*. Their
situation bristles with difficulties (unequal birth, hostile parents, unassail-
able tower, rival lover) but the unifying emphasis is not on their
experience so much as on the pathetic loveliness of their attachment
in a wicked world and on their touching child-like loyalty to one
another. Towards the end of the tale this feeling reaches its climax.
Blauncheflur has been sold as a slave to the 'Amyral of Babylone'.
Floris, after long search wheedles and tricks his way into the tower
where she and other maidens are locked up. But eventually, because
of the unworldly, dreamy absenteeism of Blauncheflur from her
official duties, their love is discovered and they are doomed to die;
but they excite pity in even the hardest heart:

There was noon so sterne man
That the Children loked oon,
That they ne wolde, al wel fawe,
Her jugement have withdrawe . . .
For Flores was so feire a yonglyng
And Blaunchefloure so swete a thing. (984–91)

984ff: No man who saw the children was so stern that he would not
gladly have withdrawn the sentence [of death] . . .

Eventually even the pagan Admiral's heart is touched and his anger assuaged:

> His swerd he breide out of his sheeth
> The children to have done to deeth.
> Blauncefloure put forth hur swire,
> And Florys dide her agayn to tyre,
> And seide, 'I am man; I shal byfore,
> With wrong hast thou thy lyf loore.—
> Florys forth his swerd putte,
> And Blauncheflor agayn him tytte.
> The King seide, 'dredry mot ye be,
> This routh by this Children to see.' (1014–23)

The sense of beautiful fragility, of something so precious and yet precarious that it should outweigh our normal feelings of justice and propriety, is part of our response to many romances. It is the feeling of Herrick's *To Daffodils* ('We have short time to stay . . .') transferred to the young. In *Floris and Blauncheflur* the romantic idealism is there; but it attaches itself to innocence and beauty rather than to love.

My third and last example is, again, of a romantic idealism masquerading as 'courtly love' while obstinately preserving quite other characteristics. In such cases the lover is presented as a heroic figure; but it is the love which serves the heroism, not *vice versa*. Malory's Lancelot is the supreme instance of this. In the long-drawn conclusion of the *Morte Darthur*, when everything moves towards the ineluctable catastrophe and 'the noble felyshyp of the Rounde Table ys brokyn for ever', we are indeed conscious of Lancelot's 'love' for Guenevere, but only, in effect, as an obligation of knighthood, a loyalty which over-rides all others. Lancelot finds, like other heroes whom we shall consider later, that to be true to himself and to the highest ideals of Arthurian knighthood he must be true to Guenevere. When this loyalty is forced into open conflict with his other great loyalty, to his sovereign Lord ('the most noble king that made me knight'), then the tragedy begins.

We must not fall into the error of mistaking this loyalty to the queen for love in the sense that this chapter has tried to define it.

---

breide snatched   *swire* neck   *dide her* . . . made her pull it back
I shal byfore I must go first   *loore* lost   *swerd* [*swere?*] neck   *agayn him*
tytte pulled him back   *dredry* . . . bad luck to you   *this Children* these young
people

We have never been conscious of it as a special personal experience for Lancelot, the sort of experience that springs from a moment of radiance and constitutes a 'way of life'. Malory is at his unhappiest when describing this sexual attachment. At the beginning of Book 18 (in Caxton's division), with the Grail fresh in his and his reader's minds, he speaks of it in terms which recall Andreas's reference to 'a furtive and hidden embrace':

... ever his thoughtis prevyly were on the quene, and so they loved togydirs more hotter than they dud toforehonde, and had many such prevy draughtis togydir that many in the courte spake of hit. (ii.1045)

Guenevere does indeed behave like a woman in love—in her jealousy, for instance, when Lancelot wears the red sleeve of the Fair Maiden of Astolat in a tournament. But Lancelot is more like a respectable married man who has got deeper involved than he should have with his employer's wife. At the supreme crisis of their relationship, when Lancelot is about to fight his way out of the queen's chamber, in his bare shirt against fourteen armed knights, it is his dutifulness, his loyal prowess, which he asks her to remember:

... and I at all tymes your poure knyght and trew unto my power, and as I never fayled you in ryght nor in wronge sytthyn the firste day kynge Arthur made me knyght... (iii.1166)

And it is 'Jesu Cryste', not Cupid, whom he prays to be his 'shylde' and his 'armoure'.

It is true that one could read a great deal more into these passages if one felt the whole context of the *Morte* supported it. Such support some have found in the eloquent little chapter entitled by Caxton, 'How trewe love is lykened to sommer', all the more because it is apparently one of Malory's freely invented passages. The characteristic high, but limited, moral tone is set by a discourse such as the following:

But nowadayes men cannat love sevennyght but they muste have all their desyres. That love may nat endure by reson, for where they bethe sone acorded and hasty, heete sone keelyth. And ryght so faryth the love nowadayes, sone hote sone colde. Thys ys no stabylyté. But the olde love was nat so. For men and women coude love togydirs seven yerys, and no lycoures lustis was betwyxte them, and than was love, trouthe and faythefulnes. And so in lyke wyse was used such love in Kynge Arthurs dayes. (iii.1119–20)

No more here than elsewhere can one find any feeling for the inward, shared experience of love such as Chaucer so movingly celebrates:

O blisful nyght, of hem so longe isought,
How blithe unto hem bothe two thow weere!
Why nad I swich oon with my soule ybought,
Ye, or the leeste joie that was theere?
Awey, thow foule daunger and thow feere,
And lat hem in this hevene blisse dwelle,
That is so heigh that al ne kan I telle!   (iii.1317–23)

Such an experience to Malory was mere 'prevy draughtis'; he saw romantic love at its best as a stable, abstemious, loyal friendship between two people who happened to be of opposite sex.

I have attempted in this chapter to describe some of the manifestations of the first and principal idealism of romance—the idealism of love. In the course of the discussion one striking paradox, as I see it, has emerged, that 'an intensely private experience is made the ground of social well-being'. The nature of this social well-being is of importance not only for an understanding of medieval courtly societies but also for an understanding of many romances. In the chapter which follows we shall see how many romancers, and particularly Chaucer, pondered the problem of the Lover as a social being, as a 'gentil man'.

---

daunger power of evil   *feere* fear   *al ne kan* . . . I cannot describe it fully

1. Among recent necessary correctives to the vastly influential account of C. S. Lewis in *The Allegory of Love* (1935) are those by P. Dronke in *Medieval Latin and the Rise of the European Love-Lyric* (2 vols., 1965–6), vol. i, and E. T. Donaldson, 'The Myth of Courtly Love' in *Speaking of Chaucer* (1970). But a more sceptical and questioning approach is now general. The appropriate chapters in Huizinga's classic study, *The Waning of the Middle Ages*, remain the best introduction to the phenomenon in its literary, artistic and social manifestations.

2. The historical basis in fact (or the lack of it) has been closely studied and sceptically presented by J. F. Benton, 'The Court of Champagne as a Literary Centre', *Speculum* xxxvi (1961). It should go without saying, however, that Andreas's treatise is itself a 'fact' of history and that his imaginative concerns are none the less 'real' even if they can be shown to use a fiction.

3. J. J. Parry's translation of Andreas's work—*The Art of Courtly Love*, p. 28.

4. ibid, p. 149.

5. ibid., p. 176.

6. ibid., p. 187.

7. I leave till later the deeper questions about the nature of the love portrayed in *Lancelot* and Chrétien's attitude towards it. See p. 137 below.

8. Translated into English as *The Lost Domain* by Frank Davison (World's Classics, 1959).

9. The Garden of Love has links also with (a) the Garden of Eden, a well-guarded spot and original home of sexual delight; and (b) the *hortus inclusus* of the Song of Songs: 'A garden inclosed is my sister, my spouse' (4.12).

10. The *lais* of *Yonec* and *Guigemar* are by Marie de France; the English romance of *Floris and Blauncheflur* is anonymous. For further details, see Booklist (p. 242).

11. *The Allegory of Love* (p. 12): '. . . the four marks of Humility, Courtesy, Adultery and the Religion of Love'. The fallacy of this way of putting it lies in the confusion of viewpoints. Generally it is only the *outside* moralist who will see the situation as adulterous and immoral. And if this viewpoint is taken, then 'the Religion of Love' should properly be the 'Idolatry of Love', and so forth.

12. The sense of an 'enemy' is a most important ingredient in many love-romances. The enemy varies, of course, from the physical ('the warring houses' of *Romeo and Juliet*) to the metaphysical (in *Troilus* the fundamental 'lak of stedfastnes' of all sublunary things).

13. In *Erec et Enide*, their courtship occupies the first third of the poem and culminates in their marriage. Such is their enjoyment of their mutual love that word gets around that Erec has lost his *valor* (courage and worth). Enide tells Erec of this and as a consequence is taken by him on a series of *aventures*, poorly clad, poorly horsed and under a vow of silence.

14. We know from lines 577–8 ('Y wreche, that deth hath mad all naked Of al the blysse that ever was maked') if not earlier, that the Knight's love is dead. It is only the Dreamer who is dense.

15. D. de Rougemont, *The Myths of Love* (Engl. trs., 1963), pp. 48 ff.

16. Huizinga, p. 96.

17. See, for example, the long passage from *Cligés* quoted below (p. 196) in which Alixandre and Soredamors soliloquize about love.

18. Rymenhild's speech is longer in MS Laud Misc. 108; hence the apparent discrepancy in line-numbering. McKnight's edition prints 3 parallel texts.

19. The EETS editor, G. H. McKnight, argues that the English text was not based directly on any of the now extant French versions, but on 'an older, or purer text' (Introd. p. xxxvii).

20. *Floire et Blancheflor*, Ed. Wilhelmine Wirtz.

3

MAN AND SOCIETY:

THE ROMANCE OF THE 'GENTIL' MAN

Medieval romance was, amongst other things, a great civilizing enterprise. To quote C. S. Lewis's words about Malory: it was concerned with 'the civilization of the heart (by no means of the head), a fineness and sensitivity, a voluntary rejection of all the uglier and more vulgar impulses'.[1] Chaucer, perhaps above all else, was occupied in his *Canterbury Tales* romances with 'the civilization of the heart'; and their motto might well be his own favourite line—'For pitee renneth soone in gentil herte'—since his use of the word 'pitee' is wider and more resonant than ours:[2]

> 'That pitee renneth soone in gentil herte,
> Feelynge his similitude in peynes smerte,
> Is preved alday, as men may it see,
> As wel by werk as by auctoritee;
> For gentil herte kitheth gentillesse.
> I se wel that ye han of my distresse
> Compassion, my faire Canacee,
> Of verray wommanly benignitee
> That Nature in youre principles hath set.' (*The Squire's Tale* 479–87)

But the civilizing is not to be confined to individuals as individuals. It is directed towards producing more agreeable people for society. A principal paradox of courtly love is that an idealized personal relationship is made the ground for an elaborate code of social behaviour. I have already quoted from Huizinga's classic account of the forms of

---

Feelynge his similitude experiencing his likeness   *preved alday* continuously demonstrated   *kitheth* shows   *principles* innate disposition

civilization in fifteenth-century Burgundy, *The Waning of the Middle Ages* (see p. 40 above). The passage continues, 'To formalize love is the supreme realization of the aspiration towards the life beautiful. . . . More than in pride and in strength, beauty is found in love. To formalize love is, moreover, a social necessity. . . . Only by constructing a system of forms and rules can barbarity be escaped.' The formalization of love is not confined to literature. In the 'system' of courtesy, 'literature, fashion and conversation . . . formed the means to regulate and refine erotic life'.

This argument about the civilizing function of love can be further developed as follows. The especial appropriateness of the fiction of courtly love was that it showed how life in 'middeleard', which orthodox theology taught men to despise, could be made a beautiful and worshipful thing. It gave the urge to make beautiful objects, the artistic and creative urge, a legitimate field of expression outside the Church. The Bible does not tell you whether you may pare your nails at table, kiss a lady when you meet her, or write a love-song. It tells you of your salvation, of your duties and responsibilities, of the spirit in which you should work and pray. Courtly love, on the other hand, is a gospel of leisure and pleasure. It teaches you how to behave to your peers when you all have time on your hands; not how to do them good, but how to make yourself desirable; how to 'commune', especially in mixed company, and how to please.

'Thou shalt please'—this is the great commandment in the courtly code. And it has remained a central concept in the idea of the Gentleman. Newman's description of the gentleman in one of his University discourses is the classic statement: the passage begins 'Hence it is that it is almost a definition of a gentleman to say he is one who never inflicts pain . . .' The gentleman is concerned, at all costs, to avoid unpleasantness, he wants social life to be a 'good show'—appearances must be preserved. Moreover he knows that appearances cannot be preserved without realities, and he cultivates virtues which will sustain the appearances.

The courtly situation presented a similar difficulty. The 'play' and 'disport' of courtly life required that men and women alike should be 'mery', 'debonair', full of 'fraunchise' and 'fredom'—in short, as I have said, that they should please. But how could this gallant and high-hearted atmosphere be supported? The answer was—through Love. The experience of 'falling in love' would confer on you the inestimable benefit of a 'goodly manere': Troilus

> bicom the frendlieste wight,
> The gentilest, and ek the mooste fre,
> The thriftiest and oon the beste knyght,
> That in his tyme was or myghte be.   (i.1079–82)

And the discipline of being in love, of wooing, would confirm and
strengthen you in your new life, free of 'japes' and 'cruelte', a life,
whether you won or lost, of faithful service.

The logic of love proceeds, then, like this. It starts from the observed
and fundamental truth that 'falling in love' makes a man pleasing to
others—'all the world loves a lover'. The first deduction from this is
that, if you want to please, you must allow yourself to fall in love and
remain in love. The second is that, if you want to please, and you are
not in love, you must *act the Lover*. This is why in the Middle Ages
the art of living approximates to an art of loving: and why the great
first psychology of love, the *Roman de la Rose*, is also the source and
pattern of 'curtesy' books.[3]

The *Roman de la Rose* is one of the great documents of thirteenth-
century culture. It was written in two parts—the first 4000 lines by
Guillaume de Lorris, about 1235; the last 18,000 by Jean de Meun
half a century later. The poem opens, as so many medieval poems do,
in May. The poet dreams that he comes upon a garden surrounded by
a wall, the mysterious Garden of Love:

Outside on 'the highe walles enbatailled' are depicted hateful qualities—
Felonye, Vilainye, Coveitise, Envye, Elde, and so forth. 'A mayden curteys'
opens the wicket gate for him. Her name is Ydelnesse (i.e. leisure). The lord
of the garden is Sir Myrthe; and with him is Lady Gladnesse. Lady Curtesie
invites the dreamer to join the dance in which the God of Love and his
Squire, Swete-Lokyng, are taking part, with Beauté, Richesse, Largesse, and
Fraunchise. After the dance the poet wanders through the garden and looks
into the well where Narcissus died. In its mirror he sees a rosebush; but when
he wishes he could pick a bud from it, the God of Love shoots him through
the eye into the heart. The God of Love then locks his heart with a key and
promises him help if he will keep his commandments. When the Dreamer,
soon afterwards, tries to pass the hedge and get at the Rose, he is encouraged by
'Bialacoil' (fair-welcoming) but repulsed by a churl called Daunger (standoffishness, aloofness) and chased away by Wykkid-Tunge (scandal-mongering)
and Shame (fear of disrepute). The dreamer is disconsolate. Lady Resoun
descends from her tower and advises him to forget love; but his Friend tells
him not to lose heart. Warmed by Venus's torch Bialacoil allows the Dreamer

---

thriftiest most excellent

to kiss the rose; but this puts Shame, Wikkid-Tunge and Jelousie on the alert and they soon reduce the Dreamer to desperation again.

Soon after this, Guillaume de Lorris's part of the poem breaks off; Jean de Meun's continuation, in an utterly different spirit, does not concern us here.

This brief summary of the allegory can only convey a pale notion of what Part I of the poem is like. But at least the courtly abstractions Richesse, Largesse, Fraunchise, Curtesie, should make it plain that the subject is not simply the private experience of romantic love but one that opens up reflections on the nature of the good life, the desirable life on earth. And when the God of Love counsels the Lover about the 'craft of love', the 'commandments' he gives are, many of them, of a sensible, practical, *social* kind.

Advice about how to 'act courtly' had, it is true, been incorporated earlier into even English romances. *King Horn*, which is not remarkable for its social finesse, has a typical 'instruction' of this kind; Aylmer, the king, addresses his steward:

> 'Stiwarde, tak nu here
> Mi fundlyng for to lere
> Of thine mestere,
> Of wude and of rivere,
> And tech him to harpe
> With his nayles scharpe,
> Bivore me to kerve,
> And of the cupe serve.
> Thu tech him of alle the liste
> That thu evre of wiste,
> In his feiren thou wise
> Into othere servise:
> Horn thu underfonge,
> And tech him of harpe and songe.'   (241–56)

What Horn has to learn, with the possible exception of harping, are what might be called masculine crafts—riding, hunting, carving at table, the service of his feudal lord. But the Lover in the *Roman de la Rose* is being prepared to play his part in a mixed society; he has a lady as well as a lord, and he has to acquire the polite accomplishments. He is to avoid 'vilanye', the characteristic behaviour of someone of a

---

lere teach   *mestere* craft, trade   *liste* accomplishments   *feiren* companions
wise direct   *underfonge* take in hand

lower class, a *vilain*; and he must not be 'outrageous' (immodest, insensitive, 'pushing'). The God of Love bids him

> . . . alle wymmen serve and praise
> And to thy power her honour reise (2229–30)

> . . . be wise and aqueyntable,
> Goodly of word and resonable (2213–14)

That is to say, he must learn to mix and to talk well. He must also take a care for his appearance and cleanliness:

> Of shon and bootes, newe and faire,
> Loke at the leest thou have a paire . . . (2265–6)

> Have hat of floures as fresh as May
> Chapelett of roses of Whitsonday. (2277–8)

He is to wash his hands, clean his teeth and nails. If he sings well, he must not hang back *too* long when he's invited to perform. In short,

> Whoso with Love wole goon or ride,
> He mot be curteis, and voide of pride,
> Mery, and full of jolite,
> And of largesse alosed be. (2351–4)

Love will be generous to him, so he must not be stingy when a present or a *pourboire* is called for.

The ideal society envisaged by Guillaume de Lorris is an extraordinary one. It is an earthly paradise, a parody of the religious conception of the Earthly Paradise;[4] no one ever works there, no one ever grows old, no one ever hears a bawling baby or a scolding wife. Admittedly there is rebuff as well as aspiration, pain as well as happiness, in the pursuit of love. But the general atmosphere of the Garden of Love is supremely conveyed by the Dance:

> But it to me liked right well
> That Curtesie me cleped so,
> And bad me on the daunce go. (806–8)

'The figure of very nobilite' is set out and expressed in the dance. But there is a nobility proper to each sex, and in the dance a man shows his manliness and a woman her womanliness 'in gentyl behavyng', the one to the other. It was the perfect symbol, then as in all ages, of

---

her their   *alosed* praised, commended, for

male-and-female, of sex, even if not always signifying 'matrimonie'. The dance also 'betokeneth concorde', social solidarity and youthful gaiety. The strength with which these 'meanings' were felt, if it were not immediately apparent in the context of courtly narrative, could be gathered from the extensive use of the dance as a symbol in the writings of the age. Love itself is often spoken of as a dance: 'loves daunce', 'the old daunce', 'the dance of lufe'—the image becomes a cliché of the language of love. The idea of a dance is not a simple symbol. It is, rather, a cluster of symbols. They are all present in the dance of the *Roman de la Rose* (Part I)—youth, sexual desire, gaiety, social enjoyment and 'curtesy'.[5]

The *Roman de la Rose*, then, is a *locus classicus* for this medieval conception of the ideal society as one made up of lovers—a 'court' of Love, or an 'order' of Lovers (to use their favourite images of community, secular and religious). But this paradox was not the invention of the author, Guillaume de Lorris. He did not 'socialize' love single-handed, so to speak. The romances of Chrétien de Troyes embody a similar conception: the court of King Arthur is, I think invariably, presented as a centre of gracious living, a mirror of Curtesy. King Arthur's court is lavishly praised in the opening lines of *Yvain*. It is the feast of Whitsuntide and the knights and ladies of the court are engaged in courtly pastimes; some are gossiping, others talking of love:

> Des angoisses et des dolors
> Et des granz biens, qu'an ont sovant
> Li deciple de son covant,
> Qui lors estoit riches et buens. (14–17)

(Of the miseries and pains and the very good things which are often received by the disciples of his 'order', which in those days was powerful and good)

Lors is emphatic—*in those days* love was a worthy thing, an 'order' with many 'disciples'. But now it is *mout abeissiée, tornée a fable*; those who think they love are liars, *mançonge an font*. (The notion of a golden age of love is clearly not an innovation of the fourteenth and fifteenth centuries, of Chaucer and Malory, but a feature of courtly idealism from the beginning.) Chrétien tells his listeners that his tale is going to be about things which are worth hearing, about Arthur whose fame (he agrees with the Breton jongleurs) will live for ever.

King Arthur's court, then, is not simply a handy rendezvous for the knights of the Round Table; it is the fountainhead of true loving.

And since love is the central experience in a whole bundle of experiences, the mainspring in the mechanism of *cortoisie*, the king's court is also a mirror of 'gracious living'. The passage in *Yvain* which shows this most clearly is that in which the marriage of Yvain and Laudine is celebrated. The court, as such, has no geographical location but consists, as in twelfth-century real life, in the presence of the king with his entourage; so to celebrate the marriage King Arthur confers his presence on Yvain at his castle.

> Qu'enor et joie li feroient...
> Et li rois dit, que volantiers
> Li feroit huit jorz toz antiers
> Enor et joie et conpaignie   (2305-9)

([The king and his courtiers] would do all joyous honour to Yvain ... And the king said that he would gladly confer on Yvain the honour and joy of his company for a whole week ...)

All the people of the castle ride out to meet the king and give him a royal welcome, a 'joyeuse entrée' as it was later to be called.

> Contre le roi li chastiaus tone
> De la joie, que l'an i fet   (2338-9)

(At the king's approach the castle resounds with the joy that is made)

There are carpets in the streets, curtains outdoors against the sun, music and dancing:

> Trestuit de joie se travaillent.
> Et a ceste joie reçoivent
> Le roi ...   (2356-8)

(Everyone gives themselves up to joy, and with this joy they welcome the king...)

   Yvain is far from being the only romance in which King Arthur's court is held up for admiration as the wellspring of true loving, true living and, incidentally, true justice. The scene just quoted can be paralleled elsewhere—most tellingly, for instance, at the end of Chrétien's *Erec et Enide*, when Erec's coronation is celebrated with a splendour of ceremony which quite eclipses even his own marriage feast. The climax of the description is, again, King Arthur's contribution; it makes the narrator almost speechless. Arthur made the Emperor Alexander look like a niggard; Caesar himself never gave such a feast

> come li rois Artus dona
> le jor que Erec corona. (6619–20)

(as King Arthur gave on the day he crowned Erec.)

Arthur *par franchise* (generosity of spirit) seats his royal person next to Erec and Enide and presents them with two crowns out of his *tresor*.

The key-word in courtly celebration, and (we may suppose) in the image which Chrétien's patrons formed for themselves of an ideal social existence, is *joie*. It means more than its modern counterparts, but exactly what more is not easy to define. A 'gallant and high-hearted happiness', a 'braverie', a defiant ignoring of whatever is ugly or painful, a spontaneity that keeps decorum, that delights in the obligations of polite formality and rigid hierarchy, a delighted acceptance of the claims of 'cest siécle mortel' on social beings; in short, the 'party-spirit' raised to the nth degree of idealization. *Joie* is perhaps the most intense expression of individual vitality within the forms of social life. And this is why it is inseparably linked with Youth and Love.[6]

The 'meaning' of romantic love (courtly love, *fine amors*) was not confined, then, to the interpretation of an isolated private experience but was concerned with the formation of a 'gentil' man in a 'gentil' society. To see this is to be able to enter into the spirit of the opening scene of *Sir Gawain and the Green Knight*:

> This kyng lay at Camylot upon Krystmasse
> With mony luflych lorde, ledes of the best—
> Rekenly of the Rounde Table alle tho riche brether—
> With rych revel oryght and rechles merthes.
> Ther tournayed tulkes by tymes ful mony,
> Justed ful jolilé thise gentyle knightes,
> Sythen kayred to the court, caroles to make;
> For ther the fest was ilyche ful fiften dayes,
> With alle the mete and the mirthe that men couthe avyse:
> Such glaum ande gle glorious to here,
> Dere dyn upon day, daunsyng on nyghtes—
> Al was hap upon heghe in halles and chambres
> With lordes and ladies, as levest him thoght. (37–49)

---

ledes men, princes *Rekenly* nobly *oryght* in a proper manner *rechles* carefree *tulkes* knights *kayred* rode *caroles* courtly ring-dances *ilyche* continued at the same pitch *avyse* devise *glaum ande gle* sounds of revelry *Dere dyn* delightful music *Al was hap . . .* happiness reigned *levest him thoght* seemed to them most delightful

The emphasis in this description on courtly joy expressing itself spontaneously, or at least without a care for the morrow, in courtly sports and merrymaking is there for all to see. Music and dancing ('glaum and gle', 'dere dyn', 'daunsyng on nyghtes') play an important part in the 'mirthe' of the court. The lords and ladies are the most famous and the 'lovelokkest' ever known. And coming with especial emphasis just before the 'bob' lines, 'al watz this fayre folk in her first age'—they were all young. Truly, for the medieval poet, 'Beauty is Youth, Youth Beauty'.

The whole tendency of the social thinking (if this is not too glib a phrase) in medieval romance from Chrétien to *Gawain* is towards a philosophy of an élite. Good manners and a refined way of life are not for every Jack and Jill; they are for the fortunate few.[7] The romances do not, admittedly, set out to present a realistic account of contemporary society; but the ethical qualities and the style of living which they glamorize are those that could only be afforded by the rich and well-born. It is, however, the great achievement of Chaucer, as I see it, in his *Wife of Bath's Tale* and *Franklin's Tale* to have extended and deepened the courtly concepts involved in the definition of a 'gentil' man until their class-basis, their narrowly conceived aristocratic tenor, becomes irrelevant. Chaucer's courtlines, more evidently than that of other romancers, is Christian at root.

The *Wife of Bath's Tale* has a relationship, of course, to the Wife herself. The fantasy of seeing a physically repulsive old woman turned into a glamorous young mistress would warm the cockles of her egotistic heart (for 'age, allas! that al wol envenyme/Hath me biraft my beautee and my pith', *Prologue*, 474). The appropriateness is ironical, as so often in *The Canterbury Tales*, because the Wife reads it as an illustration of 'maistrie', of the unorthodox domination of husband by wife—a very necessary thing in her view. But the essential meaning of the tale is courtly; it shows the spirit of submission and gratitude which Man must adopt before the 'graces' of the Lover's state can fall upon him. The Wife of Bath herself has little conception of true 'gentilesse'.[8]

There is some danger that we may look in *The Wife of Bath's Tale* for a complexity of personal psychology which simply is not there. The events in the action, the moods and decisions of the hero (so-called) are, in fact, no more than counters in an argument—an argument about the nature of courtliness. The tale uses romance material (the Loathly Lady; the company of 'fairy' dancers, 991) and has a

lesson to teach about courtliness; but the way it works is more like
a parable than anything else. It does not resonate imaginatively; or,
at least, it does not resonate through the personality of a central
character. The Knight of the tale is nameless and does not need a name;
he is Sir Anonymous.

I spoke of the 'graces' of the Lover's state falling upon the Knight
when he submits to the Woman, the Loathly Lady of the tale. To put
this into more modern terms, the Knight has to learn the true nature
of courtliness, the values it rests upon, and the self-abandonment that
it demands, before he can hope to reap its rewards. This, incidentally,
is surely the relevance of his exceedingly unknightly and uncourtly
action at the beginning, when he casually rapes a young woman
walking by the riverside. 'Oppressioun' can go no further in a sexual
relationship; rape is a total denial of what makes us human. (Gower,
who tells the same tale to make a different point, omits this incident.)
By the end of *The Wife of Bath's Tale* the Knight has learnt that love
is not for the taking. The process by which he learns is not presented
as one of internal illumination brought about by personal reaction to
circumstances or to the ugly old woman to whom he is bound. He
responds simply to her eloquence; she preaches an eloquent sermon,
as it were, on the nature of true courtliness, and he sees the light. He
has no more 'character' than the dummy in one of Plato's Dialogues.
His response and ours are the same—direct to the power of the idea
and the ideal.

There are three main points in the Loathly Lady's sermon and they
arise out of the Knight's insulting words:

> Thou art so loothly, and so oold also,
> And therto comen of so lough a kinde
> That litel wonder is thogh I walwe and wynde.
> So wolde God myn herte wolde breste! (1100-3)

She replies that a true gentleman honours goodness, not rank and
family; honours the poor, not just the well-to-do; and honours the old
and reverences them. These three points, as it seems to me, stand in
direct contradiction to the conceptions of courtliness as presented in
the first part of the *Roman de la Rose*. One cannot help wondering
whether Chaucer had it specifically in mind.

The first topic, then, of the Hag's sermon is 'gentilesse'. All the

---

lough a kinde base a family   *litel wonder* . . . it is not surprising if . . .   *So
wolde* . . . Would God my heart would break!

implications of the *Roman*, despite one brief statement to the contrary, are that this delightful experience of love, with the good breeding and social accomplishments that accompany it, is reserved for an élite. As the God of Love observes to the Lover, he is to the manner born:

> ... thou answerid so curteisly.
> For now I wot wel uttirly,
> That thou art gentyll by thy speche. (1985-7)

The Old Hag, however, observes that true gentilesse is a Christian quality:

> Crist wole we clayme of hym oure gentillesse
> Nat of oure eldres for hire old richesse. (1117-18)

She quotes Dante, 'the wise poete of Florence', and, near the end of this section of her discourse, Boethius, *De Consolatione Philosophiae*, a favourite book of Chaucer's:[9]

> Ther shul ye seen expres that it no drede is
> That he is gentil that dooth gentil dedis. (1169-70)

The Hag now turns to her second theme, 'poverte'. Christ himself was poor:

> The hye God, on whom that we bileeve,
> In wilful poverte cheese to lyve his lyf. (1178-9)

Still following Boethius, she observes that poverty is good in itself; it brings you back to the realities of life. Like a run of bad luck it opens your eyes; no one in his senses wants to be well off. This is in stark contrast to the presentation of Poverty amongst hateful qualities in the *Roman de la Rose*. When the Lover comes to the Garden first of all he sees that it is

> With highe walles enbatailled,
> Portraied without and wel entailled
> With many riche portraitures. (139-41)

Amongst the 'images' to be left outside as the Dreamer enters the

---

wel uttirly for sure   *Crist wole* ... Christ would wish us to trace our 'gentilesse' back to him and not to our forebears because of their inherited wealth and power   *expres* made clear   *no drede* no doubt   *wilful* deliberate   *cheese* chose   *enbatailled* embattled   *Portraied* ... with frescoes and many fine designs carved on the outside

enchanted Garden where he hopes to find his supreme happiness, are:
Hate, Vilainye, Coveitise, Envye, Sorrow, Elde (Old Age), Hypocrisy
and Poverty. If you want to be civilized, you must obey these three
commandments: 'Thou shalt not be Poor!' 'Thou shalt not be Unhappy!' and—'Thou shalt not be Old!' 'Elde' is the third head in the
Hag's discourse. It has no place inside the Garden of the Rose; but
Youth is there.

> And after daunced, as I gesse,
> Youthe, fulfilled of lustynesse,
> That nas not yit twelve yeer of age,
> With herte wylde, and thought volage.
> Nyce she was, but she ne mente
> Noon harm ne slight in hir entente,
> But oonly lust and jolyte. (1281–7)

In most courtly literature the old man, especially the Old Lover,
senex amans, has no place. This is one reason why Januarie in *The
Merchant's Tale* is so obnoxious. The Garden of the Rose

> . . . is no country for old men. The young
> In one another's arms, birds in the trees
> —Those dying generations—at their song . . . (Yeats)

The Old Hag argues that age deserves reverence—and no special
'auctoritee' is required for this. But she rather spoils her point, one
may think, with the, as it were, commercial observation that, being
'foul and old', at least no one else will want to make love to her. This
is perhaps a lapse.

   The Wife of Bath's Tale, to sum up, demolishes certain aristocratic
courtly pretensions—the pretensions of birth, of wealth and of youth.
Whether all this is imaginatively substantiated in the tale itself, one
may question. At least, one must observe, it is not substantiated,
'realized', through character and psychological interest. The force
of the ideals lies, I have suggested, in the eloquence of the climactic
speech of the Old Hag; the power is in the words as carriers of ideas:[10]

> Crist wole we clayme of him oure gentillesse . . .
> Thanne comth oure verray gentillesse of grace;
> It was no thyng biquethe us with oure place. (1163–4)

---

fulfilled full of   *wylde* restive   *volage* volatile   *Nyce* foolish. silly   *slight*
trickery   *lust* fun

How far this is beyond the Wife of Bath herself may be gauged from
the conclusion to her tale, where assuredly she speaks in character:

> . . . and Jhesu Crist us sende
> Housbondes meeke, yonge, and fressh abedde,
> And grace t'overbyde hem that we wedde;
> And eek I praye Jhesu shorte hir lyves
> That wol nat be governed by hir wyves;
> And olde and angry nygardes of dispence,
> God sende hem soone verray pestilence!   (1258–64)

It is not only in *The Wife of Bath's Tale* that Chaucer uses romance
as vehicle for ethical ideas. Elsewhere also he seems to be extending
and deepening the courtly concepts until, as I have said, their class-
basis, in an aristocratic élite, becomes irrelevant. We, too, the 'proles'
of the world, can become 'gentil-men'. And our relationships, even
if not courtly in the strictest sense, can become imbued with the
spirit of courtliness. Or, to put it another way, Chaucer seems to be
trying to show that courtly and Christian values, instead of being
opposed to each other, are, in the sphere of personal relationships
and perhaps even beyond that sphere, fully compatible. To take a
particular instance, marriage: the experience of love as a romantic
courtly experience could have not a disintegrating effect on marriage,
but a refining and civilizing influence. The brutalities of the marriage-
mart in a Christian society could be softened and sweetened. Paradoxically, courtly love could 'christianize' the behaviour of married
people. Despite popular belief to the contrary, Chaucer was doing
nothing new or unexpected in reconciling courtly love and marriage
(see p. 38 above); it is the power of his idealization that attracts us,
not its novelty, as in this well-known passage from the beginning of
The Franklin's Tale, his second social romance:

> For o thyng, sires, saufly dar I seye,
> That freendes everych oother mote obeye,
> If they wol longe holden compaignye.
> Love wol nat been constreyned by maistrye.
> Whan maistrie comth, the God of Love anon
> Beteth his wynges, and farewel, he is gon!
> Love is a thyng as any spirit free.
> Wommen, of kynde, desiren libertee,
> And nat to been constreyned as a thral;

---

overbyde outlive   *of dispence* in their expenditure   *of kynde* by their nature

> And so doon men, if I sooth seyen shal.
> Looke who that is moost pacient in love,
> He is at his avantage al above. (761-72)

Whatever *The Franklin's Tale* is 'about', it is certainly not a paean in praise of 'romantic marriage'. It simply happens that a happy balanced and mutual relationship is the necessary starting-point for what Chaucer has to say. It is the premiss from which Chaucer begins, not the conclusion to which he moves. Marriage typifies such a relation, in its happy mutuality, but it is not the exclusive condition of it. The proper relationship of friends, spouses and lovers is the same: they must obey one another, they must not try to dominate ('constreyne by maistrye'), they must respect the desire for individual freedom.

If Chaucer had simply wanted to praise marriage, would he, I wonder, have chosen a story in which the vows of marriage are overridden? The husband tells his wife, in effect, to value her promise, sportively given, to a mere acquaintance, *above* the solemn vows of marriage itself. The tale sets out to show that there are obligations of relationship which may transcend the bonds and obligations of mutual love.

> Trouthe is the hyeste thing that man may kepe. (1479)

Like Chaucer's other *Canterbury Tales* romances, *The Franklin's Tale* is a social romance in one very simple and basic way. It deals with a *question d'amour*—i.e. it is an example of 'luf-talkyng'. In *The Wife of Bath's Tale*, the 'question of love' is, we remember, 'What thing it is that women most desiren?' In *The Knight's Tale* we have to consider whether a lover who is in prison and sees his lady every day is happier or unhappier than one who is at liberty himself but can never see her. These are the kind of conversational gambits which Andreas Capellanus's treatise existed to promote. Looked at from this point of view Chaucer's romances are additions to the case-book of love, the Book of Problems for Lovers. *The Franklin's Tale* raises a problem at the end. Dorigen, persuaded by her husband, is ready to keep her promise to become Aurelius's lover if he removed all the dangerous rocks from the coast of Britanny; Aurelius, overcome by this supreme sacrifice, refuses to take advantage of it; the magician ('clerk') who engineered the removal is in his turn equally moved and

---

sooth truth   *Looke who* . . . observe the man who is most forbearing in love—he is the one who reaps the greatest advantages [i.e. is in a superior position].

releases Aurelius from his bond of payment. Which of them, the Franklin, asks, acted with the greatest generosity of spirit?

> Lordynges, this question, thanne, wol I aske now,
> Which was the mooste *fre*, as thynketh yow?   (1621-2)

The problem is thrown open for the company to solve; and its especial fascination is that it is insoluble. In this case the question is nearer the imaginative centre of the tale than it is in the other cases. The adjective *free*, *fre* (connected with *frank*, *liber-al*, *generosus*, etc.) has for noun, *fredom*, *fraunchise*.[11] It is an aspect of *gentilesse* (and, incidentally, one of the arrows shot at the Lover by Cupid in the *Roman de la Rose*) —an openheartedness, a total lack of self-seeking, a generosity of the spirit; *The Franklin's Tale* shows how this desirable quality, both civilized and Christian, can be released in the world.

The catalyst, if that is the word, in *The Franklin's Tale* is not love but *trouthe*. 'Trouthe' is a keyword of the tale and means at least four things. (To tabulate them is to seem to propound easy distinctions that Chaucer is careful to avoid.) The first three meanings, which shade into one another are:

(1) *trouthe* as a 'troth', a pledged word, the promise that you give another person;

(2) *trouthe* as integrity, the truth to your own inmost self;

(3) *trouthe* as loyalty, the bond of dependence that keeps society stable and united.

The first three of these are developed in Arveragus's exhortation to his wife, Dorigen, when she has confessed her stupid plight to him. The centre of meaning shifts from 'pledge' through 'integrity' until in the last line it means something wider still. Arveragus is now thinking in the most general terms: our truth to ourselves and to one another is the supreme claim upon us:

> 'Ye, wyf,' quod he, 'lat slepen that is stille;
> It may be wel, paraventure, yet today.
> Ye shul youre *trouthe* holden, by my fay!
> For God so wisly have mercy upon me,
> I hadde wel levere ystiked for to be

---

lat slepen that is stille do not be unnecessarily disturbed   *wisly* surely [i.e. as surely as I hope for salvation]   *I hadde wel levere* . . . I'd rather be run through the body for the true love I bear you than have you fail to keep . . .

> For verray love which that I to yow have,
> But if ye sholde your *trouthe* kepe and save.
> *Trouthe* is the hyeste thyng that man may kepe.'   (1472–9)

Behind these shifting connotations lies, finally, a much deeper concept. In Chaucer, 'trouthe' is a philosophical and religious term for the ultimate reality, the 'universal'. It is this final, transcendental Truth which gives the lesser 'truths' (of human fidelity and integrity) their validity. 'Almyghty God, of trouthe sovereyn,' asks a character in *Anelida and Arcite*, 'where is the trouthe of man?' Just as the 'harmony of the spheres' is the Ideal Music which earthly music dimly shadows, so God's Truth is the ideal for all sublunary relationships, not only human but physical as well. Truth is the universal principle by which the Universe is governed. It is, if you like, *God's* integrity, His wholeness, the stable faith which He alone can sustain. 'Stable faith' (*stabilis fides*) is the term Boethius uses in the great work which meant so much to Chaucer and his contemporaries, the *De Consolatione Philosophiae*. 'By "stable faith" the stars, the seasons, the ocean, and the land are controlled in harmony, and it is by precisely the same faith that human relations . . . should be controlled. . . . A lack of ["trouthe"] means becoming separated from the control of God, from the harmony of the divine system. . . .'[12] This 'trouthe' in another aspect is Love— the 'holy bond of things' to which Troilus sings a fine hymn in *Troilus and Criseyde*:

> Love, that of erthe and se hath governaunce,
> Love, that his hestes hath in hevenes hye,
> Love, that with an holsom alliaunce
> Halt peples joyned, as hym lest hem gye,
> Love, that knetteth lawe of compaignie,
> And couples doth in vertu for to dwelle,
> Bynd this acord, that I have told and telle.   (iii.1744–50)

This transcendental 'trouthe' has, finally, its explicitly Christian aspect too: in Christ's words, 'And ye shall know the truth and the truth shall make you free' (John viii, 32). And it is this which Chaucer refers to, obliquely, in the refrain of his most moving short poem, *Truth (Balade de Bon Conseyl)*. There is no final rest or peace in this sublunary world; we must look upwards to our true home, in heaven:

---

his hestes hath holds sway   *Halt* holds   *as hym lest hem gye* according as it pleases him to direct them   *doth . . . for to* enables to   *Bynd* i.e. let love bind

C

Hold the heye wey, and lat thy gost thee lede
And trouthe thee shal delivere, it is no drede. (20-1)

It may seem that I have digressed some way from *The Franklin's
Tale* itself, and that in trying to establish the depth of meaning and
association lying behind the climactic line, 'Trouthe is the hyeste
thyng that man may kepe', I have forgotten its dramatic setting.
The Franklin's Tale may seem, indeed, somewhat too light a structure
to need such a deep foundation. The tale is not, after all, an epic
romance like *Troilus*, nor a 'Divine Comedy', nor a Boethian tragedy;
it is a *lai*. And the qualities of the *lai* as a genre are delicate and delightful absurdity, hyperbole of pathos and sentiment, refinement rather
than power. I must, then, emphasize carefully that *The Franklin's Tale*
is not a deep philosophical poem about the ultimate realities. It is primarily what I have called 'social romance'. That is, it exists not to
describe private and individual experiences but to idealize the qualities
of *gentilesse* and *franchyse*. Chaucer seems to be trying (appropriately
through the unaristocratic Franklin) to extend the interest and relevance
of the courtly experiences which centre on love. He wants to see, if
you like, to what degree 'good breeding' and 'goodness' must overlap,
and what they both must rest on. The stable, mutual relationship
of Arveragus and Dorigen is an exemplar of *trouthe*; and it is *trouthe*
(fidelity and integrity) which is the necessary foundation for 'gentil'
behaviour, first in Dorigen, then in Arveragus and then in the magician.
To sum up, one may find genuinely in *The Franklin's Tale* what
Criseyde said she found and loved in Troilus:

'moral vertu, grounded upon trouthe' (iv.1672)

It is 'trouthe' that is the nurse of all virtues, of 'gentilesse', 'fraunchise'
and 'curtesye'.

Chaucer wrote a third 'social romance', *The Knight's Tale*. It is
even more different from *The Franklin's Tale* and *The Wife of Bath's
Tale* than they are from one other. It is, to generalize, less ethical,
more philosophical; it exists not so much to demonstrate the qualities
of a 'verray, parfit, gentil knyght' as to solemnize and celebrate the
courtly way of life in its ideal totality. Palamon and Arcite, the two
young heroes of the tale, who honour respectively the goddess Venus
and the god Mars, are not characterized as an individual lover and an
individual fighter; nor are they exemplars, precisely, of Love and

---

heye high   *gost* spirit   *drede* doubt

of Valour, since they are almost as alike as two peas. Yet it could be said that their different allegiances if not their behaviour symbolize these two complementary sides of the noble life, loving and fighting. Emilye, the heroine, 'fressher than the May with floures newe', is the Beauty who inspires the rival knights and is their proposed reward. Duke Theseus, 'lord and governour' of Athens, not only directs the action of the tale and philosophizes in a noble final speech about its meaning but also himself exemplifies a side of knightliness which does not loom large in medieval romance—he is a good ruler. (The 'education of a prince' in the exercise of wise government will become one of the obsessive themes of the courtly literature of the Renaissance, as we can see from Sidney's Arcadia. In medieval romance we find more interest in 'gentilesse' than in kingship.)[13]

Professor Muscatine, in a masterly study of The Knight's Tale, has written that it is concerned with

the general tenor of the noble life, the pomp and ceremony, the dignity and power, and particularly the repose and assurance with which the exponent of nobility [Theseus] invokes order.[14]

Theseus must be seen as the central figure—he certainly dominates the beginning and the ending of the tale—with Palamon and Arcite as lesser, contributory figures. They 'provide the questions and the elements of variety . . . it is Theseus who expounds the resolutions'. Perhaps the most important contribution that Professor Muscatine has made to the understanding of the tale is to have observed the deep imaginative connection between the 'order' of idealized courtly life and the 'turbulence' beneath its surface and all around it.

Order, which characterizes the structure of the poem, is also the heart of its meaning. The society depicted is one in which form is full of significance, in which life is conducted at a dignified processional pace, and in which life's pattern is itself a reflection, or better, a reproduction of the order of the universe. And what gives this conception of life its perspective, its depth and its serious-ness, is its constant awareness of a formidably antagonistic element—chaos, disorder—which in life is an ever-threatening possibility, even in moments of the supremest assuredness, and which in the poem falls across the pattern of order, being clearly exemplified in the erratic reversals of the poem's plot, and deeply embedded in the poem's texture.[15]

Nowhere are the powers of darkness and disruption more in evidence than in the speech which Saturn makes, paradoxically enough, to

bring peace between Venus and Mars, who are quarrelling about the
outcome of the battle between Palamon and Arcite:

> 'My deere doghter Venus', quod Saturne,
> 'My cours, that hath so wyde for to turne,
> Hath moore power than woot any man.
> Myn is the drenchyng in the see so wan;
> Myn is the prison in the derke cote;
> Myn is the stranglyng and hangyng by the throte,
> The murmure and the cherles rebellyng,
> The groynyng and the pryvee empoysonyng;
> I do vengeance and pleyn correccioun,
> Whil I dwelle in the signe of the leoun. (2453–62)

Our first and last impression here is of formal, patterned utterance
striving with and just controlling a turbulent undercurrent of chaos
and destruction. The antagonism between order and disorder is in
the poetry itself. On the one hand, we have the formal repetition
(2456–8) of 'Myn . . ., Myn . . ., Myn . . .'; on the other, the dark,
cold and menacing images thrust upon us by rhythmic insistence—the
drowning in a lead-coloured, grey sea, the darkness of the madman's
cell, the violence of death by poison or treason.

The assertions of order, hierarchy, ceremony, on the other hand,
culminate in the speech of Theseus at the end of the tale, which I
have already mentioned. Arcite, having won the battle for Emelye
against Palamon, has died some years back from injuries received as
he fell with his charger at the moment of victory, and he has been
buried with all pomp and ceremony. The speech opens with a fine
praise of God, the Prime Mover, which Chaucer has taken not from his
narrative source, Boccaccio, but from Boethius:

> 'The Firste Moevere of the cause above,
> Whan he first made the faire cheyne of love,
> Greet was th'effect, and heigh was his entente.
> Wel wiste he why, and what thereof he mente;
> For with that faire cheyne of love he bond
> The fyr, the eyr, the water, and the lond
> In certeyn boundes, that they may nat flee. (2987–93)

---

cours . . . orbit that is so wide   Myn i.e. all these belong to me   drenchyng
drowning   prison imprisonment   cote dungeon   groynyng complaining
do vengeance . . . undertake vengeance and complete punishment   signe of
the leoun astrological 'house' of the Lion

This impressive use of Boethius, reminiscent of equally fine moments in *Troilus*, could mislead one into seeing, wrongly, strong similarities between the two poems. In *Troilus* Chaucer quotes Boethius both in order to 'magnify' the love of Troilus and Criseyde, by identifying it with 'benigne Love', the 'holy bond of thynges' (iii.1261), and also eventually to frame it, as it were, and denote the deeper reality of God's providence which alone holds the key to the mystery of pain and lost happiness. In *Troilus* the divine order is ultimately set over and against human love even at its highest. In *The Knight's Tale* the emphasis is different; the tale asserts, 'The nobleness of life is to do thus. . . '. Theseus's oration, by going on to discourse at length and weightily about our life in time in the setting of God's stable and eternal perfection, does not diminish but enhance the value of this life properly lived and properly laid down:

'That same Prince and that Moevere,' quod he,
'Hath stablissed in this wrecched world adoun
Certeyne dayes and duracioun
To al that is engendred in this place,
Over the whiche day they may nat pace,
Al mowe they yet tho dayes wel abregge.
Ther nedeth noght noon auctoritee t'allegge,
For it is preeved by experience,
But that me list declaren my sentence.
Thanne may men by this ordre wel discerne
That thilke Moevere stable is and eterne . . .
   Considereth eek how that the harde stoon
Under oure feet, on which we trede and goon,
Yet wasteth it as it lyth by the weye.
The brode ryver somtyme wexeth dreye;
The grete tounes se we wane and wende.
Thanne may ye se that al this thyng hath ende.
   Of man and womman seen we wel also
That nedes, in oon of thise termes two,
This is to seyn, in youthe or elles age,
He moot be deed, the kyng as shal a page;
Som in his bed, som in the depe see,
Som in the large feeld as men may see;

Prince, Moevere i.e. God *pace* pass *Al mowe they* . . . although they can shorten the days [of their life] *Ther nedeth* . . . it is not necessary to adduce authority . . . *preeved* demonstrated *sentence* meaning *wane and wende* decay and disappear *nedes* of necessity *termes* periods [of life] *som . . . som* one . . . another

Ther helpeth noght, al goth that ilke weye.
Thanne may I seyn that al this thyng moot deye.
   What maketh this but Juppiter, the kyng,
That is prince and cause of alle thyng,
Convertynge al unto his propre welle
From which it is dirryved, sooth to telle?
And heer-agayns no creature on lyve,
Of no degree, availleth for to stryve.   (2994-3040)

It would not be misleading to say that in the last analysis *The Knight's Tale* is, like *Troilus*, about 'Mutabilitie', 'lak of stedfastnes' in this world. But—and here lies the great difference between it and *Troilus*—the Knight does not urge us, even at the end, to forsake this world, whereas in the epilogue to *Troilus* we find this exhortation:

Repeyreth hom fro worldly vanyte
And of youre herte upcasteth the visage
To thilke God that after his ymage
Yow made   (v.1837-40)

All Theseus says is: this life is mortal, it may be short; it behoves us therefore to live and die in it nobly—'He moot be deed, the kyng as shal a page.'

Thanne is it wysdom, as it thynketh me,
To maken vertu of necessitee
And take it weel that we may nat eschue.   (3041-3)

The fact of death is nothing, for death comes to all. What matters is to die with honour:

Why grucchen we, why have we hevynesse,
That good Arcite, of chivalrie the flour,
Departed is with duetee and honour
Out of this foule prisoun of this lyf?   (3058-61)

The Knight's Tale finally transcends 'social romance' and celebrates in tones unusually solemn and sombre the essential dignity of man. But to produce such a man a whole society and a whole constellation of qualities were required:

Ther helpeth . . . there is no help for it   *ilke* same   *alle thyng* all things
Convertynge al . . . turning everything back to its own source   *on lyve* alive
degree station in life   *Repeyreth* return   *hom* home [i.e. to spiritual things]
upcasteth . . . turn the face of your heart up to God   *thynketh* seems   *eschue*
eschew   *grucchen* complain

That is to seyen, trouthe, honour, knyghthede,
Wysdom, humblesse, estaat, and heigh kynrede,
Fredom, and al that longeth to that art.   (2789-91)

---

estaat rank   *Fredom* generosity of mind (see p. 64)

1. C. S. Lewis, 'The English Prose *Morte*' in *Essays on Malory*, Ed. J. A. W. Bennett (1963), p. 9.

2. 'Pitee': the word is associated with religious feeling through Latin *pietas* and Old French *pitié*, *pieté*, on the one hand, and with courtly manners (it is coupled with 'debonairtee', 'gentilesse' and 'womanly benignitee') on the other.

3. These paragraphs (pp. 51-2) are quoted from my *Music and Poetry in the Early Tudor Court*, pp. 155-6, by kind permission of Methuen and Co.

4. i.e. the primeval Paradise, the Garden of Eden, as depicted, for instance, in the Anglo-Norman *Play of Adam* (twelfth century).

5. It is a striking fact in itself that the allegory for a private experience of love is a courtly, social, festive scene. In the *Roman de la Rose* the dance and the dancers symbolize different facets of the Dreamer's mental state; but at the same time they give it a wider, more-than-personal meaning. The paragraph is from my *Music and Poetry*, pp. 168-9.

6. Guillaume IX, the first of the troubadours, says one of his songs will be *totz mesclatz d'amor e de joy e de joven* ('mixed of love and joy and youthfulness').

7. See *Erec*, 6850-1, describing the Coronation Mass for Erec and Enid: 'no lowborn fellow (*vilains*) was allowed in, only lords and ladies'.

8. We find the same kind of ironical relationship between tale and teller in, for example, the case of the Merchant. He thinks he is telling a story to demonstrate the fickleness of young wives; its deeper meaning reflects on the blindness, physical and moral, of an old man. To limit the truth of the tale to what the teller could consciously have meant by it would be quite stultifying.

9. The relevant passage in Boethius is in Book III, prosa 6. Part of Chaucer's translation runs: 'For which thing it folweth that yif thou ne have no gentilesse of thiself (that is to seyn, prys that cometh of thy desert), foreyn gentilesse ne maketh the nat gentil.' Chaucer also developed the theme in a short poem, or 'moral balade', entitled *Gentilesse*.

10. See Chapter 9, 'Realism and Romance: Discourse of Love', *passim*.

11. See C. S. Lewis, *Studies in Words*, ch. 5.

12. B. L. Jefferson, *Chaucer and the Consolation of Philosophy of Boethius* (1917).

13. See, however, the discussion of the alliterative *Morte Arthure*, pp. 91-4.

14. Muscatine, p. 181.

15. ibid.

4

MAN AND SUPERMAN:

THE ROMANCE OF THE SELF

Chrétien de Troyes's *Yvain* is the only one of his poems which was translated into Middle English. In its original form (not in the bowdlerized, shorter English version) it is the most complex in interest and baffling in tone, I think, of all.

It tells the story of how Yvain won the love of a lady called Laudine after having killed her husband, the Knight of the Fountain, only a few weeks before. Almost immediately after his marriage to Laudine, Yvain is persuaded by Gawain to return with him to Arthur's court to lead a life of manly adventures in order to keep up his reputation for prowess. Laudine gives him a year's leave of absence; but Yvain overstays it for a further full year, so absorbed is he in feats of arms. One day a maiden appears from his mistress, who returns his ring, declares his utter worthlessness and renounces their marriage. Yvain is struck dumb. Mad with remorse and self-loathing, he retreats from the world into a forest where he lives like a wild beast until his discovery by a lady and her damsels leads to a long process of healing and regeneration.

At an early stage in his recovery Yvain hears as he travels *un cri mout dolereus et haut*; it is a lion whom a serpent holds by the tail:

> ... et si li ardoit
> Trestoz les rains de flame ardant. (3350-1)

(and was burning all his loins with scorching fire.)

Yvain wonders which side to take in this combat; he chooses the lion's because one should not help a *felon*:

> Qu'a venimeus et a felon
> Ne doit an feire se mal non.
> Et li serpanz est venimeus,
> Si li saut par la boche feus,
> Tant est de felenie plains. (3357-61)

(for a poisonous, wicked creature asks only to have evil done to him. And the serpent is poisonous, and fire flicks out of his mouth, so full he is of wickedness.)

The terms used (*venimeus, felon*) have already put an allegorical colouring on the encounter. Without consulting our bestiaries we know that Yvain is faced with a moral choice which is also a courtly one. He chooses the noble beast (*jantil et franche*) and the beast responds nobly:

> Oëz, que fist li lions donques!
> Con fist que frans et de bon' eire
> Que il li comança a feire
> Sanblant, que a lui se randoit,
> Et ses piez joinz li estandoit
> Et vers terre ancline sa chiere,
> S'estut sor les deus piez deriere;
> Et puis si se ragenoilloit
> Et tote sa face moilloit
> De lermes par humilité.
> Mes sire Yvains par verité
> Set, que li lions l'an mercie
> Et que devant lui s'umelie
> Por le serpant, qu'il avoit mort,
> Et lui delivré de la mort
> Si li plest mout ceste avanture. (3392-407)

(Just hear now what the lion did! He acted nobly and as one well-bred; for he began to make it evident that he yielded himself to him, by standing upon his two hind-feet and bowing his face to the earth, with his fore-feet joined and stretched out toward him. Then he fell on his knees again, and all his face was wet with the tears of humility. My lord Yvain knows for a truth that the lion is thanking him and doing him homage because of the serpent which he had killed, thereby delivering him from death. He was greatly pleased by this *avanture*.)[1]

Beneath the comedy of this mock-feudal scene, in itself a parody of the way a vassal would with joined hands render homage to his lord, there are hints of something more serious. Yvain has made a moral choice *for himself*; he significantly wipes the venom of the serpent off his sword. From this moment onward he never looks back. The lion walks close to his side:

> Que ja mes ne s'an partira,
> Tos jorz mes avuec li ira;
> Que servir et garder le viaut.   (3413–15)

([The lion] will never part from him but will go along with him the whole time ready to serve and protect him.)

One of the most delightful, absurd and yet moving episodes in the poem occurs quite early in Yvain's acquaintance with this lion. They have been wandering, 'questing', for a fortnight when suddenly they find themselves at the Fountain (3490); it vividly recalls Yvain's lost love. He swoons; and, as he swoons, his sword falling from the scabbard pierces his chainmail at the neck:

> Li lions cuide mort veoir
> Son conpaignon et son seignor.
> Ains de rien nule duel greignor
> N'oïstes conter ne retreire,
> Come il an comança a feire!
> Il se detort et grate et crie
> Et s'a talant, que il s'ocie
> De l'espee, don li est vis,
> Qu'ele et son buen seignor ocis.
> A ses danz l'espee li oste
> Et sor un fust gisant l'acoste
> Et deriere a un tronc l'apuie,
> Qu'ele ne ganchisse ne fuie,
> Quant il i hurtera del piz.   (3506–19)

(Then the lion thinks that he sees his master and companion dead. You never heard greater grief narrated or told about anything than he now began to show. He casts himself about, and scratches and cries, and has the wish to kill himself with the sword with which he thinks his master has killed himself. Taking the sword from ⟨his master⟩ with his teeth he lays it on a fallen tree, and steadies it on a trunk behind, so that it will not slip or give way, when he hurls his breast against it.)[2]

It is only Yvain's sudden recovery from his faint that prevents this, perhaps unique, attempt at animal suicide from being successful.

We must pass over the extraordinary sophistication of this scene, with its elegant blend of the heroic and the mock-heroic, its core of significance behind the slight, comic grace. One point only needs to be made. The lion, who remains with Yvain to the end and helps him out of many difficulties, is not, as one might think, Yvain's vital powers, his brute strength, but rather the opposite. The lion is Yvain's lost 'trouthe', his loyalty; and their inseparable companionship, their identity in battle, seems to symbolize in Yvain after his madness (a truly and pitifully animal condition) the reintegration of the powers of man. The lion is his lost self, his 'lion' heart.

The slightly catchpenny title I have given this chapter, 'Man and Superman', could well be replaced by the title 'Man and Himself', because the Superman is that Ideal Self which Man aspires to be and which he feels he is always liable to betray.

> To thine own self be true,
> Thou canst not then be false to any man.

Polonius's wise advice, wiser than himself, could serve as an epigraph for romantic heroism, and serve also to distinguish it from epic heroism.

It is not easy to define the quality at issue. The word 'heroism' slightly narrows and colours it. It is not, in romance, simply a question of valour, of the courage which shows its true quality on the battlefield —though this can be a great part of it. It is integrity in a wider sense, or (to use the medieval word) 'trouthe', loyalty to the Ideal Self (see p. 64 above). In keeping with the whole trend of romance-writing, this 'trouthe' is seen in the final instance to be an inward *personal* quality, individual only in the sense of belonging to Man Alone, single and solitary. The narrator of Conrad's *Lord Jim* uses two words to describe the quality of Jim; he stresses the power of his *truthfulness* and his *loneliness* of soul:

From the moment the sheer *truthfulness* of his last three years of life carries the day against the ignorance, the fear, and the anger of men, he appears no longer to me as I saw him last—a white speck catching all the dim light left upon a sombre coast and the darkened sea—but greater and more pitiful in the *loneliness* of his soul.[3]

The end of *Sir Gawain and the Green Knight* demonstrates in softer tones the loneliness of the hero. Just as Gawain had been physically alone in the time of his greatest afflictions, the wintry journey to Bertilak's castle and the encounter at 'the devil's chapel', so at the end of the poem he is mentally alone with his shame:

> The nirt in the nek he naked hem schewed
> That he laght for his unleuté at the leudes hondes
>   for blame.
> He tened when he schulde telle;
> He groned for gref and grame.
> The blod in his face con melle,
> When he hit schulde schewe, for shame.   (2498-504)

Gawain tells the court:

> This is the lathe and the losse that I laght have
> Of couardise and covetyse, that I haf caght thare;
> This is the token of untrawthe that I am tan inne
> And I mot nedez hit were wyle I may last.   (2507-10)

The whole court then decide that they will each of them wear a green
'bauderyk', not as a mark of sharing the shame he feels but, it appears,
to record their very proper pride and delight at Gawain's safe return.
The narrator makes no comment. The lines are:

> The kyng comfortes the knyght, and alle the court als
> Laghen loude therat, and luflyly acorden
> That lordes and ladis that longed to the Table,
> Uche burne of the brotherhede, a bauderyk schulde have . . .
> . . . for sake of that segge, in suete to were.   (2513-18)

Even though truly courtly 'lordes and ladis' could hardly do otherwise
than reassure him, Gawain seems to be as alone at this moment as he
has ever been.

It is paradoxical that the hero of romance, the individualist, survives
and returns to the community he belongs to, while the epic hero,
much less of an individualist, characteristically dies. But even when
the epic hero is alone, the last fighter on the field, we feel the solidity
of the community behind him. The death of Roland, in the Norman
chanson de geste, the early twelfth-century epic that bears his name,
Le Chanson de Roland, is of this kind.[4] Roland, the sole survivor of
a bloody affray against a huge pagan army, is dying on the battlefield.
He is undefeated, since no one is great enough to overcome him;
and his death is due to his having burst a blood-vessel whilst blowing

---

nirt cut   *That he laght* . . . 'which he received at the knight's hands as a
reproach for his faithlessness' (Waldron)   *tened* sorrowed   *grame* vexation
con melle mingled [i.e. he blushed]   *lathe* hurt   *untrawthe* . . . disloyalty in
which I have been discovered   *were* wear   *last* live   *als* also   *luflyly* . . .
courteously agree   *burne* knight   *segge* knight   *in suete* to match his

his great horn to summon Charlemagne's army. Everything he does is designed to protect his reputation, his honour (i.e. what his king and his countrymen will think of him), not simply for his own sake but because his honour is one of their greatest possessions. The death of Roland could never be a private matter.

Roland's great problem is the disposal of his sword, and his *olifans*, the horn. The sword symbolizes to him the great conquests he has made on Charlemagne's behalf, not in random *aventures* such as a knight might have but in systematic conquest of the known world. He makes three attempts to shatter Durendal, this heroic sword:

> .x. colps i fiert par doel e par rancune.
> Cruist li acers, ne freint ne n'esgruignet.   (2301-2)

(Ten blows he strikes in misery and rage. The steel grates on the rock but neither breaks nor notches.)

The formula of 2302 is repeated three times to emphasize its solemn significance. For the sword, like Roland, is indomitable, indestructible. Each time he fails to break it, he bursts out into an eloquent lament:

> E! Durendal, cum es bele e clere e blanche!
> Cuntre soleill si luises e reflambes!   (2316-17)

(Oh Durendal! How beautiful, bright and white you are!
You shine so, and flame in the sunlight!)

He cannot bear the thought of its falling into pagan hands. In a last series of symbolic gestures, he has already advanced as far into Spain as he can; now he 'turns his face towards the pagan people' (2360), lying face down on the ground with his sword and *olifans* underneath him. The tableau is complete.

The contrast between the heroism of romance and epic heroism must not be exaggerated. There is an important sense in which Gawain also is being true to a communally held ideal; and in which Roland is true to himself. The difference is one of emphasis; it is not absolute. But it is significant of this difference in emphasis that Gawain can transcend his community and the shared values; Roland has only to exemplify them. The epic poet's view could be summed up by reversing Polonius's wise saw:

> To thine own *lord* [and to thine own friends, comrades-in-arms] be true,
> Thou canst not then be false to thine own *self*.

This brief attempt to define the difference in emphasis has brought
to light, we may notice, another aspect of romantic heroism. It is a
search, a search for the true self. The hero of an epic, it seems, can
never be at a loss to understand what is happening to him. He lives
and fights in a known land against declared enemies; he has learnt
his lesson and all he needs to do is to demonstrate it at the expected
crisis in the expected way. In the late Anglo-Saxon epic fragment,
The Battle of Maldon, there are no surprises. The small band of Saxons
will fight to the last against the invading Danes. Each warrior will
make a proud speech of resounding will and purpose and die beside his
lord; no one will shame himself and his lord by surviving to fight
another day.

> Raðe weard æt hilde   Offa forhēawen;
> hē hæfde ðeah geforþod   þæt hē his frēan gehēt,
> swā he bēotode ǣr   wið his bēahgifan,
> þæt hī sceoldon bēgen   on burh rīdan
> hāle to hāme,   oððe on here cringan,
> on wælstōwe   wundum sweltan;
> hē læg ðegenlīce   ðēodne gehende . . .
> Byrhtwold maþelode,   bord hafenode,
> sē wæs eald genēat,   æsc ācwehte,
> hē ful baldlīce   beornas lǣrde:
> 'Hige sceal þē heardra,   heorte þē cēnre,
> mōd sceal þē mare,   þē ūre mægen lȳtlað   (288–94, 309–13)

> (Quickly in battle   was Offa cut down.
> But he had performed   what he promised his lord,
> When he made his boast   to his bracelet-bestower,
> That both unharmed   they would ride to the borough,
> Back to their homes,   or fall in the fight
> And perish of wounds   in the place of slaughter.
> Thane-like he lay   beside his lord . . .
>   Byrhtwold encouraged them,   brandishing buckler,
> Aged companion   shaking ash-spear;
> Stout were the words   he spoke to his men:
>   'Heart must be braver,   courage the bolder,
> Mood the stouter   as our strength grows less!')[5]

The hero of an epic, then, knows the odds he is up against and
has often calculated them arithmetically; his is a desperate, doomed
enterprise. Roland and Oliver and the twelve peers in the *Chanson*

de Roland, Count Vivien in the *Chançun de Willame,* and others—they know their fate.

But the romance-hero is like a man fighting ghosts in a mist. He is ignorant of the nature of the enemy. Yvain, for instance, arrives at the *Chastel de Pesme Aventure.*[6] He is very discourteously received by the people around it; and when he asks why, they say (in the English version) 'Thou schal wit or to-morn at none'. In Chrétien's version a maiden explains that they do not mean to be rude, but they dare not be hospitable. They only want to frighten him away for his own good. She warns him that if he goes on he will never return alive:

> 'Dame!' fet il, 'Des le vos mire!
> Mes mes fos cuers leanz me tire
> Si ferai ce, que mes cuers viaut.' (5175–7)

('Lady', he says, 'God reward you for this! But my foolish heart draws me on [*literally,* within (the castle)]; and I shall do what my heart tells me to do.')

'My foolish heart draws me within . . .'. This looks, superficially, like the 'foolishness' that drives Roland into his last battle: his friend Oliver, reproaching him for not blowing his great horn to summon Charlemagne before it was too late, says

> Kar vasselage par sens nen est folie;
> Mielz valt mesure que ne fait estultie. (1724–5)

(Valour tempered with good sense is no madness;
Prudent moderation is worth more than foolhardiness.)

But there is a difference. Oliver reproves Roland for not understanding and not acting according to a prudent conception of *vasselage,* i.e. virtues inspired by the relationship between the vassal and his lord. And Roland has previously justified his decision by saying that he does not intend to bring shame on himself (1054), on his kindred (1076) and on France (1064). The *mes fos cuers* of Yvain is a much more personal affair, as the very word *cuers* suggests—'my inward being', he says, 'draws me on'.

On to what? He does not know. The next thing that he sees is a lawn enclosed with a palisade (I quote the slightly abbreviated English version):

> And many maidens thare he sese
> Wirkand silk and gold-wire;

Bot thai war al in pover atire.
Thaire clothes war reven on evil arai;
Ful tenderly al weped thai.
Thaire face war lene and als unclene
And blak smokkes had thai on bidene.   (2966–72)

When he tries to get out, the gate is locked. And the porter will not tell him what it all means. Eventually, to cut a long story short, he finds himself having to fight, not human foes, but two fiends, sons of the devil.

The heroism of romance is often and characteristically of this searching pattern: the hero is involved in a mystery; he is on a quest but does not know what he has to look for; he is engaged in a struggle but does not know who his adversary is. Where epic is static, romance is dynamic. In epic, the world around closes in, inexorably, predictably, on the hero, whereas in romance the hero goes to search for the final meaningful encounter that will crown his quest and, one often feels, enable him *to know himself*. This is why, in romance, the hero can be at a loss, can make mistakes and not understand what is happening to him. In epic this is almost impossible. An epic hero does not know the meaning of the word 'dilemma'; life presents him with no problems, intellectual or spiritual, only with struggles. He has simply to screw his courage to the sticking-place. But Perceval, for example, in Chrétien's Grail romance, is always failing and always learning. The typical crisis of epic is a battle; of romance, an *aventure* which may or may not result in actual combat. *Aventure* (literally an 'event') could perhaps be glossed as 'meaningful encounter'. At least, this is what it is in Chrétien: Calogrenant's encounter with the Giant Herdsman; Lancelot's encounter with the dwarf and the felon's cart; Erec's encounter with the knight of the Enchanted Garden; Perceval's encounter with the *graal* in the Castle of the Fisher King. Only one of these *aventures* culminates in armed combat; but they all have meaning—for the hero, and for us—even if the meaning is not fully explicit. These romances ask the question—What is Man? What is Man Alone?—and try to give an answer.

On the lowest level of the imagination, the answer to this question is: Man is a Champion. Man is just like you and me—but stronger. In English romance—to descend from the sublime to the ridiculous—the fantasy of the rippling biceps is common. *Beves of Hamtoun*,

---

reven . . . arai torn and tattered   *bidene* one and all

for instance, is a folk-saga. The story has been described as 'a heady brew of outrageous incident . . . culminating in a single-handed pitched battle [by Beves] against the massed citizenry in the streets of London'.[7] In this battle some 32,000 Londoners are slain by Beves, with the help of two heroic sons, Guy and Miles, and his equally heroic horse, Arondel. The following passage gives a fair idea of the ethos of the work. The king's false steward, who has just incensed the London populace against Beves, comes face to face with him:

> Ayilt the, treitour, thow foule thef!
> Thow havest the kinges sone islawe,
> Thow schelt ben hanged and to-drawe!'
>   Beves seide: 'Be sein Jon,
> Treitour was Y never non:
> That I schel kethe hastely,
> Er than Ich wende, sikerly!'
> A spere Beves let to him glide
> And smot him under the right side;
> Thourgh is bodi wente the dent,
> Ded a fel on the paviment.
> A sede anon after that dint:
> 'Treitour! now is the lif itint:
> Thus men schel teche file glotouns,
> That wile misaie gode barouns!'
> The folk com with grete route,
> Besette Beves al aboute;
> Beves and is sex knightes
> Defendede hem with al her mightes,
> So that in a lite stounde
> Five hondred thai broughte te gronde. (4374–94)

Beves's fantastic muscle-power is sustained, it should be added, by a simple piety—

> To Jesu he made his praiere
> And to Marie, is moder dere— (4415–16)

and this, too, is part of the meaning of the tale.

A shorter popular romance, in which the biceps ripples more

Ayilt surrender   *to-drawe* pulled apart   *kethe* show   *Er than* . . . before I leave here   *let* . . . *glide* aimed at him   *itint* destroyed   *file glotouns* foul villains   *misaie* slander   *is sex* his six   *hem* themselves   *her* their   *lite stounde* short while

credibly and which also carries a simple moral colouring along with it, is *The Tale of Gamelyn*.[8]

> Litheth, and lestneth · and herkeneth aright
> And ye schulle heere a talkyng · of a doughty knight.
> Sire Johan of Boundys · was his right name,
> He cowde of norture ynough · and mochil of game.

This opening, which establishes it as a story for oral delivery (i.e. as a minstrel's romance), is typical of its style; it uses a long line, only lightly and occasionally alliterative, with a break in the middle and couplet rhyme.

Gamelyn is the youngest of three brothers, and has been done out of his share of the inheritance by the eldest, John. Gamelyn, incensed, beats the servants who are sent to beat him. John shuts himself up in a loft and won't come out until Gamelyn has put his 'pestle' away. Gamelyn does so and they make peace. Gamelyn goes off to a wrestling match. When he comes home he finds the gate locked. The porter refuses to let him in:

> Now litheth and lestneth · bothe yong and olde,
> And ye schul heere gamen · of Gamelyn the bolde.
> Gamelyn com therto · for to have comen in,
> And than was it ischet · faste with a pyn;
> Than seyd Gamelyn · 'Porter, undo the yate
> For many good mannes sone · stondeth therate.'
> Than answerd the porter · and swor by Goddes berd,
> 'Thow ne schalt, Gamelyn · come into this yerde.'
> 'Thow lixt,' sayde Gamelyn · 'so browke I my chin!'
> He smote the wyket with his foot · and brak awey the pyn.
> The porter seyh tho · it might no better be,
> He sette foote on erthe · he bigan to flee.
> 'By my faith,' sayde Gamelyn · 'that travail is ilore,
> For I am of foot as light as thou · though thou haddest swore.'
> Gamelyn overtook the porter · and his teene wrak
> And gert him in the nekke · that the bon tobrak,
> And took him by that oon arm · and threw him in a welle,
> Seven fadmen it was deep · as I have herd telle.
> When Gamelyn the yonge · thus hadde pleyd his play,
> Alle that in the yerde were · drewen hem away; . . . (289–308)

Litheth, lestneth listen   *norture* i.e. he was a cultivated man   *game* sport, recreation   *lixt* liest   *so browke* . . . as I hope to enjoy the use of my chin!   *though thou haddest swore* though you had sworn to the contrary   *teene wrak* wreaked his anger [on him]   *gert* struck   *that oon* one of   *fadmen* fathoms   *hem* themselves

Gamelyn then lets in all his friends and they have a great feast for a whole week. His elder brother, John, pretends to make friends again, saying that he'll make Gamelyn his heir. In return, he asks Gamelyn one favour—'When you killed the porter, I swore I'd have you bound hand and foot. Please let me do this, so that I don't break my oath.' Gamelyn, like the poor simple fellow he is, agrees. John makes a good job of it and leaves Gamelyn tied to a post without food for two days. Gamelyn, realizing that something has gone wrong ('Methink I fast too long'!), enlists the help of the faithful steward, Adam Spencer, to free him.

And so it goes on with simple, rumbustious energy—for all the world like a good TV Western. Gamelyn eventually becomes 'King' of a band of outlaws; his Bad Brother becomes the persecuting Sheriff. In the final episode Gamelyn and his gang ride in force to the moot-hall to rescue his Good Brother, Sir Ote, and clean the whole place up.

The Tale of Gamelyn is, simply, an adventure story. It embodies a number of archetypes—Youngest Brother is cheated by Wicked Eldest Brother; Brave Young Hero cleans up Nasty Corrupt Town and overturns Nasty Corrupt 'Establishment'; Simple Honesty triumphs over Serpentine Guile; etc. It has close affinities with the Robin Hood ballads and a general resemblance to all frontier sagas of 'goodies' and 'baddies'. And it doubtless pandered to the recurrent fantasies of medieval listeners as warmly as it does to our own. We can all see ourselves as Gamelyn.

The borderline between fantasy and idealism is neither easy to define nor to recognize. To some extent it must be subjective. Some people's ideals may seem mere fantasies to us, and *vice versa*. It depends how big the gulf is, or looks to be, between the dream and the reality. If the dream is to be champion of Wimbledon and the reality a state of muscular atrophy, then the dream is mere fantasy. In other circumstances of fitness, training and determination, the dream might be a realizable ideal. There are certain works of literature which can only be read with a surrender to fantasy (I use the word for the moment solely in its psychological sense, to denote self-indulgent, because 'unreal', escapist day-dreaming). In this category I should include from our own day the novels of Ian Fleming with their seductive blend of fantasies of power, luxury and sexual satisfaction. But every age appears to need this opiate, even if some are less open about their need than we are. A medieval English romance (more precisely, a *lai*) which seems to take full advantage of its fantasy-hungry audience is *Sir Launfal*. We shall have occasion to return to it later. For the moment it is sufficient to note that the faerie queen, Dame Tryamours, is able to provide the hero with all the 'comforts' I have mentioned—and does so. Other romances, pandering less blatantly than *Gamelyn* to the physical, or *Sir Launfal* to the materialistic, yearnings of their audiences, still manage to combine elements of fantasy with genuine idealisms. Of such a kind is, in my opinion, the *Tristran* of Beroul.

The legend of Tristan and Isolde has acquired, like the legend of Faust, an almost mythic status for Europeans. It inspired, in the twelfth century, one of the finest of all romances—the *Tristan* of Gottfried von Strassburg, adapted by the German poet from the no less courtly version of the story by an Anglo-Norman, Thomas. Thomas 'radically revised and extended', in about 1160, 'older, or an older, versions of the story, in all probability to suit the taste of the Angevin court'.[9] The *Tristran* of the Norman poet, Beroul, survives, fragmentarily, in a single manuscript of the second half of the thirteenth century but seems to derive from one of the older versions; Beroul's poem, too, may have been written for an English audience.

I introduce it into this discussion because, so far from being a great love-story, Beroul's telling of the legend seems to stress other idealisms, idealisms in fact which I see as being more apposite to the condition of Man Alone than to the condition of Man in Love. But we may begin with his fantasies.

If *Gamelyn* gives its audience gratification for their fantasies of physical prowess, physical strength, Beroul's *Tristran* answers warmly our fantasies of mental astuteness. Tristran (and Iseut, too, when need be) is quick-witted, cunning—the kind of man who can argue his way out of any difficulty and wriggle out of any tight spot. The surviving manuscript fragment opens in the middle of a characteristically exciting episode. In the lost beginning of the poem Tristran would already have been to Ireland to fetch Iseut, Mark's bride-to-be; and on the voyage home they would have drunk the fatal potion (the *vin herbez*, the *lovendrins*) which binds them in love—not for ever, in this version of the story, but for three years. Tristran has been forbidden the *chanbre* of the king (104)—i.e. exiled from the royal presence—and has had his armour taken as a pledge for his good conduct (204). Nevertheless the lovers have an assignment to meet in the orchard one night. Mark has been warned of it and on the advice of the dwarf, Frocin, is hiding in a tree overhead. Luckily for them, Iseut sees Mark's shadow in the moonlight and is on her guard.

Instead of welcoming her lover as expected, she reproaches him bitterly:

> 'Sire Tristran, por Deu le roi,
> Si grant pechié avez de moi,
> Qui me mandez a itel ore!'
> Or fait senblant con s'ele plore.   (5–8)

('Tristran, in God's name, you've done very wrong in sending for me at a time like this!' And now she pretends to weep.)

By the end of her speech Tristran realizes that she is playing a part and acts up to it himself.

> Deu en rent graces et merci,
> Or set que ben istront de ci.   (99–100)

(He gives thanks gratefully to God; now he knows they will get out of this situation all right.)

Iseut plays the loyal wife sadly compromised by the indiscretion of a friend; Tristran plays the desperate, misjudged man of honour who needs someone to plead his case to the king if he is ever going to clear his name. The lovers' ruse, their feigned miseries, their protestations of innocence and loyalty, are totally successful. Mark reproaches himself bitterly, swears to be revenged on the dwarf and promises Tristran and Iseut complete freedom of resort (. . . *lor laira/La chanbre tot a lor voloir*, 296).

There are other verbal dexterities in the tale, of which the best known is the ambiguous oath which Iseut swears before King Arthur and King Mark; the leper she refers to is Tristran in disguise.

> 'Si m'aït Dex et saint Ylaire,
> Ces reliques, cest saintuaire,
> Totes celes qui ci ne sont
> Et tuit icil de par le mont,
> Q'entre mes cuises n'entra home,
> Fors le ladre qui fist soi some,
> Qui me porta outre les guez,
> Et li rois Marc mes esposez;
> Ces deus ost de mon soirement.
> Ge n'en ost plus de tote gent.'   (4201–10)

('So help me God and St Hilary, and by these relics, this holy place, the relics that are not here and all the relics in the world, I swear that no man ever came

between my thighs except the leper who carried me on his back across the
ford and my husband, King Mark. Those two I exclude from my oath; I
exclude no one else in the world.')[10]

Whatever else Tristran and Iseut may be, they are certainly a
crafty pair. We cannot help admiring their adroitness, savoir-faire,
and presence of mind. They give us a taste of the same amoral pleasure
as we get from the machinations of that wily fox Renart, in the comic
epic that bears his name, or from the tricksters of *fabliau*. This aspect
of Beroul's romance panders not merely to our fantasies of 'one-up-
man-ship' but, lightly, to the cynical, anti-idealistic streak we all have
in our natures.

However, Beroul's poem *is* a romance and our main engagement is
with the love between Tristran and Iseut viewed as some sort of an
ideal. I say, cautiously, 'some sort of an ideal' because it is obvious
even to a casual reader of Beroul that in his poem we find yet another
concept of courteous love, a concept that is palpably different from
Chrétien's or Thomas's or Gottfried's. Beroul has not got their depth
of insight, their depth of involvement. But he has a certain courtly
feeling. It is evident, for instance, in Mark's weeping in the tree for
his 'sin' of mistrust; and, again, in the way the three Bad Barons of
the story are invariably characterised as *feluns*, despite their entirely
just suspicions, and represented as being motivated by the worst
feelings:

> A la cort avoit trois barons
> Ainz ne veïstes plus felons. (581-2)

'You never saw such villains as they were!' Their status as wicked men
is driven home continuously. One climax is reached in the scene
at King Arthur's court (Arthur is a type of Justice and Courtliness)
where three worthy knights, Gawain, Gerflet and Evains, 'take them
on', promise personally to deal with them in no very knightly terms:

> 'Ge li feroie asez ennui
> Et lui pëndre an un haut pui.' (3469-70)

('I would give him something to think about and then hang him on the top
of a hill.')

says Gawain of Ganelon. Beroul's courtliness does not issue in refinement or delicacy of feeling. It is difficult to imagine one of Chrétien's
heroines, for instance, laughing to see even her worst enemies suffo-

cating in a bog—*joie en a grant, rit et envoise* (3827); or one of his heroes disguised as a leper and joking about the diseases which follow from sexual intercourse.

However, Beroul's courtliness does not simply consist in labelling all enemies of Tristran and Iseut as *felun* and degrading them by grotesque brutalities. It has its positive side also. Just as *traïson* is the word for those who oppose love, so *loial* is the word for those who uphold it. *Bone foi* is used as an epithet for Iseut.[11] And when Brengain (Brangwen, Iseut's attendant) hears about the lovers' lucky escape in the orchard, she praises God for rewarding loyalty:

> 'Granz miracles vos a fait Dex,
> Il est verais peres et tex
> Qu'il n'a cure de faire mal
> A ceus qui sont buen e loial.' (377–80)

('God has done great miracles on your behalf. He is the true Father of all, a God who never acts harshly to those who are good and true.')

God is always prepared to 'do a miracle' for true lovers (they are 'loial', surely, to each other not to Him). Later, Tristran and Iseut are about to be burned at the stake, *a grant honte*; the fire is built up; then —a dramatic divine intervention—

> Oez, seignors, de Damledé
> Conment il est plains de pité;
> Ne vieat pas mort de pecheor. (909–11)

(Now, listen and hear how merciful God is; he does not wish the death of a sinner.)

Tristran escapes, first, showing superhuman agility and cunning, and subsequently rescues Iseut. Loyalty is the prime virtue not only of Tristran and Iseut but of Tristran's *mestre*, Governal, and even of his dog, Husdent, who tracks the lovers down in their forest retreat:

> Quant son seignor vit et connut,
> Le chief hoque, la queue crole. (1542–3)

(When he sees his master and recognizes him he shakes his head and wags his tail.)

As we reflect on the poem we realize, moreover, that we have been told comparatively little about what the lovers feel for each other, apart from loyalty. We know something about their love, viewed

as an entity apart—it was always fated because of the love-drink
(*Itel fu nostre destinee*, 2302) but virtually nothing about their personal,
imaginative and emotional, experience. The potion in Beroul's
Tristran is not what it is in Gottfried's, a symbol for a passion so
deep that it is an eternal intoxication, a death; it is simply a charm,
a pre-destined spell. When it wears off, after three years, the lovers,
although still bound by a loyal bond of love, are able to take a straight
look at their situation and realize that by living like outlaws on acorns
and grass they are missing the good things of life. Tristran, out hunting,
suddenly reflects on their graceless condition (his own first!):

> Oublié ai chevalerie
> A seure cort et baronie   (2165–6)

(I have forgotten the ways of knighthood, courtliness and baronial custom.)

Iseut ought to be

> En beles chanbres, o son estre,
> Portendues de dras de soie.   (2182–3)

(In fine chambers hung with silken tapestries, with her entourage.)

One line sums it up:

> En mal uson nostre jovente.   (2222)

(In pain [misfortune?] we are spending our youth)

Their youth (youthfulness, the gay potentiality of life) is being
miserably wasted. They decide to approach Mark in the hope of a
reconciliation. This episode ought to read like a recantation, a turning-
away from love and its values. But it does not. The reason is that we
have scarcely been aware of a private mutuality in their love, only
of an innate worth in them both as representatives of courtly virtue.
In this courtly virtue we believe because God and King Mark are for
it, the Bad Barons and the deceitful dwarf against it.

Beroul's *Tristran* is a curious hybrid. At some risk of over-
simplification, I would say that it blends, or bends, an 'epic' morality
into the frame of a traditional romantic story. The love of Tristran and
Iseut and the loyalties it commands are the 'good' which in epic
would be brotherhood in arms and loyalty to the king. Their love is
more of an institution to be kept up than a deep imaginative experience.
Beroul's answer to the question, 'What is Man?' seems to be, 'Man is
a hero, brave, resourceful and, above all, loyal'.

If the only criterion of heroic romance is *inner* adventure and its dominant mode a search for 'the final meaningful encounter' which will crown the hero's quest and 'enable him to know himself', then clearly Beroul's *Tristran* does not qualify. Nor will most romances written for Englishmen, whether in English or French. Perhaps it is true to say that in English, at least, only the Gawain-poet and Chaucer followed Chrétien in the development of a self-conscious hero who realizes *in himself* the question at issue. In most cases the answer comes directly from the poet who presents us with an idealism (or merely a fantasy) of his creating, often without himself even formulating the question.

Beroul's *Tristran* is a complex work; it embodies, as we have seen, a somewhat mixed answer to the question, 'What is Man?'. This, does not mean, of course, that the poet had deliberate questions in mind, intellectually framed; but simply that a number of different feelings and attitudes became combined in, ran together in the telling of the story. Beroul's poem is not the only romance of love, so-called, which is in effect a romance of heroism. Malory's telling of the love of Lancelot and Guenevere is, I have already argued, another. It is 'truth' and 'stability' that Malory honours and celebrates in their love—basic, human qualities which go to make up the integrity of the self in *any* situation, in *any* relationship (see p. 46).

Chaucer is apparently not greatly interested in the nature of Man Alone, questing man in search of the supreme test that will enable him to know himself. In *The Knight's Tale*, valour is assumed to be part of the 'character' of both Palamon and Arcite, as it is in the 'character' of the Knight himself.

> At mortal batailles hadde he been fiftene,
> And foughten for oure feith at Tramyssene
> In listes thries, and ay slayn his foo . . . (*Gen. Prol.* 61–3)

But Chaucer, in his synthesizing way, stresses the harmony which this valour made, in the Knight's character, with other qualities— his sense of religious duty and service, his 'curtesye', his modest demeanour and 'gentil' speech.

> And though that he were worthy, he was wys,
> And of his port as meeke as is a mayde.
> He nevere yet no vileynye ne sayde
> In al his lyf unto no maner wight.
> He was a verray, parfit gentil knyght. (*Gen. Prol.* 68–72)

---

worthy i.e. good as a knight   *port* demeanour   *verray* true, loyal

And in *The Knight's Tale* itself, valour and love, 'trouthe and honour, fredom and curteisye', are all brought together in a paean of praise for the noble life.

Earlier in this chapter I attempted some broad generalizations which would distinguish romance from epic. It is evident now, I believe, that these are only valid for the 'classic' examples of the genres: the *Chanson de Roland* and Chrétien's *Yvain*, for example, are very easily distinguished. But there are a great number of romances (it would be perverse to call them anything else) whose classification is far more difficult. Fortunately, it is ultimately unimportant. Classification is only important as an aid to understanding; it is not an end in itself. Uncommonly hard to classify, but uncommonly rewarding in the attempt, is the alliterative *Morte Arthure*, the finest alliterative poem in Middle English outside the works of the *Gawain*-poet. I use it, briefly, as a final text for this chapter.

The alliterative *Morte Arthure*, written probably in the late fourteenth century, tells roughly the same story as the Norman, Wace, and the Englishman, Layamon, had told some two centuries earlier.

King Arthur is holding a feast. A Senator, sent by the Emperor Lucius at Rome, enters, demanding tribute and submission. Arthur entertains the embassy sumptuously, before sending back defiance and denial to Rome. At a council, individual British knights take vows to support Arthur's stand and to do deeds of individual prowess. Arthur then sets out for France with his army. He dreams of a dragon (himself) who kills a bear (the Emperor of Rome). In Brittany he kills the giant of Mont St Michel and rescues the Duchess of Brittany. In a great battle against the Emperor Lucius, Kay is killed; but Arthur kills Lucius. There follows the siege of Metz and Gawain's foraging expedition against Sir Priamus. Arthur receives the surrender of the Romans at Viterbo. But on the night after his greatest triumph he dreams of Fortune's Wheel. Of the Nine Worthies, six have already 'fallen'; Arthur's own 'fall' is impending. News presently arrives of Mordred's treachery and Guinevere's adultery. Arthur returns to England and defeats Mordred's navy in a great sea-fight. Gawain dashes recklessly with a small band of men into the midst of Mordred's army on shore. He is killed. Arthur eloquently mourns his death and vows revenge. In the final battle Mordred is killed but also mortally wounds Arthur, who is buried in the Isle of Avalon at Glastonbury.

> Thus endis kyng Arthure, as auctors alegges,
> That was of Ectores blude, the kynge sone of Troye.

---

the kynge sone the son of the king of Troy

There is no other Arthurian romance in which King Arthur is so important and so impressive. He is more or less continuously at the centre of the action and our interpretation of the poem is very much bound up with our interpretation of his role. He is, to begin with, in certain obvious senses the 'hero' of the poem. He accepts the challenge from Rome and, in performing it, encounters at least one major *aventure*—the battle with the giant of Mont St Michel. His doom-laden dream is the turning-point of the poem, 'from wele to wo'. And his personal determination to revenge the death of Gawain leads to the final victory and his own death.

But Arthur does not stand for Man Alone in the way that, for example, Chrétien's Lancelot does, or the English Gawain in *Sir Gawain and the Green Knight*. Apart from anything else, he seldom is alone, except on Mont St Michel; he usually has a huge army in support; the central action of the poem is a campaign not a quest. These and similar features have led some readers to see the alliterative *Morte Arthure* as a sort of English *chanson de geste*. Dr Finlayson writes:

The nearest comparable work is the Old French *chanson de geste*, the *Chanson de Roland*. The sentiments of our poem are almost purely heroic: the emphasis on the loyalty of his men to Arthur and of Arthur to them; the attitudes to war and battle, which are almost identical with those in *Beowulf* and the battle of Maldon; the close relationship of Arthur to Gawain, which parallels Charlemagne's relationship to Roland; the almost total absence of 'love-interest', despite the dominance of courtly love in contemporary literature; the stereotyped laments by Arthur on the death of Gawain which closely resemble that of Charlemagne for Roland—these are all clear indications that we are in the heroic, not the romantic world. The English poem bears a great similarity in subject matter, attitude and structure to the *chansons de geste* of the Charlemagne cycle.[12]

There is much in this view of the poem which is undeniably true; and yet, if the parallel is pressed too hard, it takes much of the individuality and colour out of the *Morte*. Heroism is, after all, an essential feature of many romances as well as of the epic; and a sense of shared values, too. The *Morte Arthure* is, indeed, 'an isolated poem' (Finlayson). But there are features in it which isolate it as surely from the *chanson de geste* as from the romance of individual heroism. Arthur is a hero but he is also a king. We have here, perhaps, the romance of heroism broadening out to be a romance of society in which the society is represented by, and its values embodied in, the person of the king:

> He may be chosyne cheftayne, cheefe of all other,
> Bathe be chauncez of armes and chevallrye noble,
> For whyeseste, and worthyeste, and wyghteste of hanndez:
> Of all the wyes thate I watte in this werlde ryche . . .
> The comlyeste of knyghtehode that undyre Cryste lyffes! (530-7)

Just as the values and qualities of the courtly lover could in the hands of Chaucer be made to take on an extra social dimension, so the valour, loyalty, largesse and magnaminity of the Christian knight could be epitomized in the royal person of the 'comlyeste of knyghtehode'. In so far as valour, loyalty, religious fervour are also qualities of the epic hero, the parallel with epic is helpful. But where the parallel obscures the issue is, I think, in the balance between individual and social values. The essential difference between the ethos of the *Chanson de Roland* and that of the *Morte Arthure* is this—in the former the individual (Roland, particularly) is, as it were, carried by the community, which has in an important sense created him; in the latter, the individual (Arthur) is the fountain and well-head of the community, the Round Table, which he has himself created:

> Thus on ryalle araye he helde his Rounde Table,
> With semblaunt and solace and selcouthe metes. (74-5)

The difference becomes the more obvious if we consider the contrasting roles of Charlemagne and Arthur, or of Roland and Gawain. *Carles li magnes* is very important in the *Chanson*; it is he who is left groaning at the end of the poem about the unremitting cares and burdens of a Christian emperor. But it is Roland whose heroic fight and death form the mainspring of the action. In the *Morte*, on the other hand, King Arthur's royal heroism is not simply the frame but, as I have said, the very centre of the poem; Gawain, however deeply his loss may be lamented, is a quite subsidiary figure.

Paradoxically, it is the *Chanson de Roland* which tells us more of individual heroism than the English poem, for Roland carries the responsibilities of individual decision and exercises them as only a hero could. Arthur's responsibilities are almost always communal; he acts and decides not as an individual (except perhaps when he goes out alone to fight the giant of Mont St Michel) but as the embodiment of Britain, as warrior-chief, religious leader, patriotic conqueror and courteous king.[13]

---

whyeseste wisest   *wyghteste* mightiest   *wyes* men   *watte* know
ryalle royal   *semblaunt* splendour   *selcouthe metes* exotic dishes

There is much more feeling in this poem than in the *chanson de geste* for the richness of life, for the values which exist beside war. This is not simply a matter of the poet's sensitive feeling for the natural world, which comes through even apparently conventional descriptions:

> Of the nyghtgale notez the noisez was swette,
> They threpide wyth the throstills, thre hundreth at ones!
> That swete swowynge of watyre and syngynge of byrdez,
> It myghte salve hym of sore that sounde was nevere! (929–32)

It is more that we feel behind and around the person of Arthur, a civilization of a sort. In the *Chanson de Roland*, the alternative to fighting is home-life in *la douce France*. We catch a glimpse once, early in the poem, of what it means to the French not to be on the battlefield: they sit on white silks, the old and grave playing chess, the nimble young men fencing together. But this is nothing compared with the rich, ceremonial activity that surrounds Arthur; when he receives the ambassadors from Rome, he tells Sir Cayons

> 'Spare for no spycerye, bot spende what the lykys,
> That there be largesce on lofte, and no lake founden;
> If thou my wyrchipe wayte, wy, be my trouthe,
> Thou sall have gersoms full grett, that gayne sall the ever.'[14] (162–5)

The description of their entertainment and of the great banquet that was served occupies over eighty lines (156–242) and it culminates in the truly regal description of Arthur and praise of his courteous speech:

> And the conquerour hymselven, so clenly arayede,
> In colours of clene golde cleede, wyth his knyghttys,
> Drissid with his dyademe one his deesse ryche,
> Fore he was demyde the doughtyeste that duellyde in erthe.
> Thane the conquerour kyndly carpede to those lordes,
> Rehetede the Romaynes with realle speche. (216–21)

This noble act of hospitality is intended, of course, to impress the

---

threpide strove   *swowynge* soughing sound   *salve* . . . heal the sickness of an incurable   *spycerye* delicacy   *largesce on lofte* generous hospitality 'on high'   *no lake* . . . nothing found wanting   *If thou my wyrchipe* . . . if you look to my honour, my man, by my truth, you shall have plentiful rewards to your everlasting profit   *clen, clenly* splendid(ly), brightly   *deesse* dais   *carpede* spoke   *Rehetede* gladdened   *realle* royal

Roman embassy, but this does not diminish its significance. Arthur is not just acting a sumptuous part; he is being more intensely and ostentatiously what he is and what everyone wants a royal hero to be.

A thought-provoking distinction has been drawn in discussion of the *Morte Arthure* between 'a heightened view of reality' and 'a dream of life'—'Like most heroic as opposed to romantic poems, *Morte Arthure* presents only a heightened view of reality not a dream of life.'[15] The observation is strikingly relevant to the episode just described; the entertainment might have been described in somewhat similar terms by a chronicler, if it had been a historical event. That such lavishly extravagantly ceremonious receptions were given, with semi-political motives behind them, is a matter of historical fact. But the distinction between 'dream' and 'reality' will not altogether hold. The 'dreams' that romance characteristically provides, whether of love, heroism or gracious living, are most satisfying, and not merely gratifying, when they embody aspirations, genuine human aspirations, related to the world we live in and the people we live with. So the difference between the alliterative *Morte* and other romances is not absolute; it resides in the kind and quality of the 'reality' which is heightened into 'dream', or (as I should prefer to say) idealized. The ideal is, indeed, of a 'Christian warrior-king' but one who also embodies the virtues of chivalry and knighthood.

This quality of life, the sense we have of 'wealth, power and civilization' behind Arthur, reminds us, finally, how arbitrary and easily confounded are the categories which I have established in order to describe the rich variety of medieval romance. Like the romance of love, the romance of heroism or integrity is capable of magnification, as I have already said, until it becomes in its own way a romance of society itself.

1. Trans. Comfort, pp. 224 ff.

2. ibid.

3. Penguin ed., pp. 331–2.

4. The earliest surviving MS is usually dated the first half of the twelfth century; the poem in some form must be earlier.

5. Trans. Kennedy, pp. 168–9.

6. Lines 5107ff. In the ME version the Chastel de Pesme Aventure (Castle of Evil Happening) is called, less imaginatively, 'The Castel of Hevy Sorow'.

7. Pearsall, 'The Development of Middle English Romance'.

8. It was printed by Skeat in an appendix to *The Canterbury Tales*. In several manuscripts of the tales it is actually inserted and given to the Cook. It cannot conceivably be by Chaucer, though perhaps he thought of working it over for the Cook. The text here quoted is from French and Hale.

9. The quotation is from Hatto's introduction, p. 9. See also Legge, *Anglo-Norman Literature*, p. 59, and Loomis, *Arthurian Literature*, p. 135 (Whitehead). Beroul's *Tristran* has been dated 'after 1191'—which would put it a generation *after* Thomas's in composition. In general, one should be sceptical of a chronology based on 'evolutionary' assumptions about taste.

10. Trans. Fedrick, p. 141.

11. *Franche, cortoise, bone foi!* (102).

12. Finlayson, *Morte Arthure*, p. 11.

13. I disagree with Finlayson who says Arthur has 'unfolded before our eyes both as conqueror and as man' (p. 14) and speaks of 'the gradual exposition of the nature of the hero'.

14. Finlayson, p. 25, comments on Arthur's feasting of the Roman ambassadors that the magnificence of the scene adds to our already growing sense of the wealth, power and civilization which Arthur represents.

15. Finlayson, note to line 2275; the other phrases, below, 'Christian warrior-king' and 'wealth, power and civilization', are quoted, also, from his edition of the poem. I am much indebted to his stimulating introduction and notes.

5

MAN AND SUPERNATURE:

THE MARVELLOUS IN ROMANCE

There is a striking passage in Chrétien's romance, *Perceval* (*le conte du graal*). Perceval has been adventuring for some time. In an early episode of his story he had wrongly, almost callously, left his old mother in a faint and ridden off to become a knight. Now, a proven knight but repentant, he is on his way back to find her. To do this he has left his newly-found, newly-won sweetheart Blancheflor. As he journeys on a wintry day, a falcon attacks a flock of wild geese flying over the countryside. One of them is wounded and falls on the snow before Perceval. When it recovers and flies off, it leaves on the white snow three drops of scarlet blood. When Perceval saw this:

> Si s'apoia desor sa lance
> Por esgarder cele samblance;
> Que li sanz et la nois ensamble
> La fresche color li resamble
> Qui ert en la face s'amie,
> Si pense tant que il s'oblie,
> Qu'autresi estoit en son vis
> Li vermels sor le blanc assis
> Com ces trois goutes de sanc furent,
> Qui sor le blance noif parurent.
> En l'esgarder que il faisoit,
> Li ert avis, tant li plaisoit,
> Qu'il veïst la color novele
> De la face s'amie bele.
> Perchevax sor les goutes muse,
> Tote la matinee i use. (4197–212)

([He] leant on his lance to observe this appearance, for the blood and the snow together remind him of his sweetheart's fresh complexion. He falls into a trance as he deeply ponders the resemblance between the red and white in her face and the three drops of blood on the snow. In the delight of his meditation he imagined that he actually saw the fresh colours in the beauty of his lady's face. Perceval muses on the drops of blood and spends the whole morning in meditation.)

Two of Arthur's knights, Sagremor and Kay, try brusquely to rouse Perceval from his trance. It is only Gawain who realizes that Perceval must not be rudely disturbed and waits until the sun has caused the drops of blood to evaporate. For, as Gawain observes:

> Cist pensers n'estoit pas vilains,
> Ainz estoit molt cortois et dols;
> Et cil estoit fel et estols
> Qui vostre cuer en romovoit.   (4458–61)

(That was not at all a boorish fancy, but on the contrary full of sweet courtesy. He who tried to shift your settled heart was rude and unfeeling.)[1]

The full meaning of this episode is never discussed by Chrétien, who has supremely the tact of leaving things alone for the imagination to work upon, as poets in all ages do and must. Its immediate interest for us now is to show that, despite the title of this chapter, the experience of the supernatural and the encounter with the marvellous are not the same thing. On the one hand, the world of everyday, a few drops of blood on the winter's snow, can carry a meaning beyond the commonplace; on the other, the most fantastic 'marvels' in the hands of a prosaic fiction-monger can leave the heart as cold and unresponsive as a piece of fish on a stone slab. The meaning is not in the marvel but in the experience which it may or may not carry. There is often a sense in the greater romancers that quite ordinary events, ordinary things, have a significance quite beyond themselves, a supernatural significance. This all-pervading sense of the world of phenomena as a *speculum* (mirror), *umbra* (shadow), *figura* (type, symbol) of transcendental truth I shall discuss later (p. 150). Our present subject is 'the marvellous'—things 'out of nature', things (like the Green Knight) which do not obey the rules.

Many romances move on a superhuman rather than on a supernatural plane. Marvels are present because they are a necessary concomitant of the hero's heroism, its necessary dramatic setting. Man cannot effectively be a *superman* in a world of bowler-hats, rolled

D

umbrellas and regular trains to the city. In the alliterative *Morte*,
Arthur's encounter with the giant of Mont St Michel is an essential
means of enhancing him, Arthur. The hero must have an antagonist
worthy of him—and he has. This giant has a famous kyrtle, woven
in Spain, and 'bordered with the berdez of burlyche kyngez'; he has
long wished to add Arthur's beard to his collection. The giant's
description in this poem is the most detailed in medieval English
literature:

> Than glopnede the gloton   and glorede unfaire,
> He grennede as a grewhounde   with grysly tuskes;
> He gapede, he groned faste,   with grucchande latez
> For grefe of the gude kynge,   that hym with grame gretez.
> His fax and his foretoppe   was filterede togeders
> And owte of his face fome   ane halfe fote large;
> His frount and his forhevede,   all was it over,
> As the fell of a froske,   and fraknede it semede,
> Huke-nebbyde as a hawke,   and a hore berde,
> And herede to the eyghn-holes   with hyngande browes;
> Harske as a hunde-fisch,   hardly who so lukez,
> So was the hyde of that hulke   hally al over.
> Erne had he full huge   and ugly to schewe,
> With eghne full horreble   and ardaunt for sothe;
> Flatt-mowthede as a fluke   with fleryande lyppys,
> And the flesche in his fortethe   fowly as a bere.
> His berde was brothy and blake,   that till his brest rechede;
> Grassede as a mereswyne   with corkes full huge,
> And all falterde the flesche   in his foule lippys,
> Ilke wrethe as a wolfe-hevede,   it wraythe owtt at ones!
> Bullenekkyde was that bierne   and brade in the scholders,
> Brok-brestede as a brawne   with brustils full large,
> Ruyd armes as an ake   with rusclede sydes,
> Lym and leskes full lothyn,   leve ye for sothe:
> Schovell-fotede was that schalke   and schaylande hym semyde
> With schankez unschaply,   schowand togedyrs;
> Thykke theese as a thursse   and thikkere in the hanche,
> Greese-growen as a galte,   full gryslych he lukez.
> Who the lenghe of the lede   lelly accountes,
> Fro the face to the fote,   was fyfe fadom lange!   (1074–103)

(Then was the glutton dismayed and glared unseemly; he grinned like a
greyhound with grisly teeth; he gaped and groaned aloud with grievous
gestures for wrath with the good king, who speaks to him in anger. His hair
and his forelock were matted together and foam came out of his face for

about half a foot. His brow and forehead were all like the skin of a frog and seemed freckled; he was hooknosed like a hawk, with a hoary beard, and was hairy round his hollow eyes with overhanging brows. Rough as a dogfish—to anyone who looked carefully—so was the skin of that giant, all over. Ears he had full huge and ugly, with horrible, burning eyes; flatmouthed like a flounder with grinning lips, and the flesh in his front teeth as foul as a bear. His beard was rough and black and reached to his breast, fat like a sea-pig with a huge carcass, and the flesh hung in shreds from his foul lips, each fold like a wolf's head it writhed out at once. Bull-necked was that giant and broad of shoulders, with a streaked breast like a boar with long bristles. Rough arms like oak branches with gnarled sides—limbs and loins right hateful to see, believe ye in truth; shovel-footed was that man and he seemed to straddle, with unshapely shanks shuffling together; thick thighs like a giant and thicker in the haunch—fat as a hog, full terrible he looks. Whoever might reckon faithfully the full length of this man, from the face to the foot, he was five fathoms long.)[2]

What is the meaning of this encounter? Does the giant exist to give Arthur superhuman stature or is there a deeper meaning? Apart from being a tyrant, an abductor, rapist, glutton, child-devourer, and all the other things that giants habitually are, there is nothing much to him. This giant does not, as it seems to me, embody a principle of supernatural evil. Dr Finlayson argues persuasively that the qualities attributed to him belong to evil animals and that we ought to see him as a personification of evil.[3] Of course he is a Bad Monster; almost all giants and dwarfs and *un*natural creatures are—the correlation between ugliness and wickedness came easily, inevitably, to all romance-writers. But he has no *reserves* of wickedness, so to speak; he has no spiritual identity, only a moral colouring. The mystery of iniquity is not in him. He is *un*natural rather than supernatural—unnatural even as a man might be.[4]

Only the context of the particular romance, as I have stressed, can determine for us how to take the marvels. But it may be helpful to establish some categories, if only to see how diverse a range of material we are alluding to when we speak of the element of the marvellous in romance.

At the nearest, the bottom end of the scale, closest to our ordinary experience, there is the *exotic*, that is the foreign, strange and remote. Strictly speaking, the exotic is not *super*natural at all; but since the natural order to which it belongs is out of our reach, out of our experience, it seems supernatural. The Middle Ages held the gorgeous East in fee, at least in imagination:

> He seyde 'The Kyng of Arabe and of Inde,
> My lige lorde, on this solempne day
> Saleweth yow, as he best can and may,
> And sendeth yow, in honour of youre feeste,
> By me, that am al redy at your heeste,
> This steede of bras . . .'   (109–14)

So, the knight-envoy who rides into Cambyuskan's court at the beginning of Chaucer's *Squire's Tale*. His provenance, from 'the Indias of spice and mine', prepares us for fantasies which will lift us out of our everyday selves. It was a great age of travellers' tales; and romance, especially the category which deals with the matter of the Orient, caters for the taste.

Next on the scale of marvels which stretches from the merely exotic to the ultimate transcendental, is a category, the largest and most basic of all, of the *marvellous* proper. If the exotic invites us to feel the thrill of fascination, of intriguing strangeness, the marvellous can be more disturbing: it astonishes, may baffle, even frighten us, as it does the heroes who confront its manifestations. The essence of marvellous objects or happenings is that they appear to defy the ordinary laws of Nature; they are irrational and in varying degrees improbable.

I broke off the above quotation from *The Squire's Tale* because at the words 'steede of bras' it was obvious that, as often, the exotic had given birth to marvellous progeny. The 'marvels' of *The Squire's Tale* are, however, of a fairly routine kind: this mechanical steed would carry you anywhere you wanted to go, within the space of twenty-four hours, in perfect safety, through the air if necessary—and you could sleep whilst travelling. There was also a magic mirror (for political foresight and amorous insight); a magic ring (enabling its wearer to talk to the birds of the air in their own language); and a magic sword which could heal the wounds it had inflicted.

In this discussion I have so far used the term 'magic' as if it were the same thing as 'marvellous'. In fact, we should distinguish at least three categories within the marvellous.

(1) The purely *mysterious*—unmotivated, unexplained and inexplicable. Such are the numerous ships without helmsmen, talking animals, and to be more specific—the Flaming Lance in Chrétien's

---

Saleweth salutes, greets   *heeste* command

Lancelot; the marvellous Fountain with the rain-making stone in his *Yvain* (and in the English *Ywain and Gawain*); the flame which comes out of Havelok's mouth; the Green Knight in all his greenness:

> Ther was lokyng on lenthe the lude to beholde,
> For uch mon had mervayle quat hit mene myght
> That a hathel and a horse myght such a hue lach,
> As growe grene as the gres . . .
>
> For fele sellyes had thay sen bot such never are;
> Forthi for fantoum and fayrye the folk there hit demed.　(232–40)

(2) The strictly *magical*. An event is magical, as I define it (according with anthropological definition), if it shows the marvellous *controlled by man*. Rings conferring invisibility or the power of tongues fit in here, with magic ointments, swords, and so forth. The 'subtil clerk' of *The Franklin's Tale* is a 'magician'. Witches, wizards, warlocks, whose habitat is our day-to-day human world belong here too—Merlin, Morgan le Fay, and their kind. They are the operators of magic, those whose skills enable them to manipulate the forces of nature in a marvellous manner. However, as Morgan's name shows, they merge into a class of 'other-worldly' beings whose nature as well as whose powers are extra-ordinary.

(3) The *miraculous*—that is to say, the marvellous *controlled by God*. Miracles are God's magic, his supernatural interventions in the natural workings of the created world. Miracles are not frequent in romance outside the Grail cycle, for obvious reasons; they disturb the self-contained, self-sufficient, imaginative world. The romance of *Amys and Amiloun* contains an angelic warning. Amiloun has undertaken, out of friendship, to deputize for Amis in a trial-by-battle:

> As he com prikand out of toun,
> Com a voice fram heven adoun,
> 　That noman herd bot he,
> And sayd, 'Thou knyght, Sir Amiloun,
> God, that suffred passioun,
> 　Sent the bode bi me;
> If thou this bataile underfong

---

on lenthe at length　*lude* man　*hathel* man　*lach* take　*fele sellyes* many marvels　*such never are* never one like this before　*Forthi for fantoum* . . . for this reason they thought it must be something supernatural　*prikand* riding *bode* message

> Thou schalt have an eventour strong
>   Within this yeres thre;
> And or this thre yere ben al gon,
> Fouler mesel nas never non
>   In the world, than thou schal be!   (1249-60)

The angel says he has been sent by Jesus to warn Amiloun. It is worth
remarking that *Amis and Amiloun* is one of the romances most closely
related to saints' lives.[5] The angelic warning in *Amis and Amiloun*
is explicitly Christian but does not, in fact, involve either the characters
or us in a religious experience. God's magic foretells the future, and
that is that.

    These broad categories—the exotic, the mysterious, the magical,
the miraculous—are all categories of the marvellous. That is to say,
they describe and distinguish events out of the ordinary which are
part of the mechanics, or, in medieval terms, the *matière*, of romance.
Marvels form a large part of the material, inherited largely from
Celtic storytellers, with which the romancer worked. We shall
consider later in more detail, and in various contexts, the nature of
this material and the broadly symbolic uses to which it can be put.
For the present, one example must suffice to show the wealth of
imaginative suggestion that a poet of genius can draw out of an
encounter with a 'marvel'.

    The incident comes from Chrétien's *Yvain* and is a tale told by one
of Arthur's knights, Calogrenant, about his meeting with the Giant
Herdsman (also known as the Monstrous Churl). It is not, he says,
a tale which redounds to his credit, but rather to the opposite, his
honte. But it acts as a spur to Yvain and sets him off on his valorous
quest. From the listener's point of view it is also a spur because its
unexplained elements provoke and tease the imagination. (The tale
is rather long and I give it in summary except for the central dialogue.)

One day, seven years ago I was travelling alone through a forest. On a heath
I came upon a castle, whose owner stood on the drawbridge, hawk on fist.
I was warmly welcomed and at the summons of a gong servants took my
horse and a maiden tended me. The maiden and I sat together on an enclosed
lawn until (alas!) the vavasour came to call me to supper. . . . In the morning
I left, after promising to return that way. Soon I came on wild bulls fighting.
To be honest I was pretty frightened. Then I saw a huge *vilain* sitting, a hideous

---

eventour Fr. *aventure*   *or* ere   *mesel* leper

creature with a club in his hand, huge head, matted hair, shaggy great ears. He was clothed in skins. When he saw me he stood up. I was on my guard, but he just stood there.

> Si m'esgarda et mot ne dist,
> Ne plus qu'une beste feïst;
> Et je cuidai que il n'eüst
> Reison ne parler ne seüst.
> Totes voies tant m'anhardi,
> Que je li dis: 'Va, car me di,
> Se tu es buene chose ou non!'
> Et il me dist: 'Je sui uns hon'.
> 'Ques hon ies tu?'—'Tes con tu voiz.
> Je ne sui autre nule foiz.'
> 'Que fes tu ci?'—'Je m'i estois,
> Si gart cez bestes par cest bois.'
> 'Gardes? Por saint Pere de Rome!
> Ja ne conoissent eles home . . .
> 'Je gart si cestes et justis,
> Que ja n'istront de cest porpris.'
> 'Et tu comant? Di m'an le voir!'
> 'N'i a celi, qui s'ost movoir . . .
> Ne nus ne s'i porroit fier
> Fors moi, s'autre eles s'estoit mis,
> Que maintenant ne fust ocis.
> Einsi sui de mes bestes sire:
> Et tu me redevroies dire,
> Ques hon tu ies et que tu quiers.'
> 'Je sui, ce voiz, uns chevaliers,
> Qui quier ce, que trover ne puis;
> Assez ai quis et rien ne truis.'
> 'Et que voldroies tu trover?'
> 'Avantures por esprover
> Ma proesce et mon hardemant,
> Or te pri et quier et demant,
> Se tu sez, que tu me consoille
> Ou d'avanture ou de mervoille.'   (323–66)

(Then he gazed at me but spoke not a word, any more than a beast would have done. And I supposed that he had not his senses or was drunk. However, I made bold to say to him: 'Come, let me know whether thou art a creature of good or not.' And he replied: 'I am a man.' 'What kind of a man art thou?' 'Such as thou seest me to be: I am by no means otherwise.' 'What dost thou here?' 'I was here, tending these cattle in this wood.' 'Wert thou really tending them? By Saint Peter of Rome! They know not the command of any man . . .' 'Well, I tend and have control of these beasts so that they will never leave this neighbourhood.' 'How dost thou do that? Come tell me now!' 'There is not one of them that dares to move . . . No one could venture here but me, for if he should go among them he would be straightway done to death. In this way I am master of my beasts. And now thou must tell me in turn what kind of man thou art, and what thou seekest here.' 'I am, as thou seest, a knight seeking for what I cannot find; long have I sought without success.' 'And what is this thou fain wouldst find?' 'Some adventure whereby to test my prowess and my bravery. Now I beg and urgently request thee to give me some counsel, if possible, concerning some adventure or marvellous thing.')[6]

The Churl replied, '*Aventures* mean nothing to me. I've never heard of them. But if you took this path, you'd come to a Fountain, shaded by a most beautiful Tree, with an iron basin hanging on it. If you pour water from the basin on to a Stone (I can't describe it but I never saw one like it), then the most almighty storm will arise, all the animals will rush out of the forest, and if you get away you'll be lucky.' I left the Churl and went to the Fountain and saw the Tree and Basin and Stone as he said. I wanted to see the storm (not a very sensible thing to do), and I did. Thank God, it was short and I wasn't killed. When calm returned a huge mass of birds came to the beautiful Tree and sang their song, their 'liturgy' (*servise*). When it was finished a knight appeared with a great deal of noise and challenged me for having caused the storm and driven him out of his house. We fought; he was bigger, my lance broke, and I was ignominiously defeated. So I returned, horseless, to the kind vavasour who said I was lucky to have escaped alive: (175–518)

> Einsi alai, einsi reving,
> Au revenir por fol me ting;
> Si vos ai conté come fos
> Ce qu'onques mes conter ne vos. (577–80)

(Thus I went, thus I returned; on my return I thought myself a fool. And, like a fool, I have told you this tale which I never wanted to tell again.)

Calogrenant's experiences are almost exactly the same as those Yvain will have when, singlehanded, he undertakes this *aventure* and forestalls King Arthur and other knights by doing so. They are recounted more briefly (lines 760–880) when Yvain, victorious in the battle, is pursuing the Knight of the Fountain to his castle. The question is what do they 'mean'? An answer to this question has sometimes been given along anthropological lines; such motifs as the Hospitable Host, the Giant Herdsman (Monstrous Churl), the Magic

Fountain, are paralleled elsewhere in Celtic and romance literature. Thus, Professor R. S. Loomis summarizes his findings on the Giant Herdsman as follows:

> The *Fer Caille* ['Man of the Wood', from 9th century Irish Saga] thus reveals a kinship with the gigantic herdsman, Curoi [a giant keeper of a fortress, in Irish myth, who 'combined traits of a sun and storm divinity' (Loomis, 208)] and the Giant Herdsmen in *Owain* and *Kulhwch* [two tales from the Welsh *Mabinogion*—*Owain* is a later analogue of *Yvain*]; while the latter in turn reveal their identity with the *vilain* of the *Mule Sans Frein* and with the Carl of Carlisle, both of whom play the part of Curoi. The dovetailing evidence, then, tends to prove that *all these herdsmen were one and the same* [my italics]. . . . Brown was therefore right in his conclusion that the Herdsman and the Hospitable Host of *Yvain* were two forms of one Otherworld being.[7]

It should not be necessary here to reiterate the truism that anthropology is not literature. Professor Loomis's remarks have great anthropological interest; they do not, as I see it, tell us anything significant about Chrétien's *Yvain*. What does it mean to say 'all these herdsmen were one and the same'? Could it mean any more than to say, for instance, that Benoît's and Boccaccio's and Chaucer's and Henryson's and Shakespeare's and Dryden's Cressidas 'were one and the same'? The various Cressidas get life and meaning from the poems and plays in which they occur; their common factors are so superficial as to be totally uninteresting. So the question remains—what do the Giant Herdsman and the Fountain 'mean' in Chrétien's poem? We have our own impressions to go on and (although it is not fully legitimate to talk of Chrétien's *intentions*) our knowledge of the kind of range of significance a twelfth-century poet might be attempting. The Giant Herdsman, by the way, appears to have no connection with the plot. If he is in any sense identifiable with the Hospitable Host (the vavasour), then the identification never comes out at all (in contrast to the analogous identification of the Green Knight with Sir Bertilak in *Sir Gawain and the Green Knight*). So he makes a good starting-point. What does he convey?

In the story, the Giant Herdsman is part, though scarcely an essential part, of the machinery for getting the challengers to the Fountain. Poetically, he initiates the suggestion of great natural forces, mysteriously controlled, and to be tampered with only at man's peril (e.g. his appearance is heralded by the fighting of *tors sauvages*). Everything about him suggests either animal or distorted man:

> . . . il ot grosse la teste
> Plus que roncins ne autre beste . . .
> Iauz de çuëte et nes de chat
> Boche fandue come los
> Danz de sangler, aguz et ros,
> Barbe noire, grenons tortiz
> Et le manton aers au piz,
> Longue eschine, torte et boçue.   (295–307)

(He had a huge head, bigger than a packhorse's or any other animal's . . . The eyes of a screech-owl, the nose of a cat, a mouth wide cleft like a wolf's, sharp yellow teeth like a boar's, a black beard with tangled hair round his lips, a chin that converged with his chest, and a long, twisted bent spine.)

Physical distortion is, as we have seen, normally symptomatic of an evil character in the romances—the *nains*, dwarf, who looks like a toad, and behaves like a *felon*, is a familiar figure. But the Giant Herdsman is not evil (329–30). He is more a Caliban; a natural, on whom 'nurture will never stick', but not a born devil. He has something of Caliban's engaging rapport with the natural world, and the same instinctive vitality. It is not his sheer brute strength which enables him to control wild beasts as if they were tame animals. Calogrenant thought he lacked the distinctive qualities of a man (*Reison ne parler ne seüst*, 326) but he turned out to be wrong—'*Je sui uns hom*'.

He is a man—but only just a man; no more. This is perhaps the point of his answer to the question 'What kind of a man are you?' 'The kind you see. I'm never any different.' It would be wrong, therefore, to give him moral significance in himself. But he serves to bring out various moral and spiritual significances in the knights—Calogrenant and Yvain. To begin with, he has no name and, thence, no true identity. He is merely *hom*—and perhaps one who does not even know how important names are for true selfhood?[8] He does not ask Calogrenant's name and is not told it. When he asks who Calogrenant is he is satisfied with the answer

> 'Je sui, ce voiz, uns chevaliers'   (358)

and proceeds to the next question.

The second point which emerges strongly from the exchange between the uncultured Monster and the accomplished Knight is what a true knight is—he is a man in search of something. His life is not like the Giant Herdsman's, an unchanging, uncomprehending

existence; it is a quest. Some lines already quoted could serve almost
as a classic definition of chivalric romance:

> 'Je sui, ce voiz, uns chevaliers
> Qui quier ce, que trover ne puis;
> Assez ai quis et rien ne truis.'
> 'Et que voldroies tu trover?'
> 'Avantures por esprover
> Ma proesce et mon hardemant.'[9]   (358–63)

The importance of *avanture* is, surely consciously, stressed by Chrétien
when the monster goes on to say that he has no notion what *avantures*
are and has never heard of them.

The Giant Herdsman is not the only monster in *Yvain*; much
later, at the castle of *Pesme Aventure*, Yvain has to fight two at once,
who really are evil and are unmistakably labelled as such: *deuz fiz
de deable*. The Herdsman, however, is the most puzzling. There is an
element of the naïve grotesque in his appearance and in his conversation (one cannot help thinking of Perceval, the crude untutored
Welsh boy, mistaking knights for angels) which is almost comic.
The comic-grotesque is a note which Chrétien strikes more than once
in *Yvain*.

To sum up, in this scene, if one may dare to articulate and define,
Chrétien seems to be asking what it is to be truly, fully human—to
be not simply *homo sapiens* endowed with 'discourse of reason' but
more. It is, he suggests, to be a seeker, a quester. In Calogrenant's
[*je*] *quier ce que trover ne puis/Assez ai quis et rien ne truis* (360) there may
even be a faint echo of the Scriptural injunction, 'Seek and ye shall find,
knock and it shall be opened unto you'. The 'aspiring mind' belonged
to the medieval knight before it belonged to the Renaissance hero.

It is clear, I hope, from this baffling and yet beautifully suggestive
passage that an encounter with a 'marvel' can be used to convey a
multitude of meanings and none of them need be 'supernatural'.
Calogrenant's encounter with the Giant Herdsman raises questions
which one might wish to call 'metaphysical'—about nature and nurture, the savage and the civilized—but not 'supernatural'. Nevertheless, there are experiences, *aventures*, in romance which clearly
do carry a supernatural significance. These include vision and dream,
in which supernatural insight or foresight is given, encounters with
fairy mistresses, and visits to the other-world which is neither heaven
nor hell. I leave for consideration in the next chapter direct experiences

of the divine, of the Christian mystery, such as the knights of the
later Grail romances undergo, or, in a different way, Troilus in the
eighth sphere after his death.

Firstly, vision and dream. Medieval dream-lore was complicated.
Even Chaucer found it confusing. All that it is necessary to say here
is that certain types of dream were thought of as carrying the authority
of truth. A *somnium* gives true information and is divinely inspired;
a *visio* gives true information about heavenly things and future events.

In the alliterative *Morte*, King Arthur at the height of his worldly
power, after the conquest of Rome, dreamt a dream which forecast
his ruin. He found himself in a wood among wild beasts, which were
licking from their teeth the blood of his knights. Then he flew to a
beautiful meadow, enclosed with mountains, and having vines of
silver and grapes of gold.

> Than discendis in the dale   down fra the clowddez
> A duches dereworthily dyghte   in dyaperde wedis.
> In a surcott of sylke   full selkouthely hewede,
> All with loyotour overlaide   lowe to the hemmes,
> And with ladily lappes   the lenghe of a yerde,
> And all redily reversside   with rebanes of golde, . . .
>   Abowte cho whirllide a whele   with hir whitte hondez,
> Overwhelme all qwayntely   the whele, as cho scholde;
> The rowell whas rede golde   with ryall stonys,
> Raylide with reches   and rubyes inewe;
> The spekes was splentide all   with speltis of silver,
> The space of a spere-lenghe   springande full faire;
> Thereone was a chayere   of chalke-whytte silver
> And chekyrde with charebocle,   chawngynge of hewes;
> Appon the compas ther clewide   kyngis one rawe
> With corowns of clere golde,   that krakede in sondire;
> Sex was of that setill   full sodaynliche fallen,
> Ilke a segge by hym selfe,   and saide theis wordez:
> 'That ever I rengnede on this rog, me rewes it ever!
> Was never roye so riche,   that regnede in erthe!
> Whene I rode in my rowte,   roughte I noghte ells
> Bot revaye and revell   and rawnson the pople.
> And thus I drife forthe my dayes,   whills I dreghe myghte,
> And therefore derflyche I am   dampnede for ever.'   (3250–77)

(Then came down into the vale from the clouds a duchess fairly clad in diapered
garments, in a bodice of silk of a very rich hue all overlaid to the hems with
embroidery and with lady-like lappets the length of a yard: and all delightfully

adorned with golden ribbons . . . She whirled a wheel about with her white hands as if deftly she were about to overturn it. The wheel was of red gold with noble jewels in it covered with ornaments and many rubies, the spokes were bedecked all over with silver bards, and stretched out full fair for the space of a spear length: thereon was a chair of chalk-white silver bedecked with carbuncles changing in hues: upon the outer circle there clung kings in a row with crowns of bright gold that burst asunder: six from that seat full suddenly fell, each man by himself and said these words: 'That ever I reigned on this rocking wheel I rue for ever! There was never so rich a king that reigned on this earth! When I rode with my company I wrought nothing else but hunting and revelling and taxing the people, and thus I spent my days as long as I lasted and therefore I am grievously damned for ever!')[10]

Arthur greeted the Duchess, who welcomed him. He was chosen to 'achieve the chair, the kingly ornaments were given to him, a sword with a bright hilt included. He was taken to the wood, and the boughs were made to yield their fruit to him. The lady drew wine for him, from the spring, and bade him drink to her. But at midday all was changed. She spoke to him fiercely and told him that he should lose his life. She whirled the wheel around, till his quarters were quashed and his chine chopped asunder by the chair.[11]

In a world where everything is figural and every created thing mirrors to us an aspect of the divine nature, what more likely than that dreams shall speak truths? Most *somnia* are allegorical; their meaning is hidden under cloudy figures which normally require the services of a clerk or a hermit to unravel. It scarcely needed a 'philosophre', however, to tell Arthur that he was in serious trouble. Even though he is so renowned that he will be chosen as one of the Nine Worthies (along with Julius Caesar, King David and Godfrey of Lorraine, etc.), his end is near. Within ten days he will hear of Mordred's treachery. The dreams of *Troilus and Criseyde*, though less elaborate than Arthur's dream, are no less significant. Criseyde, in Book II, after wrestling long with her problem, falls asleep as she listens to the song of the nightingale:

> And as she slep, anonright tho hire mette
> How that an egle, fethered whit as bon,
> Under hire brest his longe clawes sette,
> And out hire herte he rente, and that anon,
> And dide his herte into hire brest to gon,
> Of which she nought agroos, ne no thyng smerte;
> And forth he fleigh, with herte lefte for herte. (ii.915–31)

---

mette dreamt   *agroos* was afraid

Chaucer has the imaginative tact not to let anyone expound this dream. It certainly, in contrast to the 'nyghtyngale, upon a cedir grene' singing his 'lay/Of love', suggests something of the cruelty of love. The eagle is not only royal but rapacious? These serious and impressive dreams and visions bring their dreamers, sometimes unwillingly (in Criseyde's case perhaps unconsciously) into touch with a reality beyond the everyday. But this reality can be experienced also in waking life as other-worldly experience in a non-Christian form.

In so far as the marvels of romance do not simply pander to the fantasies of their heroes and readers, or, on a loftier plane, image forth their moral struggles and courtly aspirations—that is, insofar as the marvels have an objective reality—they present the reality of an experience, haunting, mysterious and powerful.[12] The larger part of the mysterious, 'other-worldly' imagery of European romance came in from the Celtic world in the twelfth century. The splendid *matière* of the Arthurian legend is only a portion of the tales told all over Europe, in the north especially, by Breton *conteors/disours*, tale-tellers. The Celts, it has been observed, changed the direction of Europe's imagination and stamped their poetic coinages on Christianity itself.[13]

Romance is not the only source for our understanding of Celtic 'other-worldly' imagery. One of the professional raconteurs of Henry II's turbulent court, Walter Map (c. 1140–c. 1210), recounts many a story, picked up perhaps in his native Wales, about outlandish beings and chilling events. It is typical that Henry II's court makes him think not of the ideal court of King Arthur as imagined by Geoffrey of Monmouth, Wace and Chrétien, but of that of King Herla, the Breton 'king of faery'. This is a summary of the story Map tells:

There arrived at his court one day riding on a huge goat a king of the pigmies; he was the size of a monkey and looked like the God Pan, with his shining face, enormous bearded head, hairy body and goat's feet. He made a proposal to King Herla: he would prepare Herla's marriage feast (Herla was getting ready to celebrate his marriage with the King of France's daughter), on condition that in return Herla would do the same for him. Herla accepted and the pigmies prepared a magnificent banquet for him. A year later the king of the dwarfs appeared to remind Herla of his covenant. He conducted Herla to his subterranean, but splendidly illuminated kingdom. . . . After a magnificent wedding, the king of the dwarfs took Herla back up to earth, having loaded him with splendid presents, horses, hounds, hunting equipment. He put one little hound in Herla's arms and said—'Carry it in your arms all the time! And see that neither you nor any of your courtiers dismounts before it jumps down itself.' Herla rode on for sometime. Then he stopped to ask a shepherd for news of the queen, whom he had left only three days before. The shepherd, a Saxon, had difficulty in understanding and answered that he didn't know her but he had heard tell of a queen, wife of King Herla (King of the Bretons who were chased out by the Saxons) who had disappeared 200 years ago. At these words some of the courtiers leapt angrily from their horses to seize hold of the maniac; they were instantly reduced to dust. The king, terrified, threatened death to anyone who got off his horse before the little hound leapt down. But the hound never did. And the king from that day onward wanders with his company through the woods. The first year of Henry II's reign he began to be seen less often; indeed, some Welshmen saw his company sinking into the River Wye, near Hereford, and no one saw him again.[14]

Stories of mysterious other-world beings and the sinister spells they could cast on humans who fell into their power found their way from Celtic story, either through romance, or directly, into folk-balladry. Many traditional folk-ballads describe encounters between mortals and 'faery' beings. *Tam Lin*, for example, tells of sweet Janet's love for a mortal lover, Tam Lin, and how she wins him back from the other-world which has claimed him.[15] These are the verses in which Tam Lin tells Janet of his meeting with the 'Queen o Fairies':

st.23   'And ance it fell upon a day,
       A cauld day and a snell,
     When we were frae the hunting come
       That frae my horse I fell;
     The Queen o Fairies she caught me
       In yon green hill to dwell.

24   'And pleasant is the fairy land,
       But, an eerie tale to tell,
     Ay at the end of seven years
       We pay a tiend to hell;
     I am sae fair and fu' o flesh
       I'm feard it be mysel.

25   'But the night is Halloween, lady,
       The Morn is Hallowday.
     Then win me, win me, an ye will,
       For weel I wat ye may.

---

snell keen   *tiend* tithe

26 'Just at the mirk and midnight hour
　　The fairy folk will ride,
　And they that wad their true-love win,
　　At Miles Cross they maun bide.

Tam Lin tells her to pull down the rider of the milk-white horse, who has a glove on his right hand, not on his left,—and to hold tight to him:

st.31 'They'll turn me in your arms, lady,
　　　Into an esk and adder;
　　But hold me fast, and fear me not,
　　　I am your bairn's father.

32 'They'll turn me to a bear sae grim
　　And then a lion bold;
　But hold me fast, and fear me not,
　　As ye shall love your child.

33 'Again they'll turn me in your arms
　　To a red het gaud of airn;
　But hold me fast, and fear me not,
　　I'll do to you nae harm.

34 'And last they'll turn me in your arms
　　Into the burning gleed;
　Then throw me into the well water,
　　O throw me in wi speed.

35 'And then I'll be your ain true-love,
　　I'll turn a naked knight;
　Then cover me wi' your green mantle,
　　And cover me out o sight.

Sweet Janet does as Tam Lin tells her and wins him back, much to the disgust of the Queen of Fairies who vents her anger and frustration on them both—but impotently:

42 'But had I kend, Tam Lin,' she says,
　　'What now this night I see,
　I wad hae taen out thy twa grey een
　　And put in twa een o tree.'

Another folk-ballad which tells of an encounter between a man and his fairy mistress, whom he mistakes for the Virgin Mary, is *Thomas*

---

esk newt　*gaud of airn* rod of iron　*gleed* glowing coal　*een* eyes　*tree* wood *the Rymer.* The *three* spiritual realms of Heaven, Hell and 'fair Elfland' are very clearly distinguished in it.

The great romance-writers, Chrétien de Troyes, Gottfried von Strassbourg, Marie de France (despite her miniature scale), the author of *Sir Gawain and the Green Knight*, transform the Celtic marvels and magic into something fully civilized, fully medieval. It is in the lesser works that we can feel the more authentic thrill, the *frisson* of an encounter with the Other. Such a work is the anonymous *lai* of *Guingamor*:[16]

Guingamor, nephew of the king and heir to the throne, rebuffs the advances of the queen. In revenge the queen issues a challenge to the court that no one will be so brave as to undertake *l'aventure de la forest*; she knows well that Guingamor will take it up. He does. He encounters a fairy mistress, who promises him three days of delight and lets him go about three hundred years later, a Rip van Winkle figure, a stranger from the past.

The *matière* of this tale is most compelling: the motif of the *blans pors* (usually a hart, or hind—*Guigemar, Graalant,* etc.) which leads the hero to the faery mistress, the motif of the other-world (here a land of Eternal Youth), and the motif of the deserted city, are of a kind to haunt the imagination. The author does not weld them into a unity, and artistically speaking the result is an imaginative and emotional jumble. But as a consequence of this jumble *we* can sense the mystery. This sensing is not part of Guingamor's experience; it is not mediated to us modified, transformed. It comes directly from the images to us. Insofar as it can be described, the impact of the other-world seems, paradoxically, to be cold and uncompromising, and yet mysteriously seductive, even possessively grasping—at best, indifferent; at worst, hostile.

I suggested above that it is characteristic of the most impressive and truly creative writers of romance in the Middle Ages to transform the supernatural images of Celtic legend into something entirely their own. But to have said 'fully courtly, fully medieval' was in some instances perhaps to overstate. There are passages in Marie de France, for example, which make us aware of something unexplained and inexplicable, a residue of the mystery which belongs to a world beyond the everyday. Such a passage occurs in her *lai* of *Yonec.* The lady's princely lover, who in the guise of a great bird has been visiting her in her solitary tower, has been betrayed and trapped by the *viel gelus,* her husband. She leaps from her tower and half-naked 'follows the tracks of his blood along the road and through a *hoge* (evidently some kind of hollow hill, since there was *nule clarté* inside); thence across a meadow into a city made all of silver. The city is apparently deserted; she enters the castle. In the first room is a knight asleep; in the second room another; in the third room she finds her *ami* on his richly ornate bed, wounded to death.'[17] The authoress makes no comment of any sort on the detail of this quest, with its familiar suggestion of an entry into the other-world and the motif of the deserted palace where the lights are burning night and day. The laconic power of this episode is strangely akin to the power of folk-poetry at its best. It would be possible, certainly, to rationalize some of the unexplained detail; emotional meanings could be attached for instance to the combined loneliness and lit-up quality of the scene. But such an exercise in courtly explication would leave the heart of the mystery untouched. It is this heart, however, of *Yonec* which seems to survive in a well-loved folk-carol, the *Corpus Christi* carol. Among the shared images and motifs are the falcon, who 'bears away' someone else's 'make' (mate, sweetheart); the flight suggested by verse 1; the richly hung hall; the knight lying on his death-bed with bleeding wounds; the maiden weeping at his side:

> Lully, lulley; lully, lulley;
> The fawcon hath born my mak away.

1 He bare hym up, he bare hym down;
   He bare hym into an orchard brown.

2 In that orchard ther was an hall,
   That was hangid with purpill and pall.

3 And in that hall ther was a bede;
   Hit was hanged with gold so rede.

4 And yn that bed ther lythe a knyght,
   His wowndes bledyng day and nyght.

5 By that bedes side ther kneleth a may,
   And she wepeth both nyght and day.

6 And by that beddes side ther stondith a ston,
   'Corpus Christi' wretyn theron.[18]

The words 'Corpus Christi' have given commentators rich matter for speculation. If the carol has anything directly to do with *Yonec*, they could be a garbled remembrance of the 'sacrament test' which the bird-lover has to take—*Corpus domini aportot/Li chevaler l'ad receü* (He [the priest] brought Our Lord's Body; the Knight received it)—to prove that though a shape-shifter he is not diabolical.

The argument does not rest, of course, on any connection, actual or hypothetical, between *Yonec* and the *Corpus Christi* carol. I wish only to establish the kinship between the strange, fascinating but forbidding supernatural world of folk-poetry and the world which lies submerged, sometimes only partially submerged, behind the images of romance. There is, finally, one most telling English poem which depicts the other-world—the lay of *Sir Orfeo*, based ultimately upon the Greek myth of Orpheus.

We cannot consider here the full import of this tale of 'ferli thing'. But there are two passages in it which, more vividly than anything else in English, capture what I have called the 'cold and uncompromising, and yet mysteriously seductive' quality of a world beyond our world. The first occurs during the long and weary years which Orfeo spends wandering in search of his queen, Dame Heurodis (Eurydice), who has been abducted by the 'king of fairy':

> He might se him bisides
> (Oft in hot under-tides)
> The King o fairy with his rout
> Com to hunt him al about
> With dim cri and bloweing,
> And houndes also with him berking;
> Ac no best thai no nome,
> No never he nist whider thai bi-come.
> And other while he might him se
> As a gret ost bi him te,
> Wel atourned, ten hundred knightes,
> Ich y-armed to his rightes,
> Of cuntenaunce stout and fers,
> With mani desplaid baners,
> And ich his sword y-drawe hold
> —Ac never he nist whider thai wold.
> And other while he seiye other thing:
> Knightes and leuedis com daunceing

---

under-tides noon-tides *rout* company *him* (284) i.e. the king of fairy *Ac no best . . .* but they did not catch a single animal *nist* did not know *whider . . .* where they were going *te* go *atourned* equipped *to his rightes* in a fitting manner

In queynt atire, gisely,
Queynt pas and softly;
Tabours and trunpes yede hem bi,
And al maner menstraci.   (281–302)

This passage catches memorably the elusive, unfulfilled quality
of life in the other-world. In a way the inhabitants are solid enough,
and they engage in the favourite pastimes of live courtiers. Yet, where
they are going, Orfeo does not know; they hunt—but catch nothing; they are armed for battle—but have no enemy in sight; even
the elegant dancers seem subdued. All in all, and despite the 'tabours
and trunpes', the dominant impression is that 'round and round the
ghosts of beauty glide'; they are, as it were, the mysterious reflections
of well-known, well-loved persons.

Finally, a passage which strikes a more sinister note. One day Orfeo
meets a troop of ladies and sees his lost queen amongst them. He follows
them 'in at a roche' (? a cave, a hill, like the *hoge* in *Yonec*) and emerges
into a 'fair cuntray'.[19] Disguised as a minstrel, he gets entrance into a
magnificent castle, which seems to him like 'the proude court of
Paradis' itself (376); it is a place of perpetual light, illuminated continuously by the splendour of 'riche stones'. But, once inside,

Than he gan bihold about al
And seiye liggeand within the wal
Of folk that were thider y-brought,
And thought dede, and nare nought.
Sum stode withouten hade,
And sum non armes nade,
And sum thurth the bodi hadde wounde,
And sum lay wode, y-bounde,
And sum armed on hors sete,
And sum astrangled as thai ete;
And sum were in water adreynt,
And sum with fire al for-schreynt.
Wives they lay on child-bedde,
Sum ded and sum awedde,
And wonder fele ther lay bisides:

---

queynt elegant   *gisely* skilfully   *pas* pace   *Tabours* . . . drums and trumpets
accompanied them and all kinds of music   *about al* all around   *seiye liggeand*
saw lying   *thought* seemed   *nare* were not   *hade* head   *nade* had not
wode mad   *adreynt* drowned   *for-schreynt* shrivelled up   *awedde* gone mad
wonder fele a huge number

Right as thai slepe her undertides
Eche was thus in this warld y-nome
With fairi thider y-come.   (387–404)

There is an unresolved paradox in this sombre vision: are they dead, or not? The poet states specifically in line 4 that they only appeared to be dead and reverts to the idea at the end (they were carried off in their noon-day sleep). And yet some have been drowned, others strangled or shrivelled in the fire. It is logically puzzling. And yet, surely, imaginatively right. The 'death-in-life and life-in-death' quality of this other-world scene, however it may fit into the poem as a whole, is full of its own power.

---

slepe slept *y-nome* seized *fairi* enchantment

1. The key-words, *vilains, fel, cortois*, are quite untranslatable.

2. Trans. amended from Lucy A. Paton in *Morte Arthur: Two Early English Romances*, Everyman's Library (1912).

3. '. . . the giant is described mainly in terms of wild or savage animals. In medieval bestiaries animals were frequently given moral *significacio*: the frog and the toad represented anger, the hawk and the shark rapacity, the bear cruelty and sloth, the wolf bloodthirsty rapacity (a shape often taken by the devil), the bull and the boar ferocity.' (Finlayson, *Morte*, p. 51, fn.)

4. This creature should be compared and contrasted with two others in particular —the Green Knight in *Sir Gawain and the Green Knight* and the Giant Herdsman in *Yvain* (see p. 102).

5. This tale of sworn brothers and the testing of friendship was a real chameleon of a tale. Apart from the folk-tale versions, there are Latin versions in verse and prose; a French *chanson de geste*, and a miracle play; romances in Anglo-Norman and Middle English; and saints' lives in almost every European language. (See Leach's introduction to his edition, pp. ix–xxxii.)

6. Trans. Comfort.

7. Loomis, *Arthurian Tradition*, p. 287.

8. On the importance of names and naming in romance, see especially Bezzola, *Le sens de l'aventure*, pp. 33–62. Chrétien keeps us waiting until line 3575 of *Conte del graal* for the name 'Perceval' and until line 3676 of *Roman de la charrette* for the name 'Lancelot'.

9. For trans. see above, p. 104.

10. Trans. Paton, see note 2 above.

11. The summary is taken, slightly modified, from Brock's side-notes. See his edition.

12. The strangeness of the experience seems often to come directly from text to reader (or listener); the protagonists themselves, though perhaps not the author, accept the mystery as a matter of course.

13. On the impact of the Celtic world on Henry II's court, see Bezzola, *Les Origines*.

14. Walter Map, *De Nugis Curiatium* (*Concerning the Trifles of Courtiers*), pp. 13ff. (Latin text), pp. 15ff. (translation by Tupper and Ogle). Map does not tell this story merely for the fun and fascination of it. He sardonically suggests that it looks as if Herla had passed on to Henry his habit of ceaseless travelling around.

15. The ballad is printed entire in Child's *English and Scottish Popular Ballads*, no. 39 (one-volume edition by Kittredge, p. 68).

16. Sometimes attributed to Marie de France. I discuss the attribution and *a priori* reasons for rejecting it in *Patterns of Love*, Ed. Lawlor, pp. 11–15.

17. Summary from *Patterns of Love*, Ed. Lawlor, p. 9.

18. This late medieval text is printed by R. L. Greene, *Early English Carols* (1935), no. 322A. The carol has been widely discussed, in connection with the Grail Legend, Anne Boleyn etc; Greene gives full references. See also his additions in *A Selection of English Carols* (1962), pp. 230–1. The parallel with *Yonec* has not, to my knowledge, been remarked.

19. On this and other other-world motifs, see H. R. Patch's comprehensive study, *The Other World* (1950), especially ch. 7, 'The Romances'.

6

MAN AND GOD:

RELIGION AND ROMANCE

In an earlier chapter I quoted Kierkegaard as saying that 'the absurdity of amorous inclination reaches a divine understanding with the absurdity of religious feeling'. This understanding, if not the absurdity, was not unknown to the Middle Ages themselves; thus, in one *conte*, a bird philosophizes:

> Dieus et Amors sont d'un acort:
> Dieus aime onor et cortoisie
> Et fine Amors ne les het mie;
> Dieus het orgueil et fausseté,
> Et Amors les tient en vilté;
> Dieus escoute bele proiére,
> Amors ne la met pas arriére.

(God and Love are in agreement: God loves honour and *cortoisie*, and courteous love does not in the least hate them. God hates pride and falsity, and Love holds them in disdain. God listens to sweet prayer, and Love does not neglect it.)[1]

God and the god of love are of one mind.

In Chapter 2 I described the way in which the experience of romantic love (*fine amors*, 'courtly love' in medieval aristocratic society) is marked and defined by a moment of illumination, a 'conversion' analogous to religious conversion—'Blissed be love, that kan thus folk converte', says the Narrator in *Troilus and Criseyde* (i.306). No one who has read at all widely in medieval romance can fail to be struck by the general interpenetration of religious with romantic experiences. And this is what I wish to discuss in the present chapter.

The romance, or, rather, cluster of romances, which describes the
Quest of the Grail, provides the most striking as well as the most
familiar instance of the medieval blend of religion with romance. In
the following episode from Malory's version of the story, Lancelot
approaches as close to the Holy Grail as he ever will. Although he is
acknowledged the greatest of earthly knights, and the father of Sir
Galahad, he has not the sanctity of Galahad, Bors and Percivale; he
leads the field, so to speak, of those who do not and cannot achieve the
Grail:

Than he enforced hym myckyll to undo the doore. Than he lystened and
herde a voice whych sange so swetly that hit semede none erthely thynge,
and hym thought the voice seyde, 'Joy and honoure be to the Fadir of Hevyn'.
Than sir Launcelot kneled adowne tofore the chambir dore, for well wyst he
that there was the Sankgreall within that chambir. Than seyde he, 'Fayre
swete Fadir, Jesu Cryste! If ever I dud thynge that plesed The, Lorde, for Thy
pité ne have me nat in dispite for my synnes done byforetyme, and that Thou
shew me somthynge of that I seke.'

And with that he saw the chambir dore opyn, and there cam oute a grete
clerenesse, that the house was as bryght as all the tourcheis of the worlde
had bene there. So cam he to the chambir doore and wolde have entird. And
anone a voice seyde unto him, 'Sir Launcelot, flee and entir nat, for thou
ought nat to do hit! For and if thou entir thou shalt forthynke hit.' Than he
withdrew hym aback ryght hevy.

Than loked he up into the myddis of the chambir and saw a table of sylver,
and the holy vessell coverde with rede samyte, and many angels aboute hit,
whereof one hylde a candylle of wexe brennynge and the other hylde a
crosse and the ornementis of an awter. And before the holy vessell he saw a
good man clothed as a pryste, and hit semed that he was at the sakerynge of
the masse. And hit semed to sir Launcelot that above the prystis hondys were
three men, whereof the two put the yongyste by lyknes betwene the prystes
hondis; and so he lyffte hym up ryght hyghe, and hit semed to shew so to the
peple.

And than sir Launcelot mervayled nat a litill, for hym thought the pryst
was so gretly charged of the fygoure that hym semed that he sholde falle to the
erth. And whan he saw none aboute hym that wolde helpe hym, than cam he
to the door a grete pace and seyde, 'Fayre Fadir, Jesu Cryste, ne take hit for
no synne, if I helpe the good man whych hath grete nede of helpe.'

Ryght so entird he into the chambir and cam toward the table of sylver,
and whan he cam nyghe hit he felte a breeth that hym thought hit was en-
tromedled with fyre, which smote hym so sore in the vysayge that hym

---

forthynke repent   *sakerynge* consecration

thought hit brente hys vysayge. And therewith he felle to the earthe and had
no power to aryse, as he that was so araged that had loste the power of hys
body and hys hyrynge and syght. Than felte he many hondys whych toke
hym up and bare hym oute of the chambir doore and leffte hym there semynge
dede to all people. (ii.1015)

After this partial vision Lancelot lies in a coma for twenty-four days,
one day for each year of his sinful life. When he recovers, he is the
welcome guest of King Pelles for four days. On the fifth, just before he
is to leave :

Ryght so as they sate at her dyner in the chyff halle, hit befylle that the San-
greall had fulfylled the table with all metis that ony harte myght thynke.
And as they sate they saw all the doorys of the paleyse and wyndowes shutte
withoute mannys honde. So were all abaysshed [and none wyste what to
doo]. (ii.1018)

A courtly feast is here blended with a sacramental communion—the
closed doors perhaps bring echoes also of Christ's appearance to his
disciples after the Resurrection—and both the courtly and the numin-
ous are conveyed through symbols taken from the fund of Irish and
Welsh stories recounted by the Breton *conteurs*. The blend is absolutely
characteristic of the developed Grail stories and Malory did not invent
it. Quite the opposite, in fact. The 'graal', it is held, derives as a symbolic object from Welsh stories of a Miraculous Platter (*dysgyl*)—
'whatever food one wished thereon was instantly obtained'.[2] The
gradual identification of the *graal* with the chalice of the Sacrament (the
vessel of the Last Supper) containing Christ's blood was the work of a
series of French romancers who used Chrétien's unfinished *Conte du
Graal* (=*Perceval*) as a starting-point. Malory, as has often been pointed
out, was in reaction against the religious mysticism of his immediate
source, *La Queste del Saint Graal*, written two centuries earlier (*c.* 1220)
by a Cistercian monk.[3]

 It is important to realize how fully this episode shares the traditions,
and is acted within the conventions, of chivalric romance. Lancelot
is faced with an *aventure* within the greater *aventure*, or quest, of the
Grail. He has to act, but first he must decide how to act. Or, perhaps,
'decide' is not the right word. He acts intuitively as a knight should. He
has been forbidden to enter the chamber, but when he sees the 'good
man' labouring under his burden, he instinctively feels that he should
offer his humble service. He does so, and pays the cost. But we cannot
feel he has acted wrongly because it has been from generosity of heart,

'gentilnesse' and 'fraunchise'—'Fayre Fadir, Jesu Cryste, ne take hit for
no synne if I helpe the good man whych hath grete nede of helpe'.
Lancelot is a questing knight who meets with an *aventure*; and he acts
with the spontaneous generosity of heart which a knight should feel.
Professor Vinaver has well observed that Malory's attitude is

> that of a man to whom the quest of the Grail was primarily an *Arthurian*
> adventure and who regarded the intrusion of the Grail upon Arthur's kingdom
> not as a means of contrasting earthly and divine chivalry and condemning the
> former, but as an opportunity offered to the knights of the Round Table to
> achieve still greater glory in *this* world. (iii.1535)

Even in the passage quoted Malory, whether deliberately or (as I
believe) through unconscious choice, omits two sentences which in the
French *Queste* redress the potential imbalance. The French author
specifically points out that Lancelot's action was the result of forgetful
disobedience—*il ne li sovient del deffens qui li avoit esté fet* (he does not
remember the prohibition which had been laid on him); and, later,
when Lancelot is unconscious, his hosts remark that it must be *aucune
venjance ou aucun demostrement de Nostre Seignor*.[4]

Yet, paradoxically, Malory's telling of the Grail story is, after
Chrétien's, the most memorable and has been the most influential. Let
us follow it to the climax. The full vision of the Grail, which comes
shortly after Lancelot's experience, is granted only to Galahad, Percivale
and Bors. It takes the form of a celebration of the Eucharist by 'Joseph,
the firste bysshop of Crystendom', with angels acting as servers ('and
two bare candils of wexe, and the thirde bare a towell, and the fourth
a speare which bled mervaylously, that the droppis felle within a boxe
which he hylde with hys othir hande'). The bishop lifts up the sacramental bread, the 'ubblie', *oblatio*:

> And at the lyftyng up there cam a figoure in lyknesse of a chylde, and the
> vysayge was as rede and as bryght os ony fyre, and smote hymselff into the
> brede, that all they saw hit that the brede was fourmed of a fleyshely man.
> And than he put hit into the holy vessel agayne, and than he ded that longed
> to a preste to do masse.
>
> And than he wente to Sir Galahad and kyssed hym, and bade hym go and
> kysse hys felowis. And so he ded anone.
>
> 'Now', seyde he, 'the servauntes of Jesu Cryste, ye shull be fedde afore
> thys table with swete metis that never knyghtes yet tasted.'
>
> And whan he had seyde he vanysshed away. And they sette hem at the
> table in grete drede and made their prayers. Than loked they and saw a man

com oute of the holy vessell that had all the sygnes of the Passion of Jesu
Cryste bledynge all opynly, and seyde, 'My knyghtes and my servauntes and
my trew chyldren which bene com oute of dedly lyff into the spirituall lyff,
I woll no lenger cover me frome you, but ye shall se now a parte of my secretes
and of my hydde thynges. Now holdith and resseyvith the hyghe order and
mete whych ye have so much desired.'

Than toke He hymselff the holy vessell and cam to sir Galahad. And he
kneled adowne and resseyved hys Saveoure. Aftir hym so ressayved all hys
felowis, and they thoughte hit so swete that hit was mervaylous to telle.[5]

In this episode the symbolism of the Grail is made explicit; every
detail is spelt out for us so that we shall not miss any point. The wonder
is, particularly in view of Malory's personal inadequacies (or disinclina-
tions), that the whole thing is not desiccated, mechanical and flat. The
miracle of transubstantiation is made visible in the most naïve physical
terms; a heavenly infant actually enters the holy bread,[6] and Christ
actually emerges from the holy vessel of the Grail. ' "Thys ys," seyde
he, "the holy dysshe wherein I ete the lambe on Estir Daye." ' There
are, I believe, at least two reasons why this succeeds in moving us.
One is, that behind the 'semblaunt' of the Eucharist, there are the
still valent symbols of the older *graal* (the mysterious dish-of-plenty)
and of the bleeding lance (which recalls to us the legend of the blind
Longinus, who was healed when he pierced the side of Christ as he hung
on the cross). Their primitive power is reinforced in the next scene
when Galahad 'went anone to the speare which lay uppon the
table and towched the bloode with hys fyngirs, and cam aftir to the
maymed knyght [the Fisher King] and anoynted his legges and hys
body'.[7]

The second reason why the climactic scenes of the Quest move us is
connected with the sheer quality of Malory's prose. It has a quality
which we would now, perhaps, call 'Biblical', certainly 'liturgical'; it
seems to derive its cadences from the same sources as the Elizabethan
prayer-book and the Authorized Version of the Bible. This passage
gives the impression of being written in a liturgical high style entirely
consonant with the quasi-liturgical, ceremonial occasion which it
celebrates. The question is a difficult one. But perhaps we should begin
by qualifying our partially formed view of Malory's capacity for
religious experience. This episode provides no evidence, one must affirm,
that Malory understood, or sympathized with, the meaning of the
French *Queste*. Spiritual chivalry is not even imaginable as an alternative to 'erthely worship'; a fully *personal* religious commitment seems

to be outside his ken. But this passage alone provides evidence that
Malory was moved and could move others with the beauty of religious
ceremony. His 'solempne' vernacular style is fully capable of conveying
the deep sense of order and propriety, of awe and of serenity, which
exalts the merely personal into a *corporate* religious act. To put it in
extreme terms, the achievement of the Grail is a ritual rather than an
experience. But it is a ritual which the term 'Arthurian', quoted earlier,
does not fully cover; rather, we should be reminded of the elaborate
'dubbing' ceremonies, liturgical ceremonies, through which a knight
was initiated in the 'felawschyp' of all goodly knights and into the
service of God and his fellow men. The beginning and consummation
of knighthood is a liturgical action.

I have tended to imply, so far, a rather one-way relationship and to
speak as if all the influence flowed in one direction—*from* religious *to*
romantic experience. But, as the passages from Malory suggest, the
traffic is in both directions. European experience of Christianity itself
was decisively changed by the romantic 'event' which awakened the
twelfth century. Gerard Manley Hopkins could never have written the
triumphant last stanza of *The Wreck of the Deutschland* without the
chivalry of Jesuitism behind him:

> Our King back, Oh, upon English souls!
> Let him easter in us, be a dayspring to the dimness of us,
>   be a crimson-cresseted east,
> More brightening her, rare-dear Britain, as his reign rolls,
> Pride, rose, prince, hero of us, high-priest,
> Our hearts' charity's hearth's fire, our thoughts' chivalry's
>   throng's Lord.

In the thirteenth century the monastic author of *La Queste del Saint
Graal* does all he may to supplant earthly chivalry with the chivalry
of Christ and to put Carbonek in the place of Camelot. But even his
Christianity is deeply modified by the chivalry he rejects.

Every age remakes Christianity in its own image. The decisive re-
making during the course of the Middle Ages could be demonstrated
in a dozen ways; but the general point will emerge, I think, from a
comparison of the death of Roland in the old French *Chanson de Roland*
(and, going further back, the representation of Christ as a feudal, epic
hero in the Anglo-Saxon poem *The Dream of the Rood*) with a chivalric
allegory from a later devotional treatise, the *Ancrene Wisse*.

In the *Chanson de Roland* (copied *c.* 1125–50) the hero dies alone, but supreme and victorious, on the battlefield. As his end approaches, he makes his confession to God:

> 'Deus, meie culpe vers les tues vertuz!
> De mes pecchez, des granz e des menuz . . .' (2369-70)

('O God, in the face of your almightiness I say *mea culpa*! for my sins both big and small . . .')

But what he recalls, in fact, is not his sin, his unworthiness, but his victories, his country, his fellow barons, and the great services he has done for his Emperor Charlemagne and thereby, by implication, for God, the supreme feudal lord of all earthly vassals:

> De plusurs choses a remembrer li prist:
> De tantes teres cum li bers conquist,
> De dulce France, des humes de sun lign,
> De Carlemagne, sun seignor ki.l nurrit; . . . (2377-80)

(He began to call many things to mind: the vast realms that he had conquered as a warrior; sweet France and the men of his kindred; and Charlemagne, his lord who had cared for him.)

And when he dies it is in supreme assurance that God, his *seignor*, will accept the surrender of his earthly fief and reward him as a lord does properly reward his faithful vassal:

> Sun destre guant a Deu en puroffrit,
> Seint Gabriel de sa main l'ad pris.
> Desur sun braz teneit le chef enclin,
> Juntes ses mains est alét a sa fin. (2389-92)

(He offers his right-hand glove to God; Saint Gabriel took it from his hand. He held his head bowed down; his hands clasped together [*sc.* in feudal homage], he went to his end.)

God sends him a worthy escort of angels and cherubim—*L'anme del cunte portent en pareis.*

In the piety of the dying Roland Christ has no part; Roland plays the role of a vassal in a vast feudal hierarchy embracing heaven and earth.[8] The Anglo-Saxon poem, equally heroic, has a different emphasis. The *Dream of the Rood* (i.e. properly speaking, the vision that the Cross had) presents a most moving picture of Christ the young warrior-hero triumphantly climbing the tree of the Cross. It is the Cross itself that speaks:

Ongyrede hine þa geong hæleđ,   þæt wæs God ælmihtig,
strang ond stiđmōd;   gestāh hē on gealgan hēanne
modig on manigra gesyhđe,   þā hē wolde mancyn lȳsan.
Bifode ic þa mē se Beorn ymbclypte;   ne dorste ic hwædre
        būgan tō eorđan,
feallan tō foldan sceatum,   ac ic sceolde fæste standan.
Rod wæs ic arǣred;   ahōf ic rīcne Cyning,
heofona Hlāford;   hyldan mē ne dorste.   (39–45)[9]

(Almighty God ungirded Him,/eager to mount the gallows,/unafraid in the
sight of many:/He would set free mankind./I shook when his arms embraced
me/but I durst not bow to the ground,/Stoop to Earth's surface./Stand fast
I must. I was reared up, a rood./I raised the great king,/liege lord of the heavens,/
dared not lean from the true.)[10]

The other side of this epic, presentation of Christ's mighty redemptive
act as an heroic gesture made proudly before all eyes—'modig on manigra geshyde'—is Satan's depiction as a *vilain*, a traitor to his lord.[11]

The more individual world of twelfth-century courtly and Christian
humanism embraced a new interpretation of the relationship between
man and God and of the salvation of mankind through Christ. In
earlier centuries, writes Professor Southern:

Man was a helpless spectator in a cosmic struggle which determined his
chances of salvation. The war was one between God and the Devil, and God
won because he proved himself the master-strategist. That God should become
Man was a great mystery, a majestic, awe-inspiring act . . . But there was
little or no place for tender compassion for the sufferings of Jesus.[12]

The 'theoretical justification' for rejecting this view was the work of
the theologian St Anselm (1033–1109); but the corresponding change
in men's hearts and emotions was brought about primarily by St
Bernard of Clairvaux (1090–1153) and the generation of monks and
preachers who followed him. As a basis for the relationship between
man and God, they substituted for feudal loyalty and service the bond
of love; and for Christ the Conqueror, Christ the Lover. One of the
central spiritual documents of this profound change is St Bernard's
Commentary on the Song of Songs; he gives expression, it has been
said, 'to an overpowering creative love, so rich and sweet that it almost
surpasses our understanding'.[13] In place of the hero whose 'royal banners
forward go' we meet, in the pages of St Bernard and of Ailred of
Rievaulx, the Man Jesus, *ebrius vino charitatis*/ 'drunk with the wine of
love'. The well-known hymn, 'Jesu, the very thought of Thee', was

written not by St Bernard himself but by a Cistercian follower; it may stand as an epitome of the new emotional warmth:

> Dulcis Jesu memoria,
> dans vera cordi gaudia,
> sed super mel et omnia
> eius dulcis praesentia.

Or, in a fourteenth-century translation:

> Jhesu, swete is the love of thee,
> Noon othir thing so swete may be;
> No thing that men may here and see
> Hath no swetnesse agens thee.[14]

This new feeling for Jesus is beautifully summed up in a well-known passage from the *Ancrene Wisse*, a work of religious instruction written early in the thirteenth century for the guidance of three young women of gentle birth who had taken vows of permanent inclosure. This *exemplum*, or parable, comes from the climax of the work, the book which treats of love.

A leafdi wes mid hire fan biset al abuten, hire lond al destruet, and heo al poure, inwith an eorthene castel. A mihti kinges luve wes thah biturnd up on hire swa unimete swithe thet he for wohlech sende hire his sonden, an efter other, ofte somet monie; sende hire beawbelez bathe feole and feire, sucurs of liveneth, help of his hehe hird to halden hire castel. Heo underfeng al as on unrecheles, and swa wes heard iheortet thet hire luve ne mahte he neaver beo the neorre. Hwet wult tu mare? He com himseolf on ende, schawde hire his feire neb, as the the wes of alle men feherest to bihalden, spec se swithe swoteliche and wordes se murie thet ha mahten deade arearen to live, wrahte feole wundres and dude muchele meistries bivoren hire ehsihthe, schawde hire his mihte, talde hire of his kinedom, bead to makien hire cwen of al thet he ahte. Al this ne heold nawt. Nes this hoker wunder? For heo nes neaver wurthe forte beon his thuften. Ah swa, thurh his deboneirte, luve hefde overcumen him thet he seide on ende: Dame, thu art iweorret and thine fan beoth se stronge thet tu ne maht nanesweis withute mi sucurs edfleon hare honden, thet ha ne don the to scheome death efter al thi weane. Ich chulle, for the luve of the, neome thet feht up o me and arudde the of ham the thi death secheth. Ich wat, thah, to sothe thet ich schal bituhen ham neomen deathes wunde; and ich hit wulle heorteliche forte ofgan thin heorte. Nu thenne biseche ich the, for the luve thet ich cuthe the, thet tu luvie me lanhure efter the ilke dede, dead, hwen thu naldest, lives. Thes king dude al thus: arudde hire of alle hire fan and wes himseolf to wundre ituket and islein on ende; thurh miracle aras, thah, from deathe to live. Nere theos ilke leafdi of uveles cunnes cunde, yef ha over alle thing ne luvede him herefter.[15]

(There was once a lady who was completely surrounded by her enemies, her land all laid waste, and she herself destitute in an earthen castle. But a king of great power loved her so much that he sent messengers to her one after another, and often several together, with many fair jewels, and with food to sustain her, and he sent his noble army to help in the holding of her castle. She accepted it all as if unthinkingly, and was so hard-hearted that he could never come any nearer to her love. What more would you? At last he went himself. He let her see the beauty of his face, the face of one who of all men was fairest to behold. He spoke so very tenderly, and spoke words of such delight that they might have raised the dead to life. He worked many wonders and brought great marvels before her eyes, revealed to her the power that he had, told her of his kingdom and asked that he might make her queen of all he possessed. All this availed nothing. Was it not strange, this disdain? For she herself was not worthy to be his handmaid. But love had so vanquished his tender heart, that at last he said, 'Lady, thou art assailed, and thine enemies are so strong that thou canst by no means escape their hands without my help, which can prevent their putting thee to a shameful death after all thy misery. For love of thee I will take this fight upon myself and deliver thee from those who seek thy death. I know without any doubt that among them I must receive my death-wound, but I will meet it gladly in order to win thy heart. Now I beseech thee, for the love I show thee, that thou shouldst love me, at least after my death has been accomplished, who wouldst not while I live.' The king carried out all this, delivered her from all her enemies, and was himself outrageously tortured and finally slain. But by a miracle he rose from death to life. Would not this lady be of an evil nature had she not loved him thereafter beyond everything else?)

The anonymous author of the *Ancrene Wisse,* deeply influenced by the new currents of spiritual thought, sees the Incarnation and Redemption not as 'that remote and majestic act of Divine Power' which filled the minds of earlier writers and artists but as an act of love, personal and even, as this anecdote has shown, 'romantic'.[16] Without much change such a passage could be made to celebrate the martyrdom of a *courtly* lover. The widespread use, too, of a tag like *quia amore langueo* is a perpetual reminder that the languages of mystical and of romantic love are largely interchangeable.

II

I hope it is clear by now that there is no simple relationship between religion and romance in the Middle Ages. Even such an apparently straightforward device as the open and deliberate use of romance story for religious purposes as we find in the *Queste del Saint Graal* raises problems which are far from straightforward. There are, besides, various other ways in which religion and romance can be combined. We find, for instance: the deliberate opposition of 'romantic' to Christian values; the imaginative enhancement of romance by the employment of religious motifs and images; the conscious valuation, or critique, of romance by outside standards; and attempts at an imaginative reconciliation of the two sets of values. These possibilities are neither exhaustive, nor always, surprising as it may seem, mutually exclusive.

The deliberate flaunting of romance values, especially the values of romantic, courtly, love, by opposing them to Christian ones, is not found as often as one might expect. But the delightful little *chante-fable* (song-story) of *Aucassin and Nicolette*, written somewhere in northern France during the thirteenth century, shows how it can be done, in a spirit of fun. The tale, part song, part prose narrative, tells of the love of two young people—Aucassin, the son of a Count, and Nicolette, a low-born, foreign girl. The Count, realizing his son's attachment, orders her guardian to send Nicolette away—if the Count lays hands on her, he'll have her burnt. Pretending that she has already gone, the guardian tells Aucassin, 'Go and marry a princess! If you make this girl, Nicolette, your mistress, you'll lose your chance of Paradise for ever.' Aucassin replies:

En paradis qu'ai-je a faire? Je n'i quier entrer, mais que j'aie Nicolete ma tresdouce amie que j'aim tant; c'en paradis ne vont fors tex gens con je vous dirai. Il i vont ci viel prestre et cil viel clop et cil manke qui tote jor et tote nuit cropent devant ces autex et en ces viés creutes, et cil a ces viés capes ereses et a ces viés tatereles vestues, qui sont nu et decauc et estrumelé, qui moeurent de faim et de soi et de froit et de mesaises; icil vont en paradis: aveuc ciax n'ai jou que faire. Mais en infer voil jou aler, car en infer vont li bel clerc, et li bel cevalier qui sont mort as tornois et as rices gueres, et li buen sergant et li franc home: aveuc ciax voil jou aler; et s'i vont les beles dames cortoises que eles ont deus amis ou trois avoc leur barons, et s'i va li ors et li argens et li vairs et li gris, et si i vont herpeor et jogleor et li roi del siecle: avoc ciax voil jou aler, mais que j'aie Nicolete ma tresdouce amie aveuc mi.[17]

E

('What should I do in Paradise? I don't want to go there unless I have Nicolette
with me, my sweetheart and beloved; for no one goes to Paradise except
those I'll describe to you—old priests, old cripples, the halt and maimed, who
spend day and night crouching in front of the altars in ancient crypts, people
with worn-out capes and old rags and tatters, naked, with no shoes or stockings,
dying of hunger and thirst, cold and disease. Those are the people who go to
heaven—I'll have nothing to do with them. It's hell I want to go to, for all
the handsome clerks go there, fine knights killed in tourneys and noble wars,
good fighting-men and gentlemen: it's them I should like to be with. Beautiful
courtly ladies go there, too—those who have two or three lovers as well as
their husbands. Gold, and silver, and good furs go in the same direction—and
harpers and minstrels, and the kings of this world. They are the people I'd like
for company, provided I can have Nicolette, my dearest sweetheart with me.')

The delicate and deliberate blasphemy of this speech is, of course,
doubly contrived: contrived by the speaker to confront, indeed affront,
Nicolette's guardian; but, further, contrived by the author, who need
be in no sense committed to it, to delight his listeners. For him probably
it is a mark of detachment; Aucassin's blasphemy is part of the absurdity
of young love (like its other hyperboles—'O shee doth teach the torches
to burne bright!') which the author feels along with its beauty.

The apotheosis of this attitude is to be found in the mid-thirteenth-
century Provençal romance, *Flamenca*. This romance, of a breath-
taking absurdity and scintillating blasphemy, must be briefly described:

The Count of Nemours marries his daughter, Flamenca, to Sir Archambaut.
Archambaut becomes jealous of the innocent attentions paid to his wife by
the King of France and shuts her up in a tower. She is only allowed out for
two purposes: to go to Church on Sundays and feast-days and to go to the town
'baths'. At church she is veiled and screened in a sort of moving cubicle; at
the baths she is locked in alone with two maid-servants.

The hero, Guillaume de Nevers, hears of her plight and falls in love with
her at once, on principle, without even seeing her. He is young, rich, handsome,
seven-foot tall, and endowed with every conceivable grace of body and mind.
His first problem is how to make himself known to this adorable and inaccessible
lady. First of all, he makes himself acquainted with the parish priest and per-
suades him to send his clerk off to study at the University, all expenses paid.
Guillaume, who is versed in liturgy and theology, takes over the clerk's duties
and thus becomes the one who during Mass, gives Flamenca the *pax* (the kiss of
peace). This enables them to talk together. Their conversation is one of the
most extraordinary in literary history.

On Sunday 7 May, Guillaume says, 'Oh dear!'; on Sunday 14 May, Flamenca asks, 'What's wrong?'. 21 May: Guillaume, 'I'm dying'. 28 May: Flamenca,

'Of what?'. Ascension Day: G. 'Of love'. 4 June, 'For whom?'. Whitsunday: 'For you.' And so they continue, two syllables at a time, until the beginning of August. (This dialogue, with the necessary psychological analysis and love-casuistry, occupies 2000 lines of text.)

Meanwhile Guillaume has been tackling the second problem—access to the 'baths'. He solves this by buying up the local inn as his private residence, importing a team of workmen from another district, and setting them to construct, in secret, an underground tunnel from the inn to directly under the 'baths'. So, finally, their problems solved, Guillaume and Flamenca (at about line 6000) meet and enjoy one another's love.[18]

Flamenca has been appropriately described as a 'romance to end all romances' and its central dialogue as 'so quintessential of the difficulties and stratagems of courtly love that it trembles on the edge of burlesque. . . . Revolving about each of these overburdened, whispered messages is a world of debate and analysis, delicately but too surely overdrawn to be taken in perfect seriousness.'[19] The justice of Professor Muscatine's comment is nowhere more apparent than in those numerous passages in the romance where the author plays with religious attitudes and motifs. Most striking is the way Guillaume's romantic hyperboles are woven into the very texture of the church service, for the central romantic encounter between Guillaume and Flamenca takes place in church during Mass, during a whole succession of Masses. The following passage describes Guillaume's sensations as he sees Flamenca for the first time at Mass; he watches as the priest sprinkles her with holy water (the rite of *Asperges*):[20]

> Le preires dis: *Asperges me*,
> Guillems si pres al *domine*
> E dis lo vers tot per entier
> Anc non cug mais qu'e cel mostier
> Fos tam ben dig; e-l preire issi
> Fora del cor . . .
> A Guillem remas totz le canz
> Et a son oste que l'ajuda;
> Mais soen gara vaus la muda
> Que del pertus los ueils non mòu.
> Le cappellas ab l'isop plòu,
> Lo sal espars per miei lo cap
> A Flamenca lo miels que sap,
> Et ill a fag un'obertura
> Dreit per mei la pelpartidura
> Per zo que mieilz lo pogues penre;

Lo cuer ac blanc e prim e tenre
E-l cris fon bell'. e resplandens.
Le soleils fes móut qu'avinens,
Car tot dreit sus, per mei aqui,
Ab un de sos rais la feri.
Quan Guillems vi la bell'ensena
Del ric tesaur qu'Amors l'ensenna
Le cors li ri totz e l'agensa
E *signum salutis* comensa;   (2470–97)

(The priest said: *Thou shalt sprinkle me*; Guillaume took it up at *O Lord* and recited the whole verse. I don't believe that it had ever been said so well before in that church. The priest then left the choir. . . . All the singing was then left to Guillaume and to his host who was helping him. Nevertheless Guillaume often gazed at the cubicle and kept his eyes on the opening [i.e. in the choir-screen]. The priest sprinkles with his sprinkler and directs the salt water as best he can towards Flamenca's head; she has made her head bare right up to the middle of her parting in order to receive it the better. Her skin was white, delicate and soft, her hair resplendently beautiful. The sun acted with perfect courtesy, for at that very moment he struck her directly with one of his rays. When Guillaume saw this fine sample of the rich treasure Love is revealing to him, his whole heart laughed with joy and he began to chant *the sign of salvation*.)

This extract is representative. The ray of sunshine falling on Flamenca's bared head is not merely a cause of joy to Guillaume but a veritable *signum salutis*, a symbol of salvation. The whole treatment of Guillaume's ecstatic amour trembles along the brink of blasphemy—so often just over the brink, in fact, that one is forced to wonder what the implications are. The chief imaginative effect, perhaps, is of a delicate flamboyance; the author teases and provokes us into wondering how far he can go. Ultimately it is the sheer extravagance and intellectual fantasy of his poem that prevent it from giving offence.

Much more in earnest is what appears to be the anti-Christian feeling of Gottfried von Strassburg's *Tristan*; 'appears' to be because, when those who are familiar with the German poem in the original cannot agree, one must be wary. Surely, however, something more serious than the intellectual pyrotechnics of *Flamenca* is going on in this German romance.[21] Amongst several there is one incident that particularly takes the reader's breath away—the Ordeal by Fire—not only for what it is but for the colouring the narrator sets upon it.

Tristan is strongly suspected by King Mark of having been in bed with his queen, Isolde; Mark resolves to put her through a judicial ordeal, not an uncommon medieval way of settling such a problem (though clergy were forbidden by the Lateran Council of 1215 to consecrate trials by ordeal). The ordeal consists of holding a red-hot iron in the bare hand: a guilty person will be burnt, an innocent will be unscathed. Isolde is bound to accept Mark's proposal.

Îsôt beleib al eine dâ
mit sorgen und mit leide:
sorg' unde leit dui beide
twungen si harte sêre.
so sorgete umbe ir êre
sô twanc si daz verholne leit,
daz si ir unwârheit
solte wârbæren
mit disen zwein swæren
enweste sî, waz ane gân:
si begunde ir swære beide lân
an der genædigen Krist,
der gehülfec in den noeten ist;
dem bevalch si harte vaste
mit gebete und mit vaste
alle ir angest unde ir nôt.
  In disen dingen hæte Îsôt
einen list ir herzen vür geleit
vil verre ûf gotes hövescheit: (15538–56)

(Isolde remained alone with her fears and sorrows,—fears and sorrows that gave her little peace. She feared for her honour and she was harassed by the secret anxiety that she would have to whitewash her falseness. With these two cares she did not know what to do: she confided them to Christ the Merciful, who is helpful when one is in trouble. With prayer and fasting she commended all her anguish most urgently to Him. Meanwhile she had propounded to her secret self a ruse which presumed very far upon her Maker's courtesy.)[22]

The ruse was this: she arranged for Tristan, disguised as a pilgrim, to be at the harbour where she would arrive. At her request this 'pilgrim' carried her ashore and, on her whispered instructions, tumbled with her to the ground, ending up by lying in the queen's arms. This enabled the queen to swear a 'true' oath to King Mark:

'That no man in the world had carnal knowledge of me or lay in my arms or beside me but you, always excepting the poor pilgrim whom, with your own eyes, you saw lying in my arms. I can offer no oath or denial concerning him . . .'

In the name of God she laid hold of the iron, carried it, and was not burned.

Thus it was made manifest and confirmed to all the world that Christ in His great virtue is pliant as a windblown sleeve [*daz der vil tugenthafte Krist/wintschaffen alse ein ermel ist*]. He falls into place and clings, whichever way you try Him, closely and smoothly, as He is bound to do. He is at the beck of every heart for honest deeds or fraud. Be it deadly earnest or a game, He is just as you would have Him. This was amply revealed in the facile queen.[23]

Mr Hatto's comment on this is: 'There is no compelling reason to regard this passage in its context as blasphemous, or heretical, or demoniac, or indeed as anything more sensational than the utterance of an intelligent and alert man who was indifferent enough in religious matters to be critical of pious excess among the ignorant.' In other words, the passage is drily ironic. Tentatively, I should question this. The irony does not read like the irony of the 'indifferent'; there is something almost passionate in the persistence with which the detail is pursued—the tone of Swift rather than of Gibbon? The rest of the work, however, does not, as it seems to me, encourage us to think that the positives of Gottfried's irony, whatever they might be, were passionately *Christian*. The puzzle remains.

A slightly later episode in the romance is just as difficult to interpret. Once again experiences of love and of religion are juxtaposed in a piquant and puzzling way. Tristan and Isolde have, finally, been banished from the court and are in exile. Tristan takes her to a cavern in the mountain-side, originally a kind of sexual retreat for giants; it is inscribed (in French) *la fossiur' a le gent amant*, The Cave of Lovers. This grotto is

round, broad, high, and perpendicular, snow-white, smooth and even, through-out its whole circumference. Above, its vault was finely keyed, and on the keystone there was a crown most beautifully adorned with goldsmith's work and encrusted with precious stones. Below, the pavement was of smooth, rich, shining marble, as green as grass. At the centre there was a Bed most perfectly cut from a slab of crystal, broad, high, well-raised from the ground, and engraved along its sides with letters, announcing that the bed was dedicated to the goddess of Love.[24]

The likeness of this cave to a Christian church, and of the allegorization which follows it to fashionable ecclesiastical allegorizations has often been noted:

Now hear their interpretations. The bar of cedar stands for the Discretion and

Understanding of Love; the other ivory for her Purity and Modesty. With these two seats, with these chaste bars, Love's house is guarded, and Deceit and Treachery locked out.[25]

Whatever the precise references, the love between Tristan and Isolde is presented in the language of Christian mysticism—'they are consumed by one another like Christ and the Soul', comments Mr Hatto, 'and, consuming, are sustained'.[26]

The problem of tone and intention is very baffling. But in the end it comes down to this: does Gottfried mean what he implies or not? It is said that it is 'unlikely that he was consciously flouting religion. Rather he was using its terms to describe what seemed to him to be the most exalted of human experiences . . . he used the only possible terms, those of Christian mysticism'. This is convincing, as far as it goes. Chaucer and Gower, to name no others, use Christian language to describe romantic, even specifically sexual, delight. But they do not leave us with the impression that Gottfried leaves with his feverish intensity of analysis; Tristan speaks of love-death:

> 'dirre tot der tuot mir wol.
> solte diu wunnecliche Isot
> iemer alsus sin min tot,
> so wolte ich gerne werben
> umb ein eweclichez sterben.'[27]

('this death pleases me well. If the lovely Isolt is always thus to be my death, then I would gladly ask for death eternal.')

Gottfried must have known what he was making Tristan say. One would give a good deal to know exactly what he meant by it.

These excerpts from Gottfried's *Tristan* show how difficult it is sometimes (especially at a distance of eight hundred years) to distinguish between romances in which the author is making a daring and provocative use of religious imagery, in order to hint at the supremacy of idealized erotic love over all other forms of love, and romances in which the author is merely enhancing love by talking about it *as if it were* a religion—with a temple, gods and goddesses, a liturgy and devotions, priests, saints and martyrs, sins, penances, sacraments, graces and all. This latter is normal romance machinery; it provides the writer with a terminology and an imagery, with a set of conventions (i.e. agreed forms), which enable him to communicate. Chaucer's highly stylized *Knight's Tale* provides numerous straightforward instances. Palamon, for instance, goes 'with hooly herte and with an heigh corage' (2213) 'to wenden on this pilgrymage/Unto the blisful Citherea benigne' and prays:

> 'Faireste of faire, O lady myn, Venus,
> Doughter to Jove, and spouse of Vulcanus . . .
> Have pitee of my bittre teeris smerte,
> And taak myn humble preyere at thyn herte . . .
> Thy temple wol I worshippe everemo
> And on thyn auter, where I ride or go,
> I wol doon sacrifice and fires beete. . . .'   (2221-53.)

This is a clear example of the imaginative enhancement of romance through religious observance. A more difficult, though fascinating, example of the same thing—a 'religion of love'—occurs in Chrétien's *Lancelot*. Queen Guenevere has been abducted by a wicked knight, Meleagaunt; Lancelot, in pursuit, is helped by a maiden. They come to a spring, and near the spring someone has left a comb with an ivory handle and a few strands of hair in it. The maiden tries to deflect Lancelot away from the fountain, but unsuccessfully. Lancelot picks up the comb; the maiden asks for it, laughing and tantalizing Lancelot by refusing to tell him whose it is. When Lancelot insists, she says, 'It's the queen's comb and her shining hair'. 'Which queen do you mean?' 'Arthur's queen, to be sure.' At this Lancelot loses his colour and his power of speech and almost swoons. With the tactful assistance of the maiden he recovers and begins to 'adore' Guenevere's hair (it is Chrétien's term, not mine) as if it were a holy relic:

> Ja mes oel d'ome ne verront
> nule chose tant enorer,
> qu'il les comance a aorer,
> et bien. c^m foiz les toche
> et a ses ialz, et a sa boche,
> et a son front, et a sa face;
> n'est joie nule qu'il n'an face:
> molt s'an fet liez, molt s'an fet riche:
> an son soing, pres del cuer, les fiche
> entre sa chemise et sa char.
> N'en preïst pas chargié un char
> d'esmeraudes ne d'escharboncles; . . .
> neïs saint Martin et saint Jasque;
> car an ces chevox tant se fie
> qu'il n'a mestier de lor aïe.   (1460-78)

---

worshippe honour   *where I ride or go* whether I ride or walk   *beete* kindle

(Never will the eye of man see anything receive such honour as when he begins to adore these tresses. A hundred thousand times he raises them to his eyes and mouth, to his forehead and face: he manifests his joy in every way, considering himself rich and happy now. He lays them in his bosom near his heart, between the shirt and the flesh. He would not exchange them for a cartload of emeralds and carbuncles . . . even for St Martin and St James [he has no need]; for he has such confidence in this hair that he requires no other aid.)[28]

A related passage occurs later in the romance. Lancelot is visiting the queen's chamber by night; he tears his way through the iron bars of the window:

> et puis vint au lit la reïne,
> si l'aore et se li ancline,
> car an nul cors saint ne croit tant. (4651-3)

(then he comes to the bed of the queen, whom he adores and before whom he kneels, holding her more dear than the relic of any saint.)

When he leaves her room, he genuflects (*soploier*):

> et fet tot autel
> con s'il fust devant un autel. (4717-18)

(and acts precisely as if it were a shrine.)[29]

The 'religion' of love could not be more explicitly invoked.

Chrétien is a highly sophisticated poet and in some respects even more baffling to the modern reader than Gottfried von Strassburg. (Did they, one wonders, write for an élite of initiates?) Not unnaturally, there are almost as many interpretations of these passages as there are critics; the three main interpretations correspond to the three main views of the poem.

One school of critics holds that it is a severely ironic diatribe against courtly love and all its works—'the religious imagery of the poem . . . is not designed to set up a "system" opposed to Christianity, but to make the significance of Lancelot's deeds apparent'. In this view, the 'adored' lock of hair is an idol, a graven image. Other critics argue that through the image or figure of secular passion, the nature of true Christian love, *caritas*, is shadowed forth. The mercy of the Lady, like the grace of God, cannot be earned; it must be freely bestowed. 'The knowledge of true love, like the knowledge of Truth, is only given to those who have gone through the long Calvary to deserve it.' The hair, then, is a sacrament of illumination, an unsought-for spiritual grace. Lastly, the romance can be seen as a supreme expression of the nature of love in the stylized conventional forms devised by medieval imaginations. It communicates 'a religion of woman-worship'; 'this religion of love also had its graces, in the ecstasies of contemplation and in the power to pass serenely through every trial'. The hair, in this interpretation, is an object for romantic, quasi-religious meditation.[30] My personal view is that Chrétien wished to do more than inculcate 'a religion of woman-worship', though he is certainly interested in the actual experience of romantic love. But what was that 'more'? Something, I believe, less explicitly Christian and theological than the second interpretation suggests.

Finally, Chaucer's *Troilus and Criseyde* provides further complex cases of the 'religion of love'; the poem is full of religious imagery. However else this imagery is used, it is used first (as by Chrétien, in his *Lancelot*) to enhance, heighten and define the experience of love; Troilus praises

> 'Benigne Love, thow holy bond of thynges,
> Whoso wol grace, and list the nought honouren,
> Lo, his desir wol fle withouten wynges.
> And noldestow of bounte hem socouren
> That serven best, and most alwey labouren,
> Yet were al lost, that dar I wel seyn certes,
> But if thi grace passed our desertes.'   (iii.1261-7)

And earlier, if Pandarus can be believed, Troilus prayed to Love:

> He seyde, 'Lord, have routhe upon my peyne,
> Al have I ben rebell in myn entente,
> Now, *mea culpa*, lord, I me repente!'   (ii.523-5)

Chaucer's *Troilus*, however, goes beyond the simple, traditional position and, I should argue, provides at once an intensification of the romantic experience and also a means of judging it, a scale of other values, a critique.

The use of a word like 'judging' is, or could be, misleading because it immediately suggests that Chaucer's attitude is essentially a moral one, whereas it could better be described (as far as this poem goes) as metaphysical. Chaucer is not passing judgment on behaviour, but looking coolly and rather sadly at *la condition humaine*:

---

list the . . . is unwilling to honour you

> Man is in love and loves what vanishes.
> What more is there to say? (Yeats)

The 'more' that Chaucer has to say is present throughout the poem in two ways—in the Boethian philosophy which forms its intellectual ground, and in the religious language which both heightens and (paradoxically) 'places' the love of Troilus and Criseyde. We shall return, inevitably, in later chapters to Chaucer's great poem, which both consummates and transcends the romance tradition. Certainly there is no other medieval English poem which displays the two loves, of religion and romance, so 'deeply interfused' and yet so finely discriminated.

1. 'Le Lai de L'Oiselet', Ed. Pauphilet, *Poètes et Romanciers*, p. 503 (cit. Dronke, *European Love-Lyric*, p. 5). According to this bird, if you maintain the 'sens, cortoisie et onors\Et loiauté' of Love, you can expect to enjoy God *and* Mammon—'Dieu et le siecle avoir poés'.

2. Loomis in *Arthurian Literature*, pp. 280, 284 ('The Origin of the Grail Legends').

3. For further details, please consult the Historical Note (p. 238).

4. *Queste*, Ed. Pauphilet, pp. 255–6. It is not known which MS of his French source Malory used. I quote the most accessible printed edition; Professor Vinaver refers to another in his commentary.

5. Vinaver, *Works*, ii.1029–30. In the first line I have changed *vigoure* to *figoure*, in accordance with Caxton's *figur* (see Vinaver's footnote, p. 1029).

6. The symbolism recalls the depiction in art (in alabaster tables, for instance) and perhaps also in drama (the Mystery cycles) of the soul as a sort of little doll which can enter and leave the head.

7. Vinaver, *Works*, ii.1031. I do not wish to imply, of course, that 'primitive' and 'Christian' meanings can here, or elsewhere, be clearly distinguished. On the 'heathenish belief that the reproductive forces of Nature were affected by, even depended on, the sexual potency of the ruler', see Loomis in *Arthurian Literature*, p. 279.

8. A different, more Christ-centred attitude is evident in the *Chançun de Willame*; the dying Vivien calls himself a scoundrel for asking to be spared from death, since Christ did not spare himself for our sake. (813–22)

9. Wyatt, *Anglo-Saxon Reader*, p. 170.

10. Trans. Alexander, p. 107.

11. e.g. in the poem known as *The Later Genesis*. See also Southern, *The Making of the Middle Ages*, p. 55, showing how deeply the Crusaders were impregnated with these conceptions; he quotes a Crusade song, 'God has brought before you his suit against the Turks and Saracens, who have done him great despite. They have seized his fiefs, where God was first served and recognized as Lord.'

12. ibid., p. 235. This short quotation does not do justice to this extremely interesting chapter.

13. Auerbach, *Literary Language*, p. 71.

14. Carleton Brown, XIV, no. 89; the English version becomes increasingly free. The Latin hymn is in *The Oxford Book of Medieval Latin Verse*, Ed. F. J. E. Raby (1959), no. 233.

15. The text is based on Geoffrey Shepherd's edition of the *Ancrene Wisse: Parts Six and Seven* (1959), 21–2; I have further modernized the orthography. Professor Shepherd's introduction is an invaluable aid towards understanding the new spirituality (especially pp. xlviii–lvi). The translation is by M. B. Salu, *The Ancrene Riwle* (1955), pp. 172–3.

16. The image of Christ the Lover pleading with his sweetheart, the World forms the theme of a number of lyrics also. See, for instance, 'Undo thi dore, my spuse dere, Allas! wy stond I loken out here?' (Carleton Brown, XIV, no. 68).

17. Ed. M. Roques, p. 6.

18. *Flamenca* is available in a parallel text edition (Provençal and modern French translation) in Bibliothèque Européenne, Ed. R. Lavaud and R. Nelli (Desclée de Brouwer, 1960). There is an English translation by H. F. M. Prescott (1930), who unacceptably attributes the romance to 'Bernadet the Troubadour'.

19. Muscatine, *Chaucer*, p. 55.

20. *Asperges me, Domine, hyssopo, et mundabor: lavabis me, et super nivem dealbabor.* Psalm L, 3: *Miserere mei, Deus, secundum magnam misericordiam tuam* (Thou shalt purge me with hyssop and I shall be clean; thou shalt wash me and I shall be whiter than snow./Have mercy upon me, O God, according to thy great mercy).

21. I am deeply indebted to Mr A. T. Hatto's translation of *Tristan* (Penguin Classics, 1960) and to his comments on it. A slightly abridged German text is edited by August Closs (Blackwell's German Texts, 1947), from which I quote the short sample passage on p. 133.

22. Trans. Hatto, p. 246.

23. ibid., pp. 247–8.

24. ibid., p. 261.

25. ibid., p. 263. As he points out in his Introduction, p. 15, other analogies have been established to link the Cave of Lovers with the 'Cubicle' ('in which the Soul suffers Union with God') and with the 'Tabernacle' (the shrine held to embody the presence of God).

26. Hatto, Introd. p. 15.

27. Text from W. T. H. Jackson in *Arthurian Literature*, p. 155, with translation. Professor Jackson's chapter should be read with Mr Hatto's introduction. Together they give a comprehensive view of the problems.

28. Trans. Comfort.

29. ibid.

30. View 1: Robertson, *Preface*, p. 452; he says, 'Lancelot is an inverted Redeemer who shows others how to live vainly without social ostracism'. View 2: Bayrav, *Symbolisme*, especially pp. 127 ff; summarized, op. 143: their love 'becomes the perfect image for divine love'. View 3: Frappier in *Arthurian Literature*, p. 180.

7

THE IMAGES OF ROMANCE

In my introductory chapter I quoted some remarks about romance by Henry James. He argued, in his preface to *The American*, that the only '*general* attribute of projected romance . . . is the fact of the kind of experience with which it deals—experience liberated, so to speak; experience disengaged, disembroiled, disencumbered, exempt from the conditions that we usually know to attach to it'. The ensuing chapters have attempted to describe those qualities which most claimed the attention of romance-writers in the Middle Ages: they are the qualities inherent in the experiences, principally, of idealized love, idealized social virtue, idealized valour and integrity and idealized religious questing. In passing it has been inevitable that something should have been said about the way romances 'work', especially in the chapter on the supernatural; the supernatural, we saw, was both in itself an experience (or could be) and also a mechanism for conveying other experiences. I should like now to consider in more detail some of the mechanisms—the modes as distinct from the themes of romance.

The modes are essentially *non*-realistic. Although realism has a function in many romances—that is, it suits the author's purpose sometimes to give us a 'slice of life'—the normal procedures are different; the experience (of love or war) is 'exempt from the conditions that we usually know to attach to it'. Thus, for example, an adulterous affair, such as Tristan's with Isolde, will be exempt from the feelings of guilt that in a Christian society would usually go with it; nor will Tristan be worried by reflections about the welfare of the body politic.[1] Or, again, the relationship between a man and a lion is untrammelled by considerations of probability in Chrétien's *Yvain*. 'Things as they are/

Are changed upon the blue guitar.' This is, in art, inevitable. In romance, doubly so, since the selection and transformation of raw material is carried further in a formal and stylized genre than in a realistic one. Amongst the various ways in which romance differs from other fictions one stands out as especially characteristic and especially interesting: the dominating use of *images*. In this discussion I shall not be using the word 'image' in quite the sense that is usual in criticism. However, rather than attempt an immediate definition, I will give an example of the technique. The example is the simplest there could be— the *lai* by Marie de France called *Laüstic*. The lady, keeping a rendez-vous at the bedroom window with her lover in the neighbouring garden, tells her exasperated and inquisitive husband:

> 'Il nen ad joïe en cest mund
> Ki n'ot le laüstic chanter.' (84–5)

('The man who doesn't listen to the nightingale's singing doesn't know what happiness is in this world.')

The husband *de ire e (de) maltalent en rist* (he laughed with anger and spite)—a vivid dramatic touch. He gets his servants to trap the bird, brutally kills it in front of her eyes—'From now on you'll be able to sleep in peace!' and throws the blood-stained corpse against her, *un poi desur le piz devant* (just a little above her breast). She sorrowfully wraps the dead bird in precious samite, embroidered in gold and *tut escrit* with the sad adventure, and sends it to her lover. He, full of courtliness— *ne fu pas vilains ne lenz* (he was not sluggishly discourteous), enshrines the dead nightingale in a golden, jewelled casket and meditates upon it every day. Or rather—and this is typical of the poet's reticence—we are left to imagine what the lover did every day; the last line of her story says simply: *Tuz jurs l'ad fet od lui porter* (he had it carried about with him continually). More important, she is totally reticent about the 'meaning' of the nightingale. She could have said, 'The nightingale signifies a beautiful innocent love; the brutality of its death signifies the cruel misapprehension that the world always affords to beauty and innocence; the rich incarceration signifies the high value which ought to be set on such a precious thing.' But there is none of this.[2]

A more complex instance of a dominant image occurs in Chrétien's *Le conte du graal*. (It is perhaps significant that it is the moderns who have agreed to call the romance by the name of its hero, *Perceval*, instead of by the name of its mysterious object.)[3] The scene in which

Perceval visits the Castle of the Grail has become one of the most famous in all romance literature, and, as we have already seen, inspired numerous 'continuators', adapters and interpreters. It is worth giving at some length for its general interest as well as its importance to the present argument.

After his long *aventure* at Biaurepaire, the castle of Blancheflor, where he has freed her from the siege of her enemies, Perceval announces his intention of going home to see his old mother, whom he had left swooning on a bridge as he rode off to become a knight. On his journey he finds a fisherman, who promises him a night's lodging and directs him to his house. On arrival Perceval is received by four young men who do all the usual things—stable his horse, disarm him, and take him to his quarters. When the *seignor* (the fisherman) arrives, Perceval is taken in to see him in the hall, where he sits before a bright fire. He apologizes for not rising to greet Perceval but he is not in good health (*je n'en sui mie aesiez*, 3108). After some small talk a squire comes in bearing a marvellous sword; it is indestructible, has a pommel of gold and a gold-embroidered sheath. It is a present to the *seignor* from his niece, who will be happy if the man it is bestowed upon puts it to good use. The *seignor* gives it to Perceval saying:

> 'Biax frere, ceste espee
> Vos fu voëe et destinee,
> Et je weil molt que vos l'aiez.'   (3167–9)

('Good friend, this sword was specifically destined for you; I am most desirous that you shall have it.')

Perceval thanks him and girds it on, draws it ('it suited him splendidly', the narrator comments), sheathes it and gives it to the *vallés* who was looking after his armour. The hall was marvellously bright:

> Et laiens avoit luminaire
> Si grant come on le pooit faire
> De chandoiles en un hostel.   (3187–9)

(And within the hall the light was the brightest that the candles of a mansion could possibly produce.)

While they talked, a *vallés* came out of an adjoining room,

> Qui une blanche lance tint
> Empoignie par le mileu
> Si passa par entre le feu
> Et cels qui el lit se soient.
> Et tot cil de laiens veoient

Le lance blanche et le fer blanc,
S'issoit une goute de sanc
Del fer de la lance en somet,
Et jusqu'a la main au vallet
Coloit cele goute vermeille.
Li vallés voit cele merveille
Qui la nuit ert laiens venus,
Si s'est de demander tenus
Coment ceste chose avenoit . . .   (3192–205)

(grasping by the middle a white lance, he passed between the fire and those
seated on the couch. All present beheld the white lance and the white point,
from which a drop of red blood ran down to the squire's hand. The youth who
had arrived that night watched this marvel, but he refrained from asking
what this meant . . .)[4]

The reason for Perceval's silence was that he had been taught, as a matter of
courtoisie, not to talk too much. Then entered two other squires holding
golden chandeliers worked in black enamel.

Li vallet estoient molt bel
Qui les chandeliers aportoient.
En chascun chandelier ardoient
Dis chandeilles a tot le mains.
Un graal entre ses deus mains
Une damoisele tenoit,
Qui avec les vallés venoit,
Bele et gente et bien acesmee.
Quant ele fu laiens entree
Atot le graal qu'ele tint
Une si grans clartez i vint
Qu'ausi perdirent les chandoiles
Lor clarté come les estoiles
Font quant solaus lieve ou la lune.
Aprés celi en revint une
Qui tint un tailleoir d'argant.
Li graaus, qui aloit devant,
De fin or esmeré estoit;
Prescïeuses pierres avoit
El graal de maintes manieres,
Des plus riches et des plus chieres
Qui en mer ne en terre soient;
Totes autres pierres passoient
Celes del graal sanz dotance.
Tout ensi com passa la lance,

Par devant le lit s'en passerent
Et d'une chambre en autre entrerent.
Et li vallés les vit passer,
Ne n'osa mie demander
Del graal cui l'en en servoit,
Que toz jors en son cuer avoit
La parole au preudome sage.   (3216–47)

(Then two other squires came in, right handsome, bearing in their hands candelabra of fine gold and niello work, and in each candelabrum were at least ten candles. A damsel came in with these squires, holding between her two hands a grail. She was beautiful, gracious, splendidly garbed, and as she entered with the grail in her hands, there was such a brilliant light that the candles lost their brightness, just as the stars do when the moon or the sun rises. After her came a damsel holding a carving platter of silver. The grail which preceded her was of refined gold; and it was set with precious stones of many kinds, the richest and the costliest that exist in the sea or in the earth. Without question those set in the grail surpassed all other jewels. Like the lance, these damsels passed before the couch and entered another chamber.

The youth watched them pass, but he did not dare to ask concerning the grail and whom one served with it, for he kept in his heart the words of the wise nobleman.)[5]

Perceval makes up his mind to enquire the next morning about what he has seen; but the next morning is too late. When he awakes the castle is completely deserted. He finds his horse ready harnessed and rides out. As he does so, the drawbridge is drawn up behind him. He calls out, but no one answers his call. He follows fresh hoof-prints through the forest which soon lead him to a lady who is lamenting the death of her lover, killed that morning by a knight. She expresses her astonishment that Perceval and his horse are so fresh when there is no lodging or hostel within 40 leagues. 'But I had an excellent lodging within earshot,' he says:

'Le meillor que jou eüsse onques.'
—'Ha! sire, vos jeüstes donques
Chiez le riche Roi Pescheor.'   (3493–5)

('the best I ever had'—'Ah, sir, then you must have lodged with the noble Fisher King.')

Perceval says he doesn't know if his host was a fisherman or a king but he treated him very well. The lady then tells Perceval about the king's dreadful wound which he got in battle:

Qu'il fu ferus d'un gavelot
Parmi les quisses ambesdeus.   (2512–13)

(For he was struck by a javelin between his two thighs.)

Furthermore, she asks him whether he saw the Bleeding Lance and the Grail, and if so whether he asked about them. When he says he kept silent, she says, 'So much the worse. What is your name?'

> Et cil qui son non ne savoit
> Devine et dist que il avoit
> Perchevax li Galois a non,
> Ne ne set s'il dist voir ou non;
> Mail il dist voir et si nel sot.   (3573–7)

(Then he who did not know his name divined it and said that his name was Perceval of Wales. He did not know whether he told the truth or not, but it was the truth though he did not know it.)[6]

The lady tells him that from now on he is *Perchevax li chaitis* (wretched). . . . *Perchevax maleürous*. He could have healed the Fisher King:

> 'Que toz eüst regaaigniez
> Ses membres et terre tenist.'   (3588–9)

'So that he might have completely regained the use of his limbs and his land.')

Now many sorrows will follow; and all is the result of Perceval's sin, the sin of leaving his mother, who, she now tells him, is dead:

> 'Por le pechié, ce saches tu,
> De ta mere t'est avenu,
> Qu'ele [est] morte del doel de toi.'   (3593–5)

('You must realize that it is because of your sin in regard to your mother that this has happened to you—for she has died of grief on your account.')

There are great and manifest differences between Marie de France's use of the 'image' of the nightingale in *Laüstic* and Chrétien's use of the *graal*. Differences of scope and magnitude, differences of intent. Marie de France wishes to be understood, though she is determined not to spell out for us exactly what we are to understand. Chrétien may have wished ultimately to be understood (in the unfinished state of the romance it is impossible to say in what terms) but the incident I have recounted clearly contains an element of deliberate mystification. Chrétien's image is also a riddle. Nevertheless, the miniature and the mural have this in common: central to the experience that each conveys, is not an idea, an attitude, a feeling, or the responses of a character, but an emphatically realized visual object which points beyond itself. This object is felt to crystallize the meaning of the scene. In the case of *Laüstic* the meaning is not difficult to grasp, though any attempt to articulate it will fall short of what the image itself 'says'. In *Perceval*, the meaning of the *graal* is only gradually and never completely unfolded —and, most important of all, again not in intellectual, conceptual terms. We learnt, for example, something about its splendour from its *grans clartez* that dimmed the branched chandeliers as the sun dims the stars; we learn, later, that it is the Fisher King's father who is served from the *graal*, and that he is so 'spiritual' a being that a single consecrated wafer suffices for his nourishment.

> 'D'une sole oiste le sert on,
> Que l'en en cel graal li porte;
> Sa vie sostient et conforte,
> Tant sainte chose est li graals.
> Et il, qui est esperitax
> Qu'a se vie plus ne covient
> Fors l'oiste qui el graal vient.
> Douze ans i a esté issi
> Que fors de la chambre n'issi
> Ou le graal veïs entrer.'   (6422–31)

('The holy man sustains and refreshes his life with a single Mass wafer. So sacred a thing is the grail, and he himself is so spiritual, that he needs no more for his sustenance than the Mass wafer which comes in the grail. Twelve years he has been thus without issuing from the chamber where you saw the grail enter.')

We feel we are getting closer (here, at last, much closer) but not through precise general statement. The hermit commits himself to one concept only, that the *graal* is *tant sainte chose*—'such a holy thing'. This merely sums up what we know already. The important questions, reiterated throughout the romance, and now partly answered, are: why does the lance bleed? and, who is served from the grail?

II

The consideration of 'images' takes us straight to the heart of the matter. We could have begun an analysis of the way romance works by thinking of character or plot or rhetoric. But the images force us towards the differences, towards those features which most clearly distinguish romance from other fictions. To a large degree the greater importance of images in romance results from the lack of a sense of space and time. Virginia Woolf wrote of Sterne's *Sentimental Journey*, 'He was travelling in France, indeed, but the road was often through his own mind, and his chief adventures were not with brigands and precipices but with the emotions of his own heart.'[7] This could be said of many of the heroes of romance; they live, move and act in a faceless landscape. It is not a *nameless* one; but the names themselves are liable to tell us more about the spiritual adventures of questing knights than about a countryside (Le Chastel de Pesme Aventure, Le Pont de l'Espee, and so forth). Since the lords and ladies of romance inhabit a land without a precise geography, the 'places' they visit, the objects they encounter and the creatures they meet take their meaning not from their relation to one another in a coherent landscape but from their relation to the experience being conveyed.[8] Even a group of images, such as those constituting Calogrenant's *aventure* in *Yvain*, do not genuinely constitute a scene—the Monstrous Herdsman, his wild animals, the Stone, the Fountain, the Storm and the liturgy of birds are an imaginative sequence, not landmarks in an itinerary.

Not only geographically but temporally, romance tends to be non-realistic. Living in an eternal spring, with 'such a day tomorrow as today', the characters scarcely seem to notice the seasons go by. In Chrétien's *Perceval* it snows, but chiefly so that the three drops of blood will have an appropriate background.[9] Gawain's famous winter journey is indeed wintry:

> For werre wrathed hym not so much that wynter nas wors,
> When the colde cler water fro the cloudes schadde
> And fres er hit falle myght to the fale erthe.
> Ner slayn wyth the slete he sleped in his yrnes,
> Mo nyghtes than innoghe, in naked rokkes
> Theras claterande fro the crest the colde borne rennes
> And henged heghe over his hede in hard iisseikkles. (726–32)

But, exceptional though this is, the landscape is not, even here, purely a physical environment. And, indeed, one might be hard put to it to find any storytelling of any age of which this statement could unreservedly be made.

It is clear that the absence of space-time connections makes other connections more important; the kind of objects and happenings which in other fictions are the necessary background and ordering of human

---

werre fighting *fres* froze *fale* colourless *yrnes* armour *Theras* where
rennes runs

experience have, in typical romance, other functions. The point need
not be laboured. Nothing could be further from romance than the
concept of *vraisemblance*, verisimilitude, so beloved of seventeenth-
century French critics:

Vraisemblance, on which the new argument for the unities was essentially based,
marks a way of thinking which found change of scene improbable and therefore objectionable because the stage was small and could never be anything
but the same stage, and rejected extension of time because of the brevity of the
performance. This notion of *vraisemblance* is typical of cultivated society. It
combines the arrogant rationalism that refuses to be taken in by imaginative
illusion with contempt for the *indocte et stupide vulgaire* which is perfectly
willing to be taken in.[10]

There is only one observation here that one might quarrel with. The
notion of *vraisemblance* was not typical of the highly cultivated societies
of the Middle Ages (and 'cultivated' indeed were the courts of Henry
II and Richard II of England, of Marie de Champagne and of Land-
grave Hermann of Thuringia, to name no others). It is worth asking why
this was so. The answer is that the habits of writers and the assumptions
of readers are intimately bound up with metaphysics. Medieval
romances have to be read in a different way from nineteenth-century
realist novels because the people who wrote them had different views
about the visible world.

In Chapter I I described the medieval way of looking at phenomena
as being, in the widest sense, symbolic and quoted a verse from Alan
of Lille:

> Omnis mundi creatura
> quasi liber et pictura
>   nobis est in speculum.[11]

The visible world is a book, a picture or a mirror in which the viewer
can see an adumbration of the truth and glory of the divine. We shall
never become good viewers, or good readers of medieval texts, while
such an exposition as the following appears merely ludicrous to us; it
comes from a medieval bestiary:

UNICORN: The unicorn is a very fierce beast with only one horn; to capture
it, a virgin maid is placed in the field. The unicorn approaches her and, resting
in her lap, is so taken. By this beast Christ is figured; by the horn his insuperable
strength is expressed. Resting in the womb of a Virgin, he was taken by the
hunters; that is, he was found in the form of a man by those who loved him.[12]

The medieval writer did not need exhorting to 'connect, only connect', because he inhabited a mental world in which all physical, mental and spiritual phenomena were enmeshed, woven together into a huge web of connections whose beginning and ending was in God. This way of looking at things is not simply a theological exercise; to allegorize from the nature of an object is both to describe and to *explain* it. Since the establishment of modern methods of empirical scientific enquiry from the seventeenth century onwards we have found it harder and harder to take other kinds of explanation seriously. We may be helped, I think, if we ponder Basil Willey's dictum that 'explanation is re-statement in terms of current assumptions'.[13] The current assumptions of the bestiary compilers were very different from those of twentieth-century zoologists.

One of the inevitable effects of the medieval type of explanation was to reduce the degree of attention given to 'things as they are', to *actual* phenomena, as we should (perhaps too sweepingly) call them. So, for example, a medieval writer wishing to describe the Blessed Virgin would not ask himself what a young Jewish working-class woman at the beginning of our era would have looked like. He might, perhaps, have envisaged her as an idealized courtly lady of his own century, thus relating her to a known ideal. But, most likely of all, he would have described her by *analogy*, or by a series of analogies relating her to objects in the natural world and in revealed truth. Thus, he would say she was like a bee, both chaste and fruitful; that she was like the fleece of Gideon, on which the dew fell when he called for it (representing the grace of God in the Annunciation); that she was like the burning bush in which Moses saw God (because in her womb God was made flesh); that she was like the ever-closed door which Ezekiel saw in a vision (she was 'closed', and no man could enter her).

This type of approach to phenomena, intellectual as it must appear, can accommodate more than one emotional attitude. Briefly, whilst believing in the interrelatedness of the created world and the Divine Reality, you can either take a Platonic view or a sacramental. According to the first (Platonic or neo-Platonic) 'the world of phenomena is only a shadow' (*umbra*, a favourite medieval metaphor); it is worth contemplating simply for what it can reveal to us of eternal truth. The second view, the sacramental, seeing the same parallels between time and eternity, insists that the single event, the single object, has inherent worth because of this; the fact that a human marriage reflects the spiritual marriage between Christ and his Church gives the human marriage not less but more validity. The Platonic view of the world leads one away from it. We ascend and kick away from beneath us the worthless ladder with its foot in the mire and clay. The sacramental, more centrally Christian, view leaves us rootedly in the everyday world where the Word was made flesh and

> Christ plays in ten thousand places,
> Lovely in limbs, and lovely in eyes not his
> To the Father through the features of men's faces.   (Hopkins)

A special term is sometimes used to denote a type of sacramentalism which is special to the Middle Ages—*figura*.

Figural interpretation establishes a connection between two events or persons, the first of which signifies not only itself but also the second, whilst the second encompasses or fulfils the first. The two poles of the figure are separate in time, but *both, being real events or figures, are within time*, within the stream of historical life.[14]

Thus Adam 'figures' Christ (so do Isaac and Samson, for different reasons); Eve 'figures' the Blessed Virgin; Noah's Flood 'figures' the Judgment; and the raising of Lazarus, the Resurrection. Erich Auerbach distinguishes the figural view of the world from the allegorical, on the one hand, and the more widely symbolical on the other. The tendency of allegory, he argues, is to strip events, natural phenomena, texts, of their concrete reality, whereas the figural interpretation depends on our experiencing them in their full actuality. The symbol, on the other hand, differs by being 'a direct interpretation of life, and originally no doubt for the most part of nature' whilst 'figural prophecy relates to an interpretation of history'.

It stands to reason that a way of looking at the world that linked all things visible and invisible into one great interlocking pattern, that reads sermons in stones, etymology and boat-building, would have an effect on the way people read books and listened to stories. 'Art', Emile Mâle has observed, was, in the Middle Ages, 'at once a script, a calculus, and a symbolic code.'[15] So, if the world itself is a Book, where he who runs may read, how much more must a book be a Book, in which lessons may be read which are not obvious to the casual observer.[16] One book in particular, it has often been said, should be our guide, and all others should be read in the same spirit—namely, God's own writ, the Bible:

> *Litera* gesta docet; Quid credas *Allegoria*;
> *Moralis* quid agas; Quo tendas *Anagogia*.

(The literal sense teaches you the story; the allegory, what you should believe; the 'morality', what you should do; and the 'anagogical' sense, your spiritual destiny.)

It is certainly interesting to know about three- or four-fold interpretation, interpretation on three or four 'levels of meaning', as we should say. But attempts to apply the method systematically to medieval vernacular poetry have only been muddling. The important thing is to be familiar with the varying ways in which medieval writers expressed their sense that there is always more to a story than a story:

Fedeil deu, entend l'estorie: asez est clere e semble nu, mais pleine est de sens et de meule. L'estoire est paille, le sens est grains; le sen est fruit, l'estorie raims. Cist livres est cum armarie des secreiz Deu.

(Faithful soul, attend to the story: it is quite straightforward and seems bare, but it is full of meaning and matter. The literal story is the chaff, the meaning is the wheat; the meaning is the fruit, the story is the branch [that bears it]. This book is like a treasure-chest containing the secrets of God.)[17]

So, the author of a twelfth-century *Livres des Rois*. Besides wheat and chaff, fruit and branch, another image is frequently used to describe the relationship between story and meaning, *littera* and *sensus*—the image of the nut: 'the external shell of falseness having been cast away, the reader may discover within the sweet kernel of truth'.[18] Some kind of antithesis is implicit in most of the metaphors used, but the sharpness of this one—shell false/kernel true—is neither necessary (except in its context, a defence of the 'fictions' of poets) nor representative.

Some comments from Reto Bezzola's book, *Le sens de l'aventure et de l'amour* will serve to sum up the foregoing argument and will also state more persuasively than I can its relevance for the reading of medieval romance. He writes that, in order to grasp the essence of a medieval work, we must extend our feeling for the symbolic nature of the world to every object and every action; and yet at the same time we must remember that these objects and actions still retain their full validity in the world of our senses—they never become *de simples images transparents*. There will be moments during a story when we can give ourselves up entirely to the charm of the narration. But suddenly there may come a passage in which things appear in an unexpected light and there is a sense of mystery; the medieval reader, accustomed to look for the reality behind the veil (*la réalité derrière le voile des phénomenes*), would pause, baffled but thoughtful, and gradually let himself be permeated by the deeper meaning of what he was reading, hearing or seeing.[19]

We may not necessarily agree with all the 'deeper meanings' that Professor Bezzola senses. In Chrétien's *Erec et Enide*, for instance, he argues that the romance as a whole is an initiation, by three stages, into the nature of *la vie du chevalier et de la dame*: the fight for the self (*le 'moi'*), the fight for the other (*le 'toi'*) and the fight for the courtly society (*la communauté*). Erec and Enide have to learn that their happiness is not an end in itself; the true happiness of love cannot be limited to their private experience but must become 'la Joie de la Cour', the happiness of the whole community.[20] This account may come to seem too precisely generalized, too tidily conceptual. On the other hand, I find it impossible to go along with Professor Vinaver, who, impressed with the difficulty of interpretation, has concluded that there is not only a distinction in romance between the *matière* and the *sens* but a positive and deliberate discrepancy, a 'duality and semi-obscurity', 'a constant tension between *conte* and *conjointure*'.[21] This, he asserts, 'offends the logic' of some modern readers but was accepted quite naturally by the learned, medieval, courtly poet. The 'duality' is not the result of incompetence, because 'while on the courtly level the coherence of the story is above reproach, on the mythological level there is simply no need for any coherent sequence'.[22] So far from believing with Bezzola that the magic and the marvels have a symbolic value in *la grande aventure de la vie*, we are to accept that 'incidents occur and magical objects appear at random'. This is to say, for example, that the moving description of the enchanted garden in 'La Joie de la Cour', the third and last *aventure* of Chrétien's *Erec et Enide*, is imaginatively irrelevant, has nothing whatever to do with Chrétien's courtly purposes.

Ultimately, the point at issue cannot be resolved by scholarship, though scholarship may illuminate it. It comes to this. Do we experience in reading 'La Joie de la Cour', and other memorable episodes in medieval romance, a sense of imaginative, of *poetic*, coherence? If so, we should not be easily put off from believing in our experience, and attempting to find words for it, either by the seeming inadequacy of past explanations, or by scholarly arguments external to the text. I hope the passages discussed in the remainder of this chapter will do something to show that centred in the 'images' of medieval romance we can find that 'lovely conformitie, or proportion, or conveniencie between the sence and the sensible' which appears to distinguish great poetry in all ages.

III

Let us start by considering an 'image' or 'images' of a quite different
kind from those in the poems of Chrétien and Marie de France. The
episode is from Malory's *Morte*. In the final stages of the Quest Sir
Galahad, Sir Percivale and Sir Bors embark (not for the first time) in
a conveniently moored Magic Ship.

And wan they com thyder they founde the shippe ryche inowghe, but they
founde nother man nor woman therein. But they founde in the ende of the
shippe two fayre lettirs wrytten, which seyde a dredefull worde and a mervaylous:
    'Thou man whych shalt entir into thys shippe, beware that thou be in
stedefaste beleve, for I am FAYTHE. And therefore beware how thou entirst
but if thou be stedfaste, for and thou fayle thereof I shall nat helpe the' . . .
    And whan they were in, hit was so mervaylous fayre and ryche that they
mervaylede. And amyddis the shippe was a fayre bedde. And anone Sir
Galahad went thereto and founde thereon a crowne of sylke. And at the feete
was a swerde, rych and fayre, and hit was drawyn out of the sheeth half a
foote and more.[23]

In the subsequent chapters Percivale's sister, who is with them on
board, tells them the history and the meaning of the sword and the
scabbard. These we must pass over. The symbolic *pièce de résistance* is
the building of the ship itself and, especially, the history of the tri-
coloured spindles on the canopy of the bed. As Malory's version is,
despite its compression from his French source (or, sometimes, because
of it), not easy to follow and still of considerable length, I quote for
convenience Jean Frappier's summary of the symbols and their meaning in his discussion of Malory's 'French book'.

[The symbolic treatment of Solomon's ship] is founded on the traditional
comparison of the Church with a ship: *Ecclesia est navis*. With this have been
combined the memory of self-propelled vessels described in Breton *lai* or
Arthurian romance and the strange legend of the wood from which the
cross was made. Solomon, builder of the Temple, the Church of the Old
Law, is the builder of the ship. Eve took with her from Paradise a branch of
the Tree of Knowledge and planted it; originally white, it turned green when
she lost her virginity, and turned red when Cain committed the first murder.
From this tree at various times were cut the three spindles which Solomon
placed in the ship in the form of a cross . . . The sword, according to the
epistle to the Ephesians, is the Word of God, the Scriptures. The hempen

girdle attached to it indicates the inferior inspiration of the Old Testament; the new girdle, made of a virgin's hair and worn by the messianic figure of Galaad, is of course the New Testament.[24]

In the compressed form of a summary these symbols and their explication read somewhat drily, to say the least. But the dryness is not all in the compression. The whole thing smells of the lamp. The passage, created by the author of *La Queste del Saint Graal* and taken over by Malory, is an elaborate example of what one may call 'retrospective allegorizing'. The archetypal symbols of Ship, Bed and Sword are not allowed to accrue their own meaning (i.e. a meaning of the kind that Marie de France's nightingale accrues, one built up from the context); instead they are 'explained' in the terms of the extraordinary legend (itself a product of the medieval synthesizing imagination) which traces the wood of the Cross back through Solomon's temple to the Tree of the Fall. In this case much of the residue of permanent meaning has been squeezed out of the symbols by the sheer intellectual complexity of the commentary needed to explicate them. Indeed, Frappier's terms 'intricate' and 'ingenious' are those that come most readily to mind. The whole thing is an extended allegorizing *after the event*—the event in this case being Chrétien's *Perceval* and the Grail stories built round it by 'continuators'.

The strength of the exegetical tradition is abundantly apparent here. Intellectual, textual commentary based on the study of the Bible is here 'applied' to another purpose. The purpose is not, in fact, so very 'other', since the mind at work is that of a Cistercian monk intent on writing a Christian gloss on the courtly gloss on the Celtic images and stories: under the knightly quest for that *sainte chose*, the grail, is hidden the eternal search of man for God and for his salvation.

Some scholars would have us believe that all medieval symbolism is of this exegetical kind, whether or not the author himself gives an exposition of his meaning. 'Between their symbolism and ours there is a great gulf, because in their case the image is in the service of the intellect and not, as in ours, of the sensibility. The symbol does not serve the purpose of expressing a sort of unique revelation such as would elude the rational intellect; rather, it simply veils a truth which has been completely grasped and which can easily be formulated in plain language.'[25] In so far as this is held applicable to medieval *literary* symbolism, the symbolism of medieval romance, it is far too sweeping. The danger lies in mistaking the conscious theorizing of any age, however impressive, as an ultimate guide either to their writings or to our reading of them. The existence of an exegetical tradition of a certain kind does not prove an intention on the author's part, nor should it constrain our approach. That is to say, we can, as they did, *reason about* symbols and 'explain' them intellectually, but this reasoning does not exhaust and may not even cover their original intention. 'Huge cloudy symbols'—the garden, the tower, the fountain—are certainly present in many medieval poems and their meaning is not limited to what theological exegesis can make of them. Because they are, indeed, 'cloudy' and in them we see, as it were, in a glass, darkly, the images of medieval romances present us with difficulties. But the prime difficulty is certainly not one of constructing an intellectual significance—Dante's procedures in *La Vita Nuova* and the adventures of some modern commentators remind us how fatally easy that can be. The difficulty is precisely the opposite—to be able to rest in our doubts and teasings and uncertainties without any irritable searchings after fact and reason.

The way the author of *La Queste* used images, in his 'retrospective allegorizing', must be distinguished from two others which we may call 'radical allegory' and 'symbolic story'. The term 'radical allegory' I borrow from C. S. Lewis's *The Allegory of Love*, and with it his definition—'a story which can be translated into literal narration . . . without confusion, but not without loss'. The principal medieval example of this, C. S. Lewis finds, is the first part of the *Roman de la Rose*:

The inner life, and specially the life of love, religion, and spiritual adventure, has therefore always been the field of true allegory; for here there are intangibles which only allegory can fix and reticences which only allegory can overcome.[26]

The distinction between 'radical allegory' and 'retrospective allegorizing' lies in the degree of coherence between the story and the signification; in 'radical allegory' they fit like hand and glove, like a man and his reflection in a mirror, whereas 'retrospective allegorizing' can hardly be achieved without duress—story and signification fit, indeed, but like a man with his straitjacket, not with his glove, much less his reflection.

In the first part of the *Roman de la Rose* we feel that the experience and the story which will fully convey it are one creation, one act of the imagination. The main outlines of the story have already been given (p. 52 above); the close examination of a single episode will, I think, show what I mean. The Lover is wandering in the garden of love full of natural delights:

> And so befyl, I rested me
> Besydes a wel, under a tree . . .
> And on the border, al withoute,
> Was written in the ston aboute,
> Letters smal, that sayden thus,
> 'Here starf the fayre Narcisus'.
>   Narcisus was a bacheler
> That Love had caught in his danger . . .   (1455–70)

The story of Narcissus and Echo follows; we hear how she died of love for him, of his coldness, and of her last prayer that he might suffer in love as she had suffered; he fell in love with his own 'shadowe' in the well and 'atte last he starf for woo'. The Lover feels inclined to withdraw, but he overcomes his reluctance:

> Unto the welle than wente I me,
> And doun I loutede for to see
> The clere water in the stoon . . .
> In world is non so cler of hewe.
> The water is evere fresh and newe . . .   (1553–60)

At the bottom of the well he sees 'two cristall stonys'. When the sun shines, the 'crystal stoon' (now singular) takes on all the colours of the spectrum. Moreover 'the merveilous crystall' has, like a mirror,

> Such strengthe that the place overall,
> Both flour, and tree, and leves grene,
> And all the yerd in it is seene . . .   (1580–2)

>   This is the mirrour perilous
> In which the proude Narcisus
> Saw all his face fair and bright,
> That made hym sithe to ligge upright.
> For whoso loketh in that mirrour,
> Ther may nothyng ben his socour
> That he ne shall ther sen somthyng
> That shal hym lede into lovyng.   (1601–8)

This is the Well of Love in which all, even the wisest of men, are caught. Venus's son, 'daun Cupido', has sown the seed of love there.

> Allway me liked for to dwelle,
> To sen the cristall in the welle,

---

befyl it happened   *al withoute* on the outside   *starf* died   *bacheler* squire
danger power   *loutede* bent   *sithe to ligge upright* afterwards to lie face upwards
[i.e. dead]   *nothyng ben* . . . nothing can prevent him seeing something there

> That shewide me full openly
> A thousand thinges faste by.
> But I may say, in sory houre
> Stode I to loken or to poure;
> For sithen have I sore siked;
> That mirrour hath me now entriked . . .
>
>   In thilke mirrour saw I tho,
> Among a thousand thinges mo,
> A roser chargid full of rosis
> That with an hegge aboute enclos is.   (1635–52)

The 'savour of the roses swote' intoxicates him and he longs to pick one. One rose-bud attracts him more than all the rest but he is deterred from putting his hand to it by the 'thesteles sharpe . . . netles, thornes and hokede breres'. Whilst he is in this plight, the God of Love takes an arrow,

> And shet att me so wondir smerte
> That thorough myn ye unto myn herte
> The takel smot, and depe it wente.   (1727–9)

C. S. Lewis, writing nearly forty years ago, was a little on the defensive when he asked his readers 'whether this passage, despite a little elaboration, is not well handled by the poet'.[27] Indeed it is. It contains a wealth of suggestion and of insight into the experience of 'falling in love' that even a lengthy analysis could not do justice to. Let us begin with a few obvious 'meanings'. The two crystals at the bottom of the well are, surely, the lady's eyes; they reflect all the beauties of the garden. These beauties, natural and artificial, have been described at length (culminating in the dance of Beauté, Richesse, Largesse and the rest); all that is best in courtly life seems 'in her summed up, in her contained'. Most marvellous of all, in her crystal eyes the Lover sees not only beauty in general (the 'roser chargid full of rosis') but something which seems particularly to invite him ('Among the knoppes I ches oon/So fair . . .'). So much for the bare bones of the allegory; but there is a lot more to it than that. There are the suggestions of the Well image itself—deep and dark, a tunnel into which he might fall, but focussing light and eternal vitality at its bottom, where the gravel

---

faste by close to   *poure* gaze steadily   *sithen* . . . since then I have sighed heavily   *tho* then   *roser* rose-bush   *shet* shot   *wondir smerte* marvellously briskly   *ye* eye   *takel* arrow   *knoppes* buds   *ches* chose

shines 'as silver fyn' and the springing grass 'ne may in wynter dye'.
The almost unnoticed shift from two crystal stones to one 'merveilous
cristal' prevents our dwelling unnecessarily on the physical parallel;
it is now the 'magic' (in every sense) of that first look which holds us
with its gift of vision enlarged (all beauty is seen in it) and yet more
concentrated too. The associations of the Rose are too well known to
need comment; but there is one subtlety that could be overlooked,
the Lover's choice of a bud that is not yet fully open. There are, finally,
two or three aspects of the 'mirrour perilous' which suggest a psychological depth which the author might not have been able fully to
formulate in abstract terms: love is, indeed, perilous, as well as inevitable (you fall in love at your own risk—even if you seem to be pushed);
it is a 'mirrour', a glass, in which you see not reality but its reflection;
and, most profound of all, the reflection you see in your lady's eyes is
your own. The choice of the Narcissus myth, superficially, serves as a
moral *exemplum*: pride in love (or, rather, in not loving) comes before
a fall. But, more deeply considered, and combined as here with the
Fontaine d'Amors, it shows how in this profound experience of
love we may be looking not for another but for the image of ourselves.[28]

I said earlier that the mechanical process which I have called 'retrospective allegorizing' would have to be distinguished not only from
'radical allegory' but also from 'symbolic story'. Some lengthy discussion of the difference between allegory and symbol might seem to be
called for in a study like the present one. We may be able to circum-
vent this if we proceed immediately with another example, the *lai* of
Guigemar by Marie de France.

Guigemar is a young prince, wise, virtuous and popular. He has only one
fault—he is impervious to love. One day he goes out hunting and shoots a
White Hind. The arrow, rebounding from her, wounds him in the thigh.
The dying hind wishes that his wound may never heal until some woman
suffers unbelievably for the love of him and he in return for her. Guigemar,
with his incurable wound, wanders off alone. In an inlet of the sea is moored
a ship with ebony rails and sails of silk. It is quite deserted. He goes aboard
and finds a bed luxuriously appointed with all the magnificence of King
Solomon. He falls asleep in it, and when he wakes up he is out at sea; there
is nothing he can do about it (*suffrir li estut l'aventure*). The ship carries him
to an ancient city where his wound will be cured. The lord of the ancient
city is an old man with a young wife, whom he guards jealously in an orchard
(*en un vergier suz le dongun*). It is enclosed on three sides by a thick wall of

green marble and on the fourth by the sea. The person who keeps the key is
an old priest, a eunuch (*les plus bas membres out perduz*). Guigemar's ship drifts
ashore, or rather is invisibly steered ashore, by the orchard. The lady and her
maid board it timorously. Guigemar is asleep and they think he is dead. He
awakes, however, and they exchange their sad life-stories; then, with some
encouragement from the maid, they declare their love for one another. Guigemar stays secretly for a year and a half. Then Fortune's wheel turns and they
fear discovery. They exchange sureties—that is to say, she ties a magic knot
in his shirt and she wears an impregnable chastity-belt. When attacked by
the *viel gelus*, her husband, Guigemar ably defends himself with a handy
clothes-horse. But he is put back, nevertheless, into his magic ship which
carries him off home. The Lady remains imprisoned and miserable until one
day she finds the gate unlocked. Making her way to the shore she discovers
the ship attached to a rock whence she had intended to drown herself. She goes
on board and is whisked away to the land of a king called Meriadu.

All the local ladies have tried unsuccessfully to undo the knot in Guigemar's
shirt; now King Meriadu and his knights try unsuccessfully to loosen the
Lady's belt. Eventually Guigemar finds himself summoned to Meriadu's
court, for reasons of war. In a scene of some length Guigemar and the Lady
unfasten their respective love-bonds and tell their tale to the company. Meriadu
objects to giving up the Lady to Guigemar, but the latter collects a great army
together and compels him.

> A grant joie s'amie en meine;
> Ore ad trespassee sa peine.

(In great delight Guigemar leads his sweetheart away; now his misery is
completely over and finished.)

The principal 'images' of this *lai* are those of the white hind, the
incurable wound, the magic ship, the enclosed garden. They are the
common stuff of fairy-tale, folk-tale, and romance. The hero of the
anonymous *lai* with similar title, *Guingamor*, chases a white boar; and
in Chrétien's *Erec et Enide* King Arthur proposes as a courtly pastime
the traditional hunting of the *blanc cerf*. It is usual for the white hart to
turn into a fairy being. The magic ship with its luxurious bed we encountered earlier in the chapter. And so forth. There is no need to go
into the history and usage of these images; it is in any case irrelevant.
The point is that the tale is dominated by them; it is from them that it
gets its particular atmosphere, mysterious yet meaningful. We need to
consider not where they come from, but of what kind they are, what
they do in their context, and of course how their context gives them

F

meaning. We need, in fact, to find their *sens, sententia*, 'sentence', significance.

Guigemar provides a striking instance of images constituting a 'mental landscape'. We considered earlier the way of medieval romancers with space and time; the sense of an actual landscape, a firmly realized locality, is very slight. We are told that the incidents of this *lai* took place in 'Britain the less', i.e. Britanny; but it does not matter and we soon forget it. The landscape is, one might almost say, 'interior'. But this is perhaps to prejudge the very question we ought to leave open for the time being. If the imagery were wholly 'interior', if it existed only to delineate 'the road through [Guigemar's] own mind', then surely we ought to call the tale an allegory? But can the tale be so translated? Or does it have an obstinately untranslatable existence of its own? Let us try it out.

Translating into abstractions we should say perhaps that Guigemar, a young man impervious to sexual attraction, becomes involved with a girl (the White Hart) whom he hurts so deeply that she dies. In misery and remorse he drifts aimlessly around (hence the Magic Ship without a steersman) hoping for the load of guilt to be removed (the wound caused by the arrow rebounding from the hart). He is lucky enough to find a woman whose husband's love is so jealously possessive (the enclosed *vergier* with the marble wall) that she longs to escape from it. This love is respectable and essentially sexless (the guard is a eunuch priest). After a mysterious encounter (the Magic Ship drifts in) and a period of secret happiness (her prison is now her seclusion) Guigemar and the Lady are separated. She contemplates suicide but is miraculously saved from it (the Magic Ship, again). And so we might go on, but with increasing difficulty—or, rather, with increasing unease and sense of dissatisfaction. The abstracted meaning seems not only too explicit but also inadequate. Perhaps no poem perfectly exemplifies continuous allegory. But the *Roman de la Rose* and *Piers Plowman* at least come a great deal closer to it than does *Guigemar*.

Yet this 'allegorization' of it is not totally absurd and contains part of the meaning of the poem. As Northrop Frye has shrewdly observed, 'It is not often realized that all commentary is allegorical interpretation, an attaching of ideas to the structure of poetic imagery.'[29] What ideas, then, may we properly attach to *Guigemar*? *Guigemar*, as it seems to me, is about a courtly experience between two young people eminently suitable to receive it. Or, to put it more precisely, it is a courtly *exemplum* about the nature of true love demonstrated by two idealized types. The lessons we have to learn about love (which is presented absolutely, unquestionedly, as the supreme earthly experience) are that it is inevitable, that it may not be forced, that loyalty raises it above the vicissitudes of fortune. Marie de France has other things to say elsewhere about the *granz biens* which is her one and only subject; the 'experience of fine feeling' has many facets and each *lai* presents a different truth about the experience. But these are the truths (or truisms) that she concentrates on here. Unlike some of the *lais*, *Guigemar*, one of the longest, finds room for discourse, general statements, about love both from the characters and from the author herself; and these, when related, give extra precision to the images. For example, one of the most memorable moments is the encounter between the hero and the white hind which culminates in Guigemar's thigh wound. This wound is later identified with the wound of love which can only be healed if it is shown:

> Mes ki ne mustre s'enferté
> A peine en peot aver santé. (481–2)

(But he who never exposes his infirmity can hardly receive a cure for it.)

The passage continues with rehearsed commonplaces and proverbs of love:[30]

> Amur est plaie dedenz cors
> E si ne piert nïent defors.
> Ceo est un mal que lunges tient
> Pur ceo que de nature vient. (483–6)

(Love is a wound within the body and never shows itself on the outside. It is long-lasting pain because it has a natural origin.)

They are nicely turned, but what gives them imaginative force, I suggest, is the memory of the earlier scene:

> En l'espeise d'un grant buissun
> Vit une bise od un foün;
> Tute fu blaunche cele beste. (89–91)

(In the heart of a big thicket he sees a hind with a fawn; she was white all over.)

(Guigemar shoots her, the arrow rebounds and wounds him in the *quisse*—thigh, sexual part?)

La bise, ke nafree esteit,
Anguissuse ert, si se plaineit;
Aprés parla en itel guise;
'Oï, lase! jo sui ocise!
E tu, vassal, ki m'as nafree,
Tel seit la tue destinee:
Jamais n'aies tu medecine!
Ne par herbe ne par racine
Ne par mire ne par pociun
N'avras tu jamés garisun
De la plaie ke as en la quisse,
De si ke cele te guarisse
Ki suffera pur tue amur
Issi grant peine e tel dolur
Ke unkes femme taunt ne suffri,
E tu referas taunt pur li
Dunt tut cil s'esmerveillerunt
Ki aiment e amé avrunt
U ki pois amerunt aprés.
Va t'en de ci! Lais m'aver pes!'   (103–32)

(The hind, wounded, was in great pain and lamented her lot. And then she spoke in these terms: 'Alas, I'm killed! And you, sir, who have wounded me, this be your destiny—may you never be cured! You will never find healing, neither in plant, nor root, neither by doctor, nor medicine, for the wound in your thigh, until a lady heal you who shall suffer for love of you such misery and grief as never woman ever suffered—and until you in your turn do as much for her as will cause all lovers, past, present and future, to be filled with wonderment. And now, go away! Leave me in peace!')

It is a mysterious encounter and baffles precise explication. The main feeling behind the passage seems to be of the integral connection between love and suffering. We can be sure that there is no feeling here for the sanctity of animal life or the cruelty of hunting. And yet at the same time we are aware of senseless pain, of something beautiful destroyed. The emotional logic holds us. Guigemar's insensitivity to love was such that everyone held him to be a lost soul (*peri*, 67). In a strange way this fault in him is made manifest in the killing of the hart (her whiteness might suggest beauty, defenceless virginity?). The innocent suffers and Guigemar's guilt can only be redeemed by love.

I should not wish to argue that the whole poem maintains this imaginative level—the knotted shirt and the chastity belt seem to me a prosaic sort of magic—but the balance between the 'image' and the doctrine of love in this part of the courtly *exemplum* which is *Guigemar* is surely a triumph. The white hart provides one of those images, so characteristic of romance at its best, that concentrate and deepen meaning.

To return to the problem shelved earlier—*Guigemar* may more usefully be described as 'symbolic story' than as allegory. Northrop Frye maintains the validity of the traditional distinction between 'symbolism' and 'allegory' developed by nineteenth-century criticism and still employed, as for instance by C. S. Lewis in *The Allegory of Love*. Professor Frye writes:

The contrast is between a 'concrete' approach to symbols [i.e. thematically significant imagery] which begins with images of actual things and works outward to ideas and propositions, and an 'abstract' approach which begins with the idea and then tries to find a concrete image to represent it.[31]

This is lucid and helpful. The only danger is that we may push the idea of 'contrast' so far that we find ourselves thinking of allegory and symbolism as 'opposites'.[32] They are opposites only in certain limited and obvious senses. If anything is abundantly clear from meditating in succession on these two passages (the Well of Narcissus and the shooting of the White Hind), it is that the two have a great deal in common—far more in common than either has with the procedures of, say, *The Unfortunate Traveller, Moll Flanders*, or *Pride and Prejudice*. The problem is to a large extent a terminological one; and it matters far more that we should be responsive to the texts in front of us than that we should be able to put them into our, at best, rough-and-ready categories.

Both 'radical allegory' and 'symbolic story' (to name the roughest-and-readiest) are deeply dependent on 'images', in the sense I have been using the word—that is, to denote any 'sensible' object or person or action endowed with a significance beyond that of everyday and seeming to concentrate in itself the meaning of an episode or theme. Of both forms we could say, with Sidney, 'the sense is given us to excite the mind'. It is perhaps chiefly the amount of scholarly energy which has been put into making the necessary distinctions that has inclined us to think of the two as poles apart. On the contrary, they are neighbouring countries on the map of fiction. They both use, for the ends of romance, as well as for other ends, a vocabulary of 'images' including (to confine ourselves for the moment to the category of objects) the tower, the ship, the bird, the castle, the rock, the well, the rose, the garden, the ring, the sword, and so on. These are, of course, the everyday objects of the medieval world. But we are struck principally not by their medievalness, nor indeed by their timelessness; rather, by their capacity to act as centres for different aspects of romantic and courtly experience, by their readiness (to adapt a fine phrase of Fulke Greville's) 'to turn the barren Philosophy [even love-philosophy] precepts into pregnant images of life'.

1. These remarks apply equally to Chrétien's *Lancelot*, though not to Malory's telling of Lancelot's story in the *Morte Darthur*.

2. I take the substance of this analysis from my essay in Lawlor, Ed. *Patterns of Love*, pp. 1–25.

3. cf. *Yvain* instead of *Le Chevalier au Lion* and *Lancelot* instead of *Le Chevalier de la Charrete*.

4. Trans. Loomis, *Medieval Romances*, p. 58.

5. ibid., pp. 58–9.

6. ibid., p. 64.

7. V. Woolf, *The Common Reader* (Second Series, 1953), p. 80.

8. Exceptions will occur to the reader of a fairly obvious kind, where the locality is named and recognizable—Gawain's journey through the Wirral; Tristan's to Cornwall; the siege of Windsor and other local references in Chrétien's *Cligés*. A totally different approach to landscape is evident in, for example, Hardy's *The Return of the Native*. Egdon Heath is a massive geographical and temporal presence in the novel, dwarfing the merely human characters. 'The great, inviolate place had an ancient permanence which the sea cannot claim. . . . The sea changed, the fields changed, the rivers, the villages and the people changed, yet Egdon remained.'

9. See p. 96 above.

10. Auerbach, 'La Cour et la Ville', in his *Scenes from the Drama of European Literature* (1959), ch. 4, p. 158.

11. See p. 27 above for the whole verse, translation and further comment.

12. Raby, *Christian-Latin Poetry*, p. 357, from Honorius, *Speculum Ecclesiæ*.

13. B. Willey, *The Seventeenth-Century Background*, p. 2.

14. Auerbach, 'Figura', op. cit. (note 10 above), ch. 1, p. 53 (my italics).

15. Mâle, *Gothic Image*, p. 22.

16. On the image of the Book, see Curtius, *European Literature*, ch. 16.

17. The quotation is from Vinaver, *Works of Malory*, i, p. lxxvi.

18. This is Nature's reply to an enquiry about the 'fictions of poets' in Alanus de Insulis, *De planctu Naturæ*: 'exteriori falsitatis abjecto putamine, dulciorem nucleum veritatis secrete intus lector inveniat' (Migne, *PL*, 210, p. 451).

19. Bezzola, *Le sens*, p. 9.

20. Bezzola, op. cit., *passim*, pp. 135–226.

21. It would be presumptuous of me to enter into the scholarly controversy concerning the much-debated term *conjointure*. The reader should consult Vinaver, *Romance*, pp. 34–7, for a detailed discussion and the persuasive suggestion that Chrétien's *bele conjointure* (*Erec*, 13–14) is modelled on Horace's *callida junctura*, 'artfully devised arrangement'. For present purposes it is enough to note that Vinaver identifies *conjointure* with the *sens*; but, significantly, he sometimes uses terms like 'superimpose' and 'add' (p. 37), whereas Chrétien speaks of 'drawing out' (*tret d'un conte d'avanture/ Un mout bele conjointure*); but see Vinaver's more precise translation on p. 34.

22. Vinaver, *Romance*, p. 42.

23. Vinaver, *Works*, ii.984–5.

24. Frappier in *Arthurian Literature*, Ed. Loomis, p. 304.

25. Marrou, *St Augustine et la fin de la culture antique* (Paris, 1938), p. 490, cit. B. F. Huppé and D. W. Robertson, *Fruyt and Chaf* (Princeton, 1963), pp. 6–7.

26. Lewis, *Allegory*, p. 166.

27. Lewis, *Allegory*, p. 129.

28. As C. S. Lewis pointed out (p. 128, note 2) the image had been tellingly used by the troubadour Bernart de Ventadorn in his song, *Can vei la lauzeta mover*, st. 3: the poet describes how he has lost himself. and power over himself, ever since he looked into his lady's eyes—*C'aissi.m perdei com perdet se/Lo bels Narcissus en la fon* (I lost myself just as did beautiful Narcissus in the well). See also F. Goldin, *The Mirror of Narcissus in the Courtly Love Lyric* (USA, 1967).

29. Frye, *Anatomy*, p. 89.

30. See, for example, *Cligés*, 687–8—the wound that does not appear on the outside.

31. *Anatomy*, p. 89.

32. Graham Hough, 'Allegorical Circle', an article to which I am much indebted, clarifies the point.

8

REALISM AND ROMANCE:
'CHARACTERS' AND TYPES

'Myth . . . is one extreme of literary design', writes Northrop Frye; 'naturalism is the other, and in between lies the whole area of romance —using that term to mean . . . the tendency to displace myth in a human direction and yet, in contrast to "realism", to conventionalize content in an idealized direction.'[1]

Professor Frye's category 'romance', 'the whole area of romance', covers a much wider field than we are immediately concerned with; but his generalization will do well to open the topic of realism in medieval romance. In *Sir Gawain*, for example, the Green Man of folklore has been humanized into the figure of the Green Knight.

> Ther hales in at the halle dor an aghlich mayster,
> On the most on the molde on mesure hyghe;
> Fro the swyre to the swange so sware and so thik,
> And his lyndes and his lymes so longe and so grete,
> Half-etayn in erde I hope that he were,
> Bot mon most I algate mynn hym to bene,
> And that the myriest in his muckel that myght ride. (136–42)

Some commentators go as far as to say that Bertilak is 'a man acting a part'. This is to go much too far in the other direction. If he were a character in a novel (it would have to be a thriller) we should probably learn before the end what he used for his green make-up and how he

---

hales passes *aghlich* terrible *mayster* lord, knight *On the most* the very biggest *molde* earth *swyre* . . . neck to the waist, sturdily built *lyndes* loins *Half-etayn* . . . 'Half a giant on earth I believe he was, but at any rate the biggest of men I declare him to be, and at the same time, the shapeliest of stature that could ride' (Davis)

performed the conjuring-trick with his head. But he is not. He is a Marvellous Man—both 'marvel' and 'man'.

Medieval romance is full of 'myth displaced in a human direction'. Another fascinating instance occurs in Chrétien's *Yvain* (and slightly more prosaically in the English *Ywain and Gawain*)—the incident of the Giant Herdsman. Calogrenant's encounter with this Calibanesque figure was described in an earlier chapter (p. 102).

The problem must now be approached from the other side. We have seen the 'myths', the mysterious images, for the most part, of Celtic mythology, 'displaced in a human direction'. Let us now consider the tendency of romance-writers 'to conventionalize content', as Northrop Frye's succinct but somewhat ugly phrase has it, 'in an idealized direction'. I have already written of the 'pregnant images of life' which characterize medieval romance in its most typical forms— the images which seem to focus the meaning and define the structure of many tales. Medieval romance, like medieval drama, is as it were a processional form; and the chief actors move from one *aventure* to another, not through a clearly defined and located countryside, but in a geographical vacuum. Specific locations (the Castle of Maidens, the Castle of the Grail, Bertilak's Castle, the *Castel de Pesme Aventure*, the Sword-Bridge, etc.) are more than anything else the necessary stage-properties for dramatized spiritual or mental experiences. Like Kafka's castle, they are not so much places as events in the mind. The 'claim of the ideal', I have argued, is the central experience of romance, and all its basic conventions have emerged, crystallized, to express it—not only conventions of setting and location, but conventions of plot and action (including the usual 'happy ending'), of characterization and of motive. It follows that, at least to begin with, one should assume all modifications of this ideal world to be attempts to make it more meaningful and to communicate it more forcibly; intended, in short, as enrichments of the ideal and not as criticisms of it.

The enrichment which is most liable to misunderstanding is the enrichment of 'character'. If the word 'character' could be avoided, I would avoid it, because it resounds with all the presuppositions of realistic fiction. However, 'persons' would raise other objections, and 'dramatis personae' others again. By the term 'characters' I mean simply and neutrally the walkers and talkers who people the imaginary world. The 'characters' of romance are white and black, good men and bad men, saints and devils. Wickedness is idealized as well as goodness; there is very little room in romance for the comfortable, smudgy greys of ordinary life, of *l'homme moyen sensuel*—no, nor woman neither. . . .

However, not everyone in romance is a perfect knight or a perfect lady. To begin with, the hero himself must not embody *achieved* perfection. If he does, as Galahad in effect does, then the suspense is lost. We know that Galahad is destined to draw the Sword from the Stone; we know that he is the peerless knight who can sit in the empty seat of the Round Table (the Siege Perillous); we know, finally, that 'Thys ys he by whom the Sankgreall shall be encheved, for there sate never none but he there but he were myscheved'.[2] The result is that we can never believe in Galahad's humanity; he is too perfect.

At least, the hero must be *unproven*, even though we suspect him of perfectibility; he must be a Beaumains or a Perceval, with much to learn and much to undergo. However—and this is the essential point— the unproven hero is already set fair; the seeds of perfection are within him and need only to grow to fruition. There are critical decisions to be made, but no changes of course, no compromises. The ideal knight is not in any sense 'lost'; he is not a wanderer but a quester; he has a vocation. Perceval, while still an untutored lad, hunting with a javelin in the Welsh hills, feels the Call before he even knows what a knight is. Perceval is, in fact, a test case. He appears in some lights to be a 'character'; he passes through stages of innocence, ignorance, inadequacy and irresponsibility. His illumination is progressive and can be charted. And this suggests inner growth; it suggests, in short, a 'character' with its inner laws, its inner life. But this might still be misleading because the growth from innocence to maturity is preconceived and there is only a limited degree of interaction between him and the world around him. The 'character' of a romance-hero is rather a rehearsed interior monologue than a meaningful and unpredictable dialogue with the outside world. To put it briefly, the hero has to realize his potential, not to come to terms with life. In the famous scene at the castle of the Grail which I described earlier, when Perceval fails to ask the crucial question—*del graal cui l'en en servoit*—he fails not so much because he does not 'adjust' to the world around him (the essence of the *aventure* is that he is given no clue at all as to his proper response), but because he is not true to his inner self, to the inner light that should have illumined his spirit at that, as at every, juncture.

Gawain, on the other hand, in *Sir Gawain and the Green Knight*, is credible as a hero in a different way. It is true we know that he will meet the challenge of the Green Knight and that, impossible as it may seem, he will emerge triumphant. But this is a different kind of 'knowing'; it depends on our literary experience of romance, not on Gawain's character. We 'know' it in the same way as we 'know' in *The Tempest* that Ferdinand will find his father and marry Miranda. We believe, dramatically, in the possibility of failure, I suppose. And we do so long before Gawain has actually exposed himself in a moment of weakness, at the taking of the girdle:

> Then kest the knyght, and hit come to his hert
> Hit were a juel for the jopardé that hym jugged were:
> When he acheved to the chapel his chek for to fech,
> Myght he haf slypped to be unslayn the sleght were noble.   (1855–8)

(Then the knight pondered, and it came to him what a splendid thing it would be in the dangerous situation before him—when he arrived at the chapel to meet his doom, it would be a nice piece of cunning to escape without being killed.)

Gawain may be a hero—but he would prefer to be a live one.

However, I am not sure that our deeper superior belief in Gawain is, in the end, a matter of feeling that he has a weak spot, that he is after all a man like we are. He so obviously is not. Rather, it has to do with the way he is, as it were, 'substantiated'. It is his superhuman *perfection* that we believe in. So perhaps the real difference between Gawain and Galahad is between a 'realized' perfection and a merely stated, un-substantiated perfection; and the difference between Gawain and Perceval, a difference between a less and a more highly stylized sub-stantiation of the perfect knight. This brings us back to the notion of 'enrichment'.

The immediate first impact of the world of marvels which was provided for the romance-poets by Celtic mythology is (as one writer has put it) of 'the tantalizing poetry of chance, irrationality and dream'. The stories in themselves have no meaning—at least, no meaning which was consciously accessible to the twelfth-century or the fourteenth-century poet, any more than it is to us. To use the medieval terms, they are simply the poet's *matière*; the *sens* is his prime concern. The *sens* of romance is, as I have said, 'the claim of the ideal'; and the prime func-tion of realism in romance is to enrich the ideal. This is why the realism is generally spasmodic and selective. The author has no desire to depict life 'as it really is' but 'as it ought to be'. But the principle of selection for the enrichment of the ideal is not simple; it is twofold. One kind of realism I shall call *consonant* (i.e. agreeing, substantiating); the other, *dissonant* (i.e. disagreeing, acting as a foil, setting off by contrast). The

most obviously realistic passages in *Sir Gawain and the Green Knight* are
completely consonant with the courtly Gawain: the detailed description of King Arthur's Christmas feasting at Camelot (37); Gawain's
speech on taking up the challenge (343); the arming of Gawain
(566); Gawain's reception at Bertilak's castle (815); Gawain's three
dialogues with the Lady (1178, 1468, 1733).

Let us take the second of these. The Green Knight has made his
astounding entry into the hall where King Arthur and the court are
just starting their New Year's Day feast.

> And al stouned at his steven and ston-stil seten
> In a swoghe sylence thurgh the sale riche.
> As al were slypped upon slepe so slaked hor lotes
>   In hye—
> I deme hit not al for doute
> Bot sum for cortaysye.   (242-7)

The Green Knight taunts the court for being so cowed (as he likes to
interpret it). 'What, is this Arthures hous. . . .?' He expected a more
manly reception. King Arthur is greatly offended ('The blod schot for
scham into his schyre face') and takes up the challenge himself. Gawain,
however, sitting by the queen, asks if he may undertake it instead.

> 'Wolde ye, worthilych lorde,' quoth Wawan to the kyng,
> 'Bid me bowe fro this benche and stonde by yow there,
> That I wythoute vylanye myght voyde this table,
> And that my legge ladye lyked not ille,
> I wolde com to your counseyl bifore your cort ryche.
> For me think hit not semly—as hit is soth knawen—
> Ther such an askyng is hevened so hyghe in your sale,
> Thagh ye yourself be talenttyf, to take hit to yourselven,
> Whil mony so bolde yow aboute on benche sytten
> That under heven I hope non hawerer of wylle
> Ne better bodyes on bent ther baret is rered.
> I am the wakkest, I wot, and of wyt feblest,

---

stouned . . . were amazed at his voice   *swoghe* dead [silence]   *sale* hall   *As al
were slypped* . . . 'their voices died away as suddenly as if they had all fallen
asleep' (Waldron)   *I deme* . . . 'I think it was not entirely owing to fear, but
partly out of courtesy' (Davis)   *Wolde ye* . . . *bid* if you were willing to command me   *bowe* come   *And that* . . . and if (the queen) were not displeased
Ther such an askyng . . . when such a request is raised   *talenttyf* desirous   *That
under heven* 'that I think nobody on earth readier in courage' (Davis)   *bodyes on
bent* . . . men 'on the field of battle' (Waldron)

> And lest lur of my lyf, who laytes the sothe.
> Bot for as much as ye are myn em, I am only to prayse;
> No bounté bot your blod I in my bodé knowe.
> And sythen this note is so nys that noght hit yow falles,
> And I have frayned hit at yow fyrst, foldes hit to me.
> And if I carp not comlyly let alle this cort rych
>   Bout blame.' (343–61)

This speech could have been written as a model in a handbook of 'cortaysye'. Gawain's problem is now to get the Green Knight's challenge, and the *aventure* which will surely follow it, transferred from the king to himself, without giving offence. To particularize— he must not abruptly leave the queen's side unless the king commands him to and the queen is willing; he must uphold the reputation of King Arthur's knights ('Ne better bodyes on bent ther baret is rered') without appearing to claim any kind of superiority over them ('I am the wakkest . . .' and, indeed, could more easily be spared than anyone else); he must not imply that the king needs his support, and he never indeed allows it to appear that he could even think such a thought; he must leave the king in such a position that he may withdraw gracefully and without loss of face ('this note is so nys . . .'—the whole affair is too trivial to warrant regal action); he must not appear to attribute any merit to himself, it is all the king's ('No bounté bot your blod I in my bodé knowe); and, finally, he must publicly allow the possibility that he has not achieved a completely courteous solution to all these problems and exonerate the rest of the court from any share in his discourtesy.

Needless to say the speech, with its syntactical convolutions and air of intensely self-conscious, almost Jamesian, qualification and modification, enables Gawain to walk the delicate tightrope he has stretched for himself. Mr Spearing has most helpfully analysed the minutiae of the 'poetry of *cortaysye*' as it appears here: its 'peculiarly circumlocutory phrases' with their 'significant indirectness' and the 'length and complexity of its sentences':

---

lest lur . . . 'my life would be the smallest loss' (Davis)   *laytes* wishes to know
Bot for as much . . . 'I am only praiseworthy in that you are my uncle'
(Waldron)   *bounté* worthiness   *this note* . . . 'this matter is so foolish'
(Waldron)   *noght* . . . *falles* it isn't appropriate to yourself   *frayned* asked
foldes hit it is fitting   *And if I carp* . . . 'even if I speak improperly, let all this
noble court be free from blame' (Davis) [various other translations of 360–1
are possible]

The complexity of the syntax suggests the subtlety of the relationships that Gawain is establishing between a number of independent factors. . . . The sense one has in moving through the passage is of the skirting of a series of obstacles, the overcoming or evading of one difficulty after another; the syntax seems to wind itself along, to move two steps sideways for every step forwards. This effect is heightened by the profusion of parenthetic phrases . . .[3]

This 'show of sinuous politeness' would have seemed to the medieval courtly listener exemplary in the fullest sense of that word—excellent in its kind and thereby providing an example for others to follow. They would not, I believe, have thought of it primarily as 'expressing the character' of Gawain. 'Demonstrating the essential characteristics' would be a less misleading phrase. The poet has indeed 'enriched' his portrait of Gawain in a remarkable speech; but he has not individualized him. We must not be so steeped in novelistic preconceptions of 'character' that we react adversely to preoccupations of medieval poets differing from our own. The editor of a recent edition of the poem praises the poet 'above all for his warm and quick appreciation of mind and motive'. This is praise which no one who has read, say, Gawain's dialogues with the Lady could possibly withhold. But there is an important qualification to be made. In those crucial scenes, as in the scene of the transferred challenge, the poet's prime concern is not the particular but the general—the nature of courtesy, not the psychology of Gawain.

A similar argument could be developed about the lesser heroes of Chaucerian romance; but to do it at length would now, I hope, be unnecessary. Palamon and Arcite are a straightforward case—paste-board and emblematic from start to finish; mouthpieces occasionally, but generally puppets moving in the courtly dance that Chaucer has devised. *The Knight's Tale* is indeed a safe place to start the study of 'characterization' in medieval romance. There is of course an important sense in which *Sir Gawain and the Green Knight* is more concerned with the individual than is *The Knight's Tale*; but this has nothing to do with individual characterization. The Gawain-poet is concerned with the nature of the Christian knight, with what goes to make up the perfect, single specimen. He must have known that all men are different; his poem implies that all men should be the same. *The Knight's Tale* by contrast is, as I have argued, 'ceremonial romance', romance of the public common life; it is a grand ennoblement of the whole enterprise, a praise of the Dance itself, not a prescription for the good dancer. *Troilus and Criseyde*, on the other hand, needs more extended consideration.

Chaucer's *Troilus* (Criseyde's name was first added to the title in the fifteenth century) is centrally 'about' Troilus—'Bothe of his joie and of his cares colde'.[4] Books 1 and 5 are above all *his* books; and long passages are devoted to describing his sensations. We shall consider some 300 lines that follow his 'fall', when he has become 'sodeynly most subgit unto love'. To deal cursorily: on receiving the 'fixe and depe impressioun' (297) of Criseyde, Troilus becomes deeply agitated, even if 'nat fullich al awhaped' (not totally stupefied); he is able on return to the palace (324) to maintain his jeering pose and his contempt for the 'ordre' of lovers (336). When he can, he escapes to the solitude of his chamber (358), sits on his bed, sighing and groaning, and meditates on his lady; he makes an 'act' of submission and gratitude to the 'god of love' (421); he loses his colour 'sexty tyme a day' (441); he longs to see her to ease his suffering but finds it intensified (448); he is obsessed with the thought of her to the exclusion of all else (453, 465) and lives his life as a warrior simply to please her (481); he loses sleep, and his appetite, and his healthy looks (484); and, although dismayed by her apparent indifference (495) and experiencing an undefined jealousy, cannot pluck up courage to speak to her. In short, Troilus knows he is caught; and he is elated, self-critical and self-pitying by turns.

It is one of Chaucer's achievements that *Troilus and Criseyde* has a density of psychological interest which is, though not unique in itself, uniquely presented. The romances of Chrétien de Troyes, such short poems as *Le Lai de L'Ombre*, *Le Châtelain de Vergi*, and Thomas's *Tristan* —not to mention the first part of the *Roman de la Rose*—contain much subtle analysis of the psychological state of being in love. But in none of these do we feel a psychological continuum to the degree that we feel it in Chaucer. For quite extended passages of Chaucer's poem we live imaginatively within the character's flux of mood and emotion; in Chrétien's romances we enter, on the whole, more static conditions. There is no point in denying Chaucer's anticipation, in this, of the novelist's technique—an observation which has often been made. We are not simply told about the inner conflicts and desires of the characters; we experience them, as it were, from inside.

The danger, of course, is not that this will fail to be understood but that it will be too simply, too exclusively, understood. Troilus, it must be said once and for all, is not 'a fully-rounded character', in the novelistic sense, and was never intended to be. He is an elaborated symbol, a 'figure', a Type; he is a sort of 'highest common factor' of courtly lovers, 'the mould of fashion, and the glass of form'; he is their epitome. In my summary account of the symptoms of love's 'maladie' which Troilus undergoes I did not draw attention to two passages which characterize his presentation: the first is the *Canticus Troili* (400–20); the second is his 'compleynte' (507–39). These are not naturalistic expressions of his 'wo'; they are extended soliloquies—the soliloquies of a Romeo rather than of a Hamlet. If we want to hear the genuine accents of a man in emotional distress, we must turn to a later stanza of dialogue between Troilus and Pandarus:

> 'How hastow thus unkyndely and longe
> Hid this fro me, thow fol?' quod Pandarus.
> 'Paraunter thow myghte after swich oon longe
> That myn avys anoon may helpen us.'
> 'This were a wonder thing', quod Troilus.
> 'Thow koudest nevere in love thiselven wisse:
> How devel maistow brynge me to blisse?' (i.617)

The *Canticus Troili*, on the other hand, is a lyrical debate, heightening the oxymoron of love, its bitter-sweet quality—'O quike deth! O swete harme so queynte!':

> 'If no love is, O God, what fele I so?
> And if love is, what thing and which is he?
> If love be good, from whennes cometh my woo?
> If it be wikke, a wonder thynketh me,
> When every torment and adversite
> That comth of hym, may to me savory thynke,
> For ay thurst I, the more that ich it drynke.' (i.400)[5]

Sometimes, as in this stanza, the intensity of the paradox is realized through the sharpening of logical argument; sometimes mere juxtaposition achieves the effect:

> 'O quike deth! O swete harme so queynte!' . . . (411)
> 'For hete of cold, for cold of hete, I dye.' (420)

This is a 'song' in the sense that a *canzone* by Dante or Petrarch is a song. The word suggests highly-wrought speech and idealized emotion, and its use here is analogous to its use by an epic poet, like Virgil or Dante, to describe the making of poetry in the high style. In such a

---

Paraunter . . . perhaps you may be longing for someone such that my counsel . . .
wisse guide   *How devel* how the devil . . . [expletive]   *wikke* evil
a wonder . . . that seems strange to me when . . .   *thynke* seem   *queynte* strange

passage as this Chaucer is telling us not about Troilus but about the
nature of Love. Chaucer is perhaps always more interested in the
universal than in the particular, in 'just representations of general
nature' than in the quirks and wriggles of an individual soul.

An American critic, Wayne Schumaker, in an essay on the Wife of
Bath, has put the doubts and questions which the *Canticus Troili* might
raise into a cogent, general form. His comments admirably sum up and
supplement the ones I have made:

. . . nowhere in the *Canterbury Tales* does Chaucer commit himself utterly
to an exploration of the implications of personality. . . . He shows an extraordinary and precious awareness of idiosyncratic appearance and behaviour.
But he does not, except by way of introduction in the General Prologue,
keep the focus very long upon *men*. About the intellectual and emotional
tensions that underlie outward eccentricity he knows chiefly what an impersonal
medieval science and philosophy have taught him. More important still, he
does not seek tirelessly by direct observation to learn more. He has no really
profound curiosity about the individual soul. His strongest interest is in the
general—in what is not (as it would have seemed to him) self-limiting and
therefore trivial. He is not a patient searcher of men's hearts, but a docile
scholar who imposes upon his perceptions, as scholars have always tended to
do, a framework of systematized notions.

In this way, no doubt, he saw Alys of Bath: at first, delightedly, with his
physical eyes and instinctive sympathies; later, with the eye of inward vision,
which strove to find in her a representative of something larger and more
important than herself.[6]

Chaucer certainly wished Troilus and Criseyde to be 'representative of
something larger and more important' than a pair of Trojan—or even
fourteenth-century courtly—lovers. Troilus is never given a superflu-
ous or inconsequential concreteness. He is wholly what his Type
demands, though he is this much more interestingly and convincingly
than most courtly lovers. And by being this he can, to our awakened
imaginations, be much more, be everyone who trembles before the
claim of an unknown and beautiful experience.

The instances of realism so far considered have been all of the
'consonant' variety; the characters have been 'realized' in such a way
as to establish and confirm what they stand for. I want now to consider the use of unidealized characters in romance as a kind of foil. The
device of contrast is, of course, basic to all fiction in which the nature of
our humanity is an important issue. Dorothea, the idealist, in *Middle-
march* is set off by the hard, brittle shallowness of Rosamond Vincy;

Isabel, a different kind of idealist, in *Portrait of a Lady*, is beautifully
defined by her brash and energetic compatriot, the female journalist
Henrietta Stackpole. It is perhaps more surprising to find such foils in
romance. One takes for granted, of course, the 'black' characters already mentioned—the devils and the really wicked, irredeemable
knights, like Meleagant in Chrétien's *Lancelot*, or Sir Breuse-sance-Pite
in Malory's rambling Tristram story. More interesting are certain not
exactly 'grey' but 'off-white' characters: Malory's Sir Dinadan;
Chrétien's Kay (Keu), the steward of Arthur's court; and Chaucer's
Pandarus. In each of these persons we note a fundamental compliance
with the accepted code, combined with a failure to realize it. They are
'dissonant' characters. In so far as they are developed they jar against
the harmony of the chivalric ideal.

Malory's presentation of Sir Dinadan I find casual and uncomprehending. We first meet him in Book IX (Caxton); he is Tristram's
comrade-in-arms and shares his exile. On their wanderings they get
news that Lancelot is to be ambushed by thirty knights:

'Now, fayre damesell', seyde sir Trystram, 'brynge me to that same place
where they shold mete with sir Launcelot'. Than seyde sir Dynadan, 'What
woll ye do? Hit ys nat for us to fyght with thirty knyghtes, and wyte you well
I woll nat thereoff! As to macche o knyght, two or three ys inow and they be
men, but for to matche fiftene knyghtes, that I woll never undirtake'. (ii.505)

Tristram scoffs at him, and threatens him; but Dinadan is resolute—
'Sir . . . I promise you to look upon and do what I may to save myself,
but I would I had not met with you.' However, when it comes to the
point, 'then came in Sir Dinadan and he did passing well'—they killed
twenty and put the other ten to flight. So, in effect, it is simply a 'ploy'.
The questioning of chivalric ideals does not go very deep and is never
expressed in action. Dinadan is no Falstaff ('What is honour? A word.
What is that word Honour? Ayre: a trim reckoning. Who hath it?
He that dy'de a Wednesday. Doth he feele it? No. Doth he heare it?
No. Is it insensible then? yea, to the dead.'). Nor is he a Thersites.
('Lechery, lechery, still warres and lechery, nothing else holds fashion.')
He is a good, loyal, second-class knight who likes to have his sceptical
little joke but is essentially a sound and respected member of the club.
As Malory himself says:

And sir Dynadan overthrew four knyghtes mo, and there he dede grete dedis
of armys, for he was a good knyght. But he was a grete skoffer and a gaper,

and the meryste knyght amonge felyship that was that tyme lyvynge: and he loved every good knyght and every good knyght loved hym. (ii.665)

The French prose romance of *Tristan* which is Malory's main source (and six times as long) portrays a Dinadan that makes much more sense than Malory's. The real point of Dinadan, the French tale makes clear, is as a social figure, one who gives himself a social role to play; he is not a serious critic of chivalry. He is the 'merriest knight among fellowship' (i.e. in company) absolutely *because* he is 'a scoffer and a japer'. He is the irritant, the disbeliever, the ironist who makes conversation run and sparkle and prevents it being a stagnant pool of assent. A striking example of this is quoted by Professor Vinaver (he, however, takes Dinadan much more seriously than I think is justified):

After dinner Guinevere requests Lancelot not to fight against Arthur's fellowship ('je ne voudroie en nule maniere du monde que courrouz montast entre vous et euls'), and turning to Dinadan asks him why she has only seen him once at the tournament. 'My lady,' says Dinadan, 'I am sure you can see me every day if only you look into your heart! The "abbesse" and all the nuns of this nunnery look so pale that I am certain they must be praying for me all day—or else they would not look as though they ate nothing but herbs and beans. But lo! how their colour has improved since my arrival here. *La vermeille coleur vous est montee ou visage, et pour ce dy je que la char vous est amendee.*' Amidst general laughter the 'abbesse', who was 'sage dame et courtoise', asks Dinadan what he would like the nuns to say in their prayers. 'Et Dinadan lui respont: "Toutes mes prieres et mes oroisons si ne sont ne mes seulement que Dieu me deffende et me gart de prison a dame et a damoiselle." . . . "Ha! Dinadan, dit la royne, ne voulés vous pas amer une belle dame et faire belles joustes et aler aux armes pour l'amour de lui! Car quant vous ceste chouse ne voulés faire, pourquoy vous feistes vous faire chevalier? . . . Vous vous deussiez estre fait ordonner a prouvoire." '[7]

('I wouldn't for the world have any ill feeling arise between you and them.'/ 'The scarlet colour has mounted to your cheeks—that's why I say you are in better health.'/'And Dinadan replied: "All my prayers are devoted to asking God to save me from becoming the prisoner of a lady, wife or maiden." . . . "Oh Dinadan, says the queen, don't you want to love a fair lady and joust nobly and live a knightly life for the love of her? Because if you don't want this why did you get yourself made a knight? . . . You ought to have been ordained priest." ')

In this scene the society in which Dinadan is acting is the fictional one of the romance itself. However, we should note that sometimes the French author, followed only half-heartedly by Malory, makes his character play to the imagined (or real) gallery of his readers (or listeners). It does not ultimately, perhaps, make much difference to the impression the scene creates.

In contrast to Sir Dinadan, who is a wit and a bit of a buffoon, Chrétien's Sir Kay (Keu) can be positively nasty. The scurrilous, exasperating Sir Kay is a recurrent feature of Chrétien's Arthurian romances. He is certainly one of the reasons why the courtliness of *Yvain*, for example, is such a curiously tangled affair. Towards the end of that romance Gawain is urgently needed as a champion but is not available because he is away on a quest—and the reason for the quest is the uncourtly behaviour of Kay, King Arthur's seneschal. Chrétien makes a cross-reference here to his *Lancelot*, which had opened with the challenge of a stranger knight: would Arthur entrust his queen, Guenevere, to a chosen champion? Kay, in his usual presumptuous way, had claimed the privilege of defending the queen and was beaten in the first battle. Gawain and, *incognito*, Lancelot, had to leave the court to win her back. Kay's single uncourtly act has affected the course of two romances.

Kay is, as I have said, a perpetual irritant, a grain of grit in the well-oiled, smooth-running courtly machine. His performance in *Yvain* gives a good idea of what he can do. It starts very early in the romance. He and some other knights are being entertained by Sir Calogrenant who is telling them

> un conte
> Non de s'enor, mes de sa honte (59–60)

(a story redounding not to his credit but to his shame)

Suddenly the queen appears amongst them. Only Calogrenant sees her coming and he leaps to his feet.

> Et Kes, qui mout fu ranposneus,
> Fel et poignanz et afiteus
> Li dist: 'Par De, Calogrenant!
> Mout vos voi or preu et saillant.' (69–72)

(And Kay, who was scurrilous by nature, unpleasantly sarcastic and insulting, said to him 'Good God, Calogrenant, what a bold, nimble fellow you are!')

'You *are* a gentleman, aren't you?' says Kay. 'And you want the queen to think we are boorish by comparison, don't you?' The queen has to reprove Kay for being *enuieus* and *vilains* and spewing out his poison (*vuidier del venin*). Kay tells the queen not to concern herself with trifles. And so it goes on. Calogrenant is not personally offended, because he knows Kay cannot help it; it is his habitual behaviour. A dunghill always stinks:

> Toz jorz doit puïr li fumiers
> Et taons poindre et maloz bruire
> Enuieus enuiier et nuire. (116–18)

(The dunghill is bound to go on stinking, the gadfly to sting and bees to buzz; similarly, those who are obnoxious will continue being so.)

It is only with difficulty that Calogrenant can be persuaded to continue his story. Later on, Kay bursts out again—this time to accuse Yvain of idle boasting because he wants to take up the quest:

> Aprés mangier sanz remuër
> Va chascuns Noradin tuër . . . (595–6)

(Anyone can be going to kill Noradin [the Sultan of Syria] without getting out of his chair after dinner.)

Yvain, he says, is only an armchair fighter. Yvain, of course, will prove abundantly that he is not, and later, when he is defending the Fountain, *incognito*, he has the pleasure of unhorsing Kay (2254). The irony is that Kay has just been carrying on about 'that coward, Yvain', who is absent from the court when there is fighting to be done.

What is all this for? A simple explanation could be that Kay, the 'cad' in the gentlemen's club, serves as a safety-valve for Chrétien or for his listeners. I am inclined to doubt this. One is irritated, often intensely, by Kay, but one does not find oneself identifying with him against the idealisms of courtliness, as one does often with Pandarus's common-sense against Troilus's starry-eyed condition. More plausibly, we can see Kay as an artistic foil: the courtly appear more so, in contrast to him. Perhaps we should see him also as an actual occasion for, and a spur to, courtliness: it is part of a true courtly frame of mind to be able to put up with such as Kay, a harder task perhaps, humanly speaking, than rescuing damsels in distress. Certainly these scenes, which can be paralleled from the other romances, increase the imaginative and emotional range of the poems.

Finally, Pandarus. Chaucer, above all medieval romancers, provides us with the deepest and most problematic example of what I have called a 'dissonant' character. Compared with Pandarus, Sir Dinadan is shallowly conceived and even Sir Kay looks sketchy.[8] For reasons of space we must confine our attention largely to Book I of *Troilus and Criseyde*.

Pandarus does not enter the scene until the courtliness of Troilus and the depth of his love-woe are fully established. But just when we are beginning to think that Troilus deserves to drown in his own salt tears (i.543),

> A frend of his, that called was Pandare,
> Com oones in unwar, and herde hym groone. (i.548–9)

His immediate response to Troilus's groans characterizes the man: he takes on a deliberate role and taunts Troilus with a 'drie mock':

> Han now thus soone Grekes maad yow leene?

> Or hastow som remors of conscience,
> And art now falle in som devocioun . . .? (i.553–5)

The manifest absurdity of the accusation of cowardice lends an additional piquancy to the insensitive worldliness of Pandarus's accusation of 'holyness'. We know that Troilus *has* fallen 'in som devocioun' ('O lord, now youres is/My spirit, which that oughte youres be'; 422–3); and the fact that Pandarus can so urbanely mock the fervours of religion prepares us to believe that he may not understand the fervours of love either. Pandarus stands at once revealed as a manipulator:

> Thise wordes seyde he for the nones alle,
> That with swich thing he myght hym angry maken,
> And with an angre don his wo to falle . . . (i.561–3)

But perhaps my comments are too acid, and make Pandarus appear so, too, for a few lines later we hear that he 'neigh malt for wo and routhe'. If a manipulator, he is at least a sympathetic, even a sentimental one.

The fact that Pandarus leaps into action, fully-equipped, as it were, without the formal *descriptio* thought necessary for the introduction of a new character in most medieval romances, is characteristic of the procedure of this section of the poem. The truths that emerge, emerge from the interaction of two 'live' characters, not from the comments of the narrator (who remains largely silent now). But the truths are, nevertheless, not to be solely about the characters as individuals; they

---

unwar unexpectedly   *for the nones alle* simply to meet the occasion   *with an angre don . . .* by making him angry cause his grief to abate

are to be at least as much about the nature of love. In this section we become aware, for the first time, that we are not, as in most romances, going to hear a story simply about love, or even about love and chivalry, but a story about *love-in-relation*—love in relation to the common-sense experience of reality, to the mysterious workings of destiny, perhaps even (though we cannot yet be sure) to the moral values of medieval Christianity.

The faculty of well-intentioned manipulation is the keynote of Pandarus's character; he is one of Nature's managers. In C. S. Lewis's words:

Everyone has met the modern equivalent of Pandarus. When you are in the hands of such a man you can travel first-class through the length and breadth of England on a third-class ticket . . .; noble first-floor bedrooms will open for you in hotels that have sworn they are absolutely full . . . And all the time, he will be such good company that he can

> make you so to laugh at his folye.
> That you for laughter wenen for to dye.

Yet he is no mere comedian: he can talk with you far into the night when the joking and the 'tales of Wade' are over, of

> many an uncouth, glad and deep matere
> As frendes doon, whan they been met y-fere.

. . . He is faithful, too, once you have won him to your side: a discreet, resourceful, indefatigable man.[9]

The sense that Pandarus, because he is inquisitive as well as kind, a busybody as well as Troilus's sturdy friend, is determined to manage Troilus's affair for him colours all he says and does. His pragmatic worldliness is apparent when he gives Troilus a good shaking at a critical moment:

> Tho gan the veyne of Troilus to blede,
> For he was hit, and wax al reed for shame.
> 'A ha!' quod Pandar, 'here bygynneth game'.
>
> And with that word, he gan him for to shake,
> And seyde: 'thef, thow shalt hyre name telle.'   (i.866-70)

Pandarus's opportunism, his calculated commonsensicalities, throw into relief the qualities for which Troilus stands, the *sancta simplicitas* of the romantic lover. There is an appealing helplessness in Troilus's idealism which is accentuated by Pandarus's common-sense and 'busy-

ness'. We ought to note, though, in passing that Chaucer greatly
strengthens the dramatic, the imaginative plausibility of Troilus by
letting Pandarus provoke some quite sharp and 'real' reactions from
him, too:

> 'Thou koudest nevere in love thiselven wisse
> How devel maistow brynge me to blisse?'   (i.622–3)

> . . . 'frend, though that I stylle lye,
> I am nat deef; now pees, and crye namore.'   (i.752–3)

Troilus has not lost all his 'proud Bayard' spirit, despite the solemn self-
pity—at which surely we are to laugh—of the first response to his
visitor:

> 'Go hennes awey: for certes my deyinge
> Wol the disese, and I mot nedes deye.'   (i.572–3)

If even Troilus is not unmixed, what are we to say of Pandarus himself, a more complex 'character'? The other side, or sides, to the presentation of Pandarus modifies the main antithesis of the whole passage
(i.550–1064) as I originally stated it—between the 'realism' of Pandarus
and the idealism of Troilus. We clearly have no simple contrast, if
Pandarus also is 'a lover, and a doctor in Love's law, a friend according
to the old, high code of friendship, and a man of sentiment'.[10] Certainly,
the principal critical difficulty in reading the second half of Book I is
to know how to take Pandarus's long speeches; there are three of them,
and together they occupy about 200 lines.

The speeches are not simply naturalistic; but, of course, they have
this side. They are the speeches of a man who talks well and likes to
hear himself talking. This much we could deduce from Troilus's
reaction:

> 'Lat be thyne olde ensaumples, I the preye.'   (i.760)

Pandarus is a bit of a bore on the subject of love; he is a Polonius-figure
'full of wise saws and modern instances'. He has clearly devoted much
time to the favourite medieval subject of 'luf-talkying', to debating
topics and 'questions' of love and to its casuistry in general. Love is a
concept to him—an intellectual idea, the proper subject for man's wit
to exercise on—not merely an experience.[11] In the first speech his texts
are:

---

disese be uncomfortable to, distress

'A fool may ek a wis-man ofte gide'   (i.630)

'Men seyn: "to wrecche is consolacioun
To have another felawe in hys peyne" '   (i.708)

He is an accomplished rhetorician; and he talks not to establish truth,
but to persuade. Words to him are tools; the emotions of his friends
are his raw materials.

After Pandarus has made Troilus quite aghast by suggesting that he
tell Troilus's lady (as yet unnamed) about his sad condition (765), he
launches forth on a further discourse, about the folly of undeclared
love. The following stanza is a fair sample of his gnomic style:

'Thow mayst allone here wepe and crye and knele,—
But love a womman that she woot it nought,
And she wol quyte it that thow shalt nat fele;
Unknowe, unkist, and lost, that is unsought.
What! many a man hath love ful deere ybought
Twenty wynter that his lady wiste,
That never yet his lady mouth he kiste.'   (i.806)

The antithetic second and third lines with their neatly patterned 'that
she', 'that thow', have the air of a rehearsed commonplace. And the
fourth line, smartly cumulative in negatives, is evidently a current
saying, a proverb of love. They contrast strangely with the simple
sincerity of Troilus's

'She nyl to noon swich wrecche as I ben wonne.'   (i.777)

Pandarus has a mastery of the second-rate and naturally gravitates to
the second-hand. His own love-affair, to which they both refer, remains shadowy and uncircumstantial—'I love oon best, and that me
smerteth sore'. Not that Pandarus cannot be sharp and pointed, telling
and persuasive, when he wishes to be; but his language, laced with
easy maxims, shows the limitations of his mind; imaginatively he is
tepid. His verbal bite is sharp but shallow. Yet Pandarus's garrulous-
ness, his piling of proverb on proverb, his multiplication of 'ensamples',
do not only reveal him as a verbal busybody; they convey directly and
tangibly to us the sense of machination which is Pandarus's stock-in-
trade. His rhetoric shows that he can manipulate words as well as

---

to wrecche . . . for one who is miserable it is consoling to have someone else to
share his pain   *love a womman* . . . love a woman in such a way that she doesn't
realize it and she will requite you in such a way that you don't feel it   *nyl* will
not

people; indeed, it is with words that this spider will entice his two flies towards the web he is spreading for them. To say that Pandarus is a 'doctor in Love's law' and that through him Chaucer provides his audience with the 'love-doctryne' which they expected, is a truth, but only a partial one. Like Shakespeare, Chaucer can both give his audience what it wants and make it mean something they never dreamt of.

Pandarus's rhetoric, then, is not just a symptom of his character but a veritable symbol of what he is in the poem. The words he weaves, like the manœuvres he performs, are part of the net of circumstances in which the lovers are caught. It is Pandarus's most dangerous illusion that he can handle this net with impeccable judgment and unfailing success. He sees himself as a fisher of men who can land his lovers unerringly in the lap of salvation. Or, to use an image of Chaucer, Pandarus is the harper and Troilus, if he escapes from the dull, 'bestial' condition of being an ass (731), will respond to his music;[12] Pandarus pipes and his puppets have to dance.

Is it fair, one might ask, at this stage of the poem to speak of Pandarus's 'dangerous illusion'? I think it is, partly because of the quality of his persuasions. They are well-meant, certainly. Pandarus wishes to be kind; he is no dark malignant Iago, no devil, no 'priest of Satan'. But there is something thick-skinned about his glib promises, a moral insensitiveness when he says Troilus can have absolutely any woman he wants ('theigh that it were Eleyne/That is thi brother wife', 677; or, 'Were it for my suster al thy sorwe,/By my wil she sholde al be thyn to-morwe', 860). Pandarus is a very confident counsellor; and if we wince slightly when he uses phrases like 'fullich in me assure' (680) or says, to encourage Troilus to confide in him,

> wolde I fayn remeve
> Thi wronge conseyte, and do the som wyght triste. (i.691–2)

it is not just because we know the story and know that he is bound to be proved wrong in the end. It is because Chaucer has already made us feel through his language that Pandarus, for all his charm, his well-bred, gentlemanly capabilities, his energy and his kindness, is not in the last resort to be trusted.

Pandarus is the supreme example in medieval romance of one stock type—the confidante, friend and go-between. But here he is brought to life and endowed by his creator with a baffling complexity of character.

---

fullich in me assure trust me absolutely   *conseyte* idea [i.e. Troilus's—that no one can be trusted]   *do the . . . triste* enable you to trust

The word 'character' can properly be used of Pandarus, provided we do not assume that Chaucer takes a psychologically conceived, novelistic interest in him. Chaucer uses Pandarus, subtly drawn as he is, to embody some of his deepest general reflections on this unstable and transitory world as well as to provide a foil for the idealistic presentation of Troilus.

We still have, perhaps, a tendency to assume that the centre of interest in a narrative fiction, even a poetic one, must be in the experience of the individual. As a result we are particularly liable, I believe, to unbalanced interpretations of what seem to be purely naturalistic features in romance characters. The chapter which follows is devoted to examining a closely related aspect of romance which also can easily be misunderstood—the author's employment of speech, talk, and discourse.

1. Frye, *Anatomy*, pp. 136–7.

2. Ed. Vinaver, ii.861.

3. Spearing, *Criticism and Medieval Poetry*, p. 46.

4. Lydgate seems to have been the first to call the poem 'Troilus and Cresseide'. See Root, introd., p. xi.

5. The *Cantus Troili* (in some MSS, *canticus*) in fact renders Petrarch's Sonnet 88, 'S'amor non è'.

6. W. Schumaker, 'Alisoun in Wanderland', *ELH* 18 (1951), 77.

7. Vinaver, *Works*, iii.1505–6.

8. This is not to imply that either Sir Dinadan or Sir Kay ought to have been any different in their contexts; Sir Kay, at any rate, is fully adequate for Chrétien's purpose.

9. Lewis, *Allegory*, p. 190; it will be seen that I do not find myself in agreement with the general conclusions of his character-sketch of Pandarus.

10. Lewis, op. cit., p. 191.

11. See pp. 190ff.

12. Root (p. 424) quotes Boethius, i. pr. 4. 1–2, 'Artow lyke an asse to the harpe?', and a fifteenth-century proverb, 'Ung asne n'entend rien en musique'.

9

REALISM AND ROMANCE:

DISCOURSE OF LOVE

There is a crucial episode in *Sir Gawain and the Green Knight* which shows us Sir Gawain and his hostess engaged in a war of wit and words. Whilst Sir Bertilak is out hunting, his wife visits Gawain in his bedchamber; he hears someone coming and peeps out through the bed-curtain:

> Hit was the ladi, loflyest to beholde,
> That drow the dor after hir ful dernly and stylle ... (1187–8)

Gawain at first pretends to be asleep. At last he opens his eyes:

> 'God moroun, Sir Gawayn,' sayde that gay lady,
> 'Ye are a sleper unslye, that mon may slyde hider.
> Now are ye tan astyt! Bot true us may schape,
> I schal bynde yow in your bedde—that be ye trayst;'
> Al laghande the lady lauced tho bourdes.
> 'Goud moroun, gay,' quoth Gawayn the blythe,
> 'Me schal worthe at your wille, and that me wel likes,
> For I yelde me yederly and yeye after grace,
> And that is the best, be my dome, for me byhoves nede!'
> (And thus he bourded agayn with mony a blythe laghter).
> 'Bot wolde ye, lady lovely, then, leve me grante
> And deprece your prysoun and pray hym to ryse,
> I wolde bowe of this bed and busk me better;
> I schulde kever the more comfort to karp yow wyth'.
> 'Nay forsothe, beau sir,' sayd that swete,
> 'Ye schal not rise of your bedde. I rych yow better:

---

drow pulled [the door] to   *dernly and stylle* stealthily and quietly

> I schal happe yow here that other half als,
> And sythen karp wyth my knyght that I kaght have.
> For I wene wel, iwysse, Sir Wowen ye are,
> That alle the worlde worchipes; quereso ye ride,
> Your honour, your hendelayk is hendely praysed
> With lordes, wyth ladyes, with alle that lyf bere.
> And now ye ar here, iwysse, and we bot oure one;
> My lorde and his ledes ar on lenthe faren,
> Other burnes in her bedde, and my burdes als,
> The dor drawen, and dit with a derf haspe;
> And sythen I have in this hous hym that al lykes,
> I schal ware my whyle wel, whyl hit lastes,
>   with tale.
>
> Ye are welcum to my cors,
> Yowre awen won to wale,
> Me behoves of fyne force
> Your servaunt be, and schale.'   (1208–40)

('Good morning, Sir Gawain,' said that fair lady, 'you are a careless sleeper if one may slip in to your room [without your knowing]. Now you are caught. Unless we can arrange a truce between us, I shall fasten you in your bed, you can be sure of that.' The lady laughed as she jested with him. 'Good morning dear lady,' said Gawain the happy man, 'I am entirely at your disposal and glad to be so, for I yield myself to you without hesitation and ask for grace. And that's the best course, I think—I have no choice!' (And thus he jested in his turn with much laughing.) 'But, fair lady, if you would give me leave and would release your prisoner and tell him to rise, I would get out of bed and get properly dressed; then I should talk more comfortably with you.' 'No, indeed no, good sir!' replied the sweet lady; 'you are not to get up out of bed; I have better advice for you. I shall imprison you here from the other side too [by leaning her arm over him?] and then talk with my knight whom I have captured. For I realize for certain that you are Sir Gawain, whom the whole world honours, wherever you may travel. Your honour and courtliness are nobly praised among lords, ladies, absolutely everyone. And now you are really here; and we are quite alone. My lord and his men are gone on a distant trip; other people are in bed, including my women; the door is shut and stoutly locked. And since I have in this house him who is pleasing to all, I shall use my time well, while it lasts, in talking. You are very welcome here, and may take your pleasure [*disputed lines, see editions*]. I must of necessity be your servant, and I shall be.')

No one could doubt for a moment that in this scene and the two following dialogues we have the reality of courtly conversation, of 'communing'—the 'clene, cortays carpe, closed from filthe' for which Gawain was especially renowned. The expectation of such talk lent an added warmth to the welcome he received from Bertilak's household:

> 'Now schal we semlych se sleghtes of thewes
> And the teccheles termes of talkyng noble . . .'   (916–17)

('Now, as is fitting, shall we see skilled demonstrations of courtliness and the faultless expressions which pertain to noble conversation.')

The lesson which everyone in the castle hopes to have and to profit by is a lesson, not in public speaking ('talkyng noble' has none of those associations) but in 'luf-talkyng', 'her dere dalyaunce of her derne wordes'. It is hard to translate this concept into modern terms without trivializing it—'the gracious exchange of private conversation between the sexes' could be a beginning but does not give enough prominence to the teasing, flirtatious side of the art of banter. A sense of delicate provocation and countering, of verbal fencing, thrust and riposte, of problems set 'in ernest or in game', this is also present. To find the art of gallant conversation re-created in other, increasingly more familiar, terms we should look at Elizabethan court-comedy (*Love's Labour's Lost*, for instance) or the social comedy of the Restoration 'wits'; and, after the demise of the long courtly tradition, in (say) Jane Austen's *Emma* (the heroine's exchanges with Frank Churchill), in Oscar Wilde's drawing-room comedy, and so on. In the *Gawain* scene the art, from the Lady's side, consisted in teasing and even blackmailing her opponent into a position from which he could not extricate himself without embarrassment or rudeness—or telling the plain truth. Gawain's skill consisted in the polish of his evasiveness. The matter of such 'dalliance', we may note, is supremely *un*original. In the encounters with the Lady we find the time-honoured gambits of war and truce, of gaoler and prisoner, of teacher and pupil. And the tone, too, is equally pre-defined: it is, above all, gay—the recurrent words are 'laghande', 'blythe', 'daynté', 'mery'.

The art of 'dalliance' is not the only discursive element in medieval romance but it is of central importance and we shall return to it. For the moment the most necessary thing to note is that such 'dalliance' is one of the pleasures of hearing (and, now, reading) romance, for two reasons. First, intellectual play is pleasurable, in itself; we enjoy using our wits. And, secondly, such discourse fills out our notion of the courtly idealisms which centre in the experiences of love and heroism but expand beyond them, as we have already seen, to embrace a whole way of life, 'a civilization of the heart'—and even somewhat of the head. I have said 'one of the *pleasures*' deliberately, not 'one of the expected features', since the latter might suggest that we could justify the prominence of discourse in medieval romance simply by an appeal to contemporary taste—'This is the sort of thing they liked, and so it had to be put in'. The recognition of period tastes in certain features of medieval literature, or art, does not in itself constitute a defence of dullness or irrelevance. We need to proceed from recognition towards judgment: is there, or is there not, underlying these features, something that, properly understood, can 'please many and please long', a 'just representation of general nature'?

Such a representation is surely to be found earlier in a short-story romance entitled *Le Lai de l'Ombre* (*c.* 1220) by Jehan Renart.[1] There is no particular reason why it should be called a *lai*, except its shortness and the general looseness of terminology which is common in medieval times. It is a romance episode which tells of a wooing. There are in effect only two characters, a Knight and a Lady, both of supreme virtue, intelligence and beauty, and both unnamed.

He falls in love with her and goes to pay court. In their first encounter he seizes on her every courteous word and gesture and construes it in his favour. He asks her to pledge him with a token which will inspire him to heights of valour. Although moved by his impassioned pleas she refuses outright. While she is lost in thought he slips a ring on to her finger without her noticing and quickly takes his leave. She soon realizes what has happened, and in a state of grave embarrassment sends for him to return. He does so, glad at heart, only to be told that she cannot and will not keep his ring. He resists as strongly as he can, until finally she says,

> 'Or vos veil jë aconjurer,
> Par la grant foi que me devez,
> Et proier que le reprenez,
> Si chier con vos avez m'amor.'　(824–7)

('Now will I conjure you by the great faith you owe me, and entreat you, as you value your love for me, to take your ring again.')[2]

Conjured thus in the name of his love to be obedient to her wishes, the Knight is in a dilemma. He takes his ring back on condition he can do what he likes with it. In the courtyard there is a well. Gazing at the Lady's shadow reflected in the well, he declares he will give the ring to *La riens que j'aing miex emprés vos* (the thing I love best after you) and he throws the ring into the water. The

Lady is deeply moved by this supremely courteous gesture. Never since Adam ate the apple was there such courtesy in a man. She addresses him:

> 'Biaus douz amis,
> Tot vostre cuer ont el mien mis
> Cil doz mot et cil plesant fet . . .'   (931–3)

('Most fair, sweet friend, your heart and mine have been made as one by these gracious words and pleasing ways . . .')[3]

She gives him her ring and they plight their troth in joy.

The *Lai de l'Ombre* helps us to set one aspect of *Sir Gawain and the Green Knight* in a tradition.[4] The *Lai* has, indeed, striking similarities to the thrice repeated encounters of Sir Gawain with his hostess. The roles are, admittedly, reversed; but in each instance the interest resides in 'the give and take, the thrust and parry of two opponents'. There is extraordinary skill in the way each author presents both the opportunism of the aggressor and the courteous evasiveness of the quarry. It is usually said of both works that the interest is almost entirely psychological; and this is true as far as it goes. But a further question needs to be asked: What is the psychology for? What purpose does it serve? We have to beware of giving a modern answer to this question. The psychology of the *Lai de l'Ombre* is, first and foremost, part of the love-casuistry; it serves the same general ends and must have pleased the same general courtly public as Andreas Capellanus's *De Amore* (see pp. 30–3 above), which, we remember, sets and solves a number of *questions d'amour*. It might not be too far from the mark to imagine a patroness setting Jehan Renart the problem that his hero is faced with: 'What should a Knight do if his Lady requires him to take back a ring which he has given her . . .? The answer Jehan Renart gives is still of interest seven centuries later, not because it is the perfect casuistical reply but, on the contrary, because it transcends casuistry. It seems to crystallize for all time an exquisite moment of courtliness; it is this which is served by the psychological interest, the Lover's demands and pleas and the Lady's elegant sidestepping, firm yet never brusque—no mere summary can do justice to the twists and turns of the dialogue. It is a meaningful human situation, certainly; but one which leads to a climax where a gesture of almost quixotic courtesy claims the Lady's surrender. The 'meaning' of the tale resides in the idealized delicacy of sentiment. Although Jehan Renart is a far more intellectual author than Marie de France, they have something in common here—to read their poems was, and is, a sentimental education.

Modern readers are possibly better equipped to read the 'images' or accept the 'characters' of medieval romance, better prepared, in fact, to accept other kinds of formalism, than to accept the formalism of speech. Our natural tendencies are still to expect speech to be closely fitted, psychologically, to character, to be disdainful of verbal play (despite our admiration for Donne and James Joyce), to dislike doctrine and didacticism, and moreover to be suspicious of too much general statement. What we must come to realize is that the discursive element in the best romances, so far from being an excrescence, is one way in which 'the claim of the ideal' is substantiated. If we had to find a single phrase to describe the nature of the formalized speech which figures so prominently in romance, it might be 'rhetoric in the service of an idealism'.

Troilus, in a moment of desolation, after the exchange of Criseyde for Antenor and her departure from Troy, goes to gaze on her empty house, with its 'dores spered alle'. Overcome with sorrow he bursts out passionately:

> 'O paleys desolat,
> O hous of houses whilom best ihight,
> O paleys empty and disconsolat,
> O thow lanterne of which queynt is the light,
> O paleys, whilom day, that now art nyght,
> Wel oughtestow to falle, and I to dye,
> Syn she is went that wont was us to gye!
>
> O paleis, whilom crowne of houses alle,
> Enlumyned with sonne of alle blisse!
> O ryng, fro which the ruby is out falle,
> O cause of wo, that cause hast ben of lisse!
> Yit, syn I may no bet, fayn wolde I kisse
> Thi colde dores, dorste I for this route;
> And farewel shryne, of which the seynt is oute!' (v.540–53)

Rethorik is the appropriate term to describe this passage for several reasons.[5] First, however, a word of general explanation. The term in medieval usage denotes the traditional techniques of communication in speech and in writing, in prose and in verse, with little distinction drawn between them. Fashions in rhetoric varied somewhat from age to age; but there was no change in the fundamental outlook. *Rethorik*

---

spered barred   *whilom best* . . . formerly called 'best'   *queynt* put out   *gye* guide
lisse joy   *bet* better   *dorste* . . . if I dared to with this crowd here

G

is an art of persuasion and its purpose 'to express thought with fluency, force and appropriateness so as to appeal to the reason [and] move the feelings'.[6] Or, to quote from the English sixteenth-century writer, George Puttenham, 'our maker or Poet is appointed not for a judge but rather for a pleader', and he seeks 'to inveigle and appassionate the mind':

Now if our presupposall be true, that the Poet is of all other the most auncient Orator, as he that by good and pleasant perswasions first reduced the wilde and beastly people into publicke societies and civilitie of life, insinuating unto them, under fictions with sweete and coloured speeches, many wholesome lessons and doctrines, then no doubt there is nothing so fitte for him, as to be furnished with all the figures that be *Rhetoricall*, and such as do most beautifie language with eloquence and sententiousness [i.e. force of expression and richness of meaning].[7]

It is possible to waste a lot of time on the detail and the technical jargon of *rethorik*, attempting to master 'the figures that be Rhetoricall'— *anaphora*, *chiasma*, *exclamatio*, *prosecutio*, *occupatio* and the rest. The results are disappointing. On the other hand, one can scarcely spend too long pondering the assumptions that lie behind this enormously influential and long-lived body of teaching. C. S. Lewis once wrote that it was 'the greatest single barrier between us and our ancestors'.

These assumptions are, principally: that there is no essential difference between the art of poetry and any other kind of verbal art (oratory, preaching, letter-writing, etc.); that it is first and last an art (that is, a skilled craft) of communication, not of self-exploration or expression; that its subject is the known truth, its natural medium the traditional story, theme or argument, its form ordered and 'artificial', its technique deliberately persuasive, and its purpose to delight and improve mankind. The aesthetic assumptions behind *rethorik*, it will be seen, are far-reaching and about as different from ours over the last two centuries as it is possible for them to be. In the hands of bad writers *rethorik* had its vices, of course; in particular, the vice of over-elaboration. 'The figures and figurative speaches, which be the flowers as it were and coulours that a Poet setteth upon his language'[8]—these could, and frequently did, get out of hand. But the abuse of ornament in *rethorik* must not blind us to its fundamental importance.

Returning now to Troilus's eloquent apostrophe, we find the comments almost make themselves. Troilus, as so often, is a mouthpiece for the ideal. One has only to contrast his utterance, totally devoid of any individual nuance, with the circumstantial detail of this personal letter from a novel:

> The house Frantz spoke of is a little two-storey private one. Mademoiselle de Galais's room must be on the first floor. The windows up there are the ones most hidden by trees, but if you walk along the pavement you can see them quite well. The curtains are drawn and you'd have to be mad to hope that one day between those curtains the face of Yvonne de Galais would appear.
>
> It's on a boulevard. It was raining a little. The trees are green already. You could hear the sharp clang of the trams which kept going by . . .
>
> When it got dark, windows all around began to show lights, but not in that house. It is certainly unoccupied. And yet Easter isn't far off.[9]

This thoroughly novelistic description is not without symbolic force; it embodies the same contrast of light and darkness as we find in Troilus's address to the 'paleys empty and disconsolat'. Yvonne's curtains are drawn; her room also is a 'lanterne of which queynt is the light'. But the symbolism is part of a fully local scene—the boulevard, the green trees, the clanging trams.

Just as Troilus before Criseyde's house is Desolation personified and not a complicatedly sentient human being, so he and other lovers are at different times eloquent mouthpieces for Mourning, Elation, Doubt, and so on. There is naturally a relation between speech and speaker; but it is frequently of this simple one-to-one kind. The real relevance of speech can, in fact, often lie elsewhere. The passages of formal discourse in romance have a variety of purposes: they can be models of right feeling (such as we have already seen in the *Lai de l'Ombre*); debates embodying genuine tensions; conflicts of thought or instinct or emotion; debates demonstrating intellectual and verbal skills, as it were in play; ethical statements or exhortations; or philosophical disquisitions.

One of the most extraordinary passages in twelfth-century romance is that which describes the falling in love of Alixandre and Soredamors; it extends over 600 lines of Chrétien's romance, *Cligés*. Alixandre has permission from his father, the emperor Alexander, to leave home and present himself at the court of King Arthur. He arrives at court with twelve companions and makes a good impression. The king accepts his offer to serve him. On an expedition to Brittany the king takes Alixandre with him in the royal ship, the queen takes a lady called Soredamors. Up to this point the narrative has been relatively straightforward, apart from a 'praise' of *largesse* from Alixandre's father, the emperor (188–213). But now the 'discourse' begins in earnest.

Soredamors (*qui desdaigneuse estoit d'amors*) has never seen a man who pleased her. But love will get his revenge on her for her pride and indifference (*orguel et dangier*). He has pierced her heart with a dart and she is stricken with love. Love has prepared a hot bath for her (*li a chaufe un baing*). She accuses her eyes of treachery: 'Eyes you have betrayed me. It pains me now that I have sight. Pains me? No! Surely I have control of my eyes. But I must be on my guard. What the eye doesn't see, the heart doesn't grieve over (*Car cui ialz ne voit cuers ne dialt*). Shall I love him if he doesn't love me? Are my eyes to blame for following my desire? No! Who then? I myself. I must be mad to wish for something which causes me pain. Does Love think he can lead me astray like others? I'll go on having nothing to do with him.' She doesn't know that Alixandre is equally smitten. The queen notices Soredamors's suffering and thinks she must be seasick. (The quibbling passage which follows must be given in the original and should really be read aloud to get the full flavour of the punning sound-play on *la mer/l'amer/l'amor/amers*):

> Ne set don ce puet avenir,
> Ne ne set por coi il le font
> Fors que por la mer ou il sont.
> Espoir bien s'an aparceüst,
> Se la mers ne la deceüst;
> Mes la mers l'angingne et deçoit
> Si qu'an la mer l'amor ne voit;
> An la mer sont, et d'amer vient,
> Et d'amors vient li max ques tient.[10]   (536–44)

(But she knows no reason why they should [grow pale and tremble], unless it be because of the sea where they are. I think she would have divined the cause, had the sea not thrown her off her guard, but the sea deceives and tricks her so that she does not discover love because of the sea. < They are on the sea > and it is from love that comes the bitter pain that distresses them.)[11]

Alixandre and Soredamors remain in mutual ignorance of their plight and are ashamed to reveal it. But the fire that is covered with ashes doesn't burn any the less fiercely. They deceive everyone but at night they suffer for it (*Mes la nuit est la plainte granz*).

The narrator says he will tell us first about Alixandre. Alixandre's 'complaint' (not a complaint in the ordinary sense of the word, but a formal lament or *planctus*) runs on for nearly 250 lines and covers every conceivable topic:

'Ought I to remain silent or not? An ill man needs help and advice. But my illness can never be cured. A doctor could have helped at first; not now. Where does the pain come from? But does Love cause pain? I thought Love was a gentleman (*dolz et debonaire*) not a *felon*. Love chastises me to teach me a lesson. Ought I to despise my master?'

And so on. Alixandre works out a string of images to do with light and heat: the eye is the mirror of the heart, and through this mirror the flame passes without breaking it; the heart in the breast is like a candle in a lantern; the eye is like a pane of glass which does not throw light of itself but only when the sun passes through it. Shortly after this we have a description of Love's arrow which is 'feathered' with the golden tresses of Soredamors, and then an itemized description of her beauty in traditional style—brow, eyes, mouth, teeth, throat, etc. The 'shaft' of the arrow, her body, was covered up. The 'complaint' ends with total submission to love.

> Granz est la conplainte Alixandre,
> Mes cele ne rest mie mandre
> Que la dameisele demainne.   (865–7)

(Long is Alexander's 'complaint', but that which the maiden utters is not a whit shorter.)

Fortunately for us we need not go into Soredamors's 'no less long' complaint in any detail. She concerns herself, in precisely the same style and tone as Alixandre, with his beauty, with the nature of love, with the lessons of love:

> Ensi se plaint et cil et cele
> Et li uns vers l'autre se cele.   (1039–40)

(Thus plain both He and She and hide the truth from one another.)

If the question that Criseyde so early asked of Troilus—'Kan he wel speke of love'?—had been asked of these two, it could confidently have been answered in the affirmative. This extravaganza of 'luf-talkyng' is enough to send most readers thankfully back to the laconic wooing style of Horn and Rymenhild:

> Knight, nu is thi time
> For to sitte bi me.
> Do nu that thu er of spake:
> To thi wif thu me take.   (565–8)

But we should not refuse our imaginative sympathy too brusquely, for these *complaintes* set the tone for the extraordinarily rarefied blend of passion and ratiocination which characterizes the amours of Alixandre and Soredamors. It is the absence for so long in this passage of any supporting image or action that differentiates it from Chrétien's usual procedure, and from later passages in the same romance. It is as if in the first bars of a concerto movement, the soloist were to go off into an elaborate cadenza. There simply is not, we feel, enough stuffing to support it. These lovers are all air and fire. Later, concrete objects and actions begin to play a part in the affair: a shirt into which Soredamors happens to have sewn a few of her golden hairs is given to Alixandre by the queen (1142). Alixandre gets to know the true, and incalculable, value of his shirt and wallows in the possession of it. He kisses it a hundred thousand times, takes it to bed with him and spends the whole night embracing it:

> Tote nuit la chemise anbrace,
> Et quant il le chevol remire,
> De tot le mont cuide estre sire.   (1618–20)

(All the night he embraces his shirt, and when he looks at the hair, he thinks he is lord of the whole world.)

The narrator comments drily *Bien fet Amors d'un sage fol* (Love easily makes a wise man mad). We should note that the substantiation of the ideal of 'clene cortays carp' does not preclude ironic comment on its basis in passionate love. But it is probably more important still to realize that the *folie* of love is one of the 'commonplaces' (*topoi*, stock themes) of courtly discourse, along with the mutual relationships of Heart and Eye; the notion of love as an illness requiring a doctor; the oxymoron of pain and pleasure; and, probably, every other talking-point in the *complaintes*.

Cligés sets before us, as strikingly as any medieval romance, the quality of dialectical virtuosity which had a part to play in the ideal of the courtier-lover, the very type of civilized man. It is hard to decide whether there is any 'objective correlative' for the discourse of Alixandre and Soredamors other than a delight in argument for its own sake and a fascination with the general, unindividualized, emotional dilemmas of courtly lovers at the beginning of their tortured careers. There may be something else, I think—a growing interest in the way people's minds work, which leads to an attempt to analyse the 'new' experience of romantic love as an imaginative condition. But the analysis exists, surely, at least as much to sustain the accepted intellectual style, to provide a frame for the gymnastics of sensibility, as for any truth that may emerge. We know, in any case, that practically all the material was pre-cast and predictable (a great number of the 'common-places' come out of Ovid, for instance); the novelty must then lie in the expertise of the poet's handling, since it certainly does not lie in the revelation of 'character' through new images and ideas.

If the *Lai de l'Ombre* used the discourse of love chiefly in order to call into being the emotional experience of *fin amors*, and *Cligés* used it in order to create a state of intellectual excitement, the talk in other romances may have a stronger moral or ethical bias. A well-known instance of a debate between different points of view in a situation involving ethical choice was quoted earlier from Chrétien's *Lancelot*—the incident of the dwarf and the cart. The whole 'debate' only occupies some fifteen lines (360 ff.) and is in indirect speech—a miniature, indeed, by Chrétien's standards (see p. 34).

A more extended, though less central, moral debate takes place later in the same romance between *Pitiez* and *Largece*. The orgulous knight who defends the Swordbridge, which Lancelot, still in pursuit of Guenevere's abductor, must cross, offers to ferry Lancelot over—for the price of his head. Lancelot not unnaturally refusing, they fight. The first 'round' ends with Lancelot un-helming his opponent. Whilst they are discussing the terms on which Lancelot might show him mercy, a distressed maiden gallops up on a mule, wishes Lancelot his heart's desire and asks for a boon. This he promises, only to discover that the boon is the head of the knight he had just defeated—*einz ne trovas/si felon ne si desleal* (there was never a knight so wicked and traitorous, 2810–11). Lancelot is now in a quandary. What should he do? Which demand should he satisfy?

> Et a cesti, et a celui
> viaut feire ce qu'il li demandent:
> largece et pitiez li comandent
> que lor boen face a enbedeus,
> qu'il estoit larges et piteus.
> Mes se cele la teste an porte,
> donc iert pitiez vaincue et morte;
> et s'ele ne l'an porte quite,
> donc iert largece desconfite. (2836–44)

(He wishes to respect the wishes of both her and him. Generosity and pity each command him to do their will; for he was both generous and tender-hearted. But if she carries off the head, then will pity be defeated, and put to death; whereas, if she does not carry off the head, generosity will be discomfited.)[12]

This problem in courtesy is debated in terms that will still be familiar four centuries later in the Elizabethan love-sonnet. Each side in the debate is personified and presents claim or counter-claim, as in Shakespeare's sonnet no. 46 'Mine eye and heart are at a mortall warre'. Chrétien's presentation is not, in the event, carried through as a mental allegory. Shortly after the passage quoted, Lancelot soliloquizes to himself, as any later hero might, to the effect that he has never before refused mercy to a defeated opponent, and the allegory is dropped.

As has been pointed out many times, the episodic 'mental allegory' of earlier romance, dramatizing internal moral and emotional tensions, may have encouraged the development of full-scale allegory, such as we find in the *Roman de la Rose*, Part I, where the state of being in love, with all its irresolutions, tensions, and setbacks, is staged as if it were as a scene in a courtly garden. Thirteenth-century writers, one must emphasize, did not in fact *need* such allegorizations in order to set out the mechanisms of the mind. A cursory reading of the contemporary devotional treatise, the *Ancrene Wisse*, with its meticulously observed and delicately notated naturalistic portraits of, for instance, slanderers and seducers should quickly dispel that illusion. But the writers evidently liked allegorizations, since they became so popular in the following centuries. It is worth while considering why. The answer, I believe, is central to the argument of this chapter—that 'discourse of love' was an admired, and must still be experienced as an integral imaginative ingredient of many a courtly romance. The allegorical presentation of an internal conflict through the personifications, *Amor*, *Raison*, *Largesse*, *Pitié*, etc., enabled a freer use of 'discourse' than did other presentations. When the 'churl' Daunger and 'dame Frauchise' argue with one another, each puts forward a 'case', each pleads. This means a continual supply of openings for the *rethorik*, the 'luf-talkyng' which they so much enjoyed and which is, as I have argued, itself an admired courtly quality:

> She seide, 'Daunger, gret wrong ye do,
> To worche this man so myche woo,
> Or pynen hym so angerly;
> It is to you gret villany.
> I can not see why, ne how,
> That he hath trespassed ageyn you,

Daunger standoffishness, aloofness [a quality of the Lady]   *pynen* torment
angerly cruelly

Save that he loveth; wherfore ye shulde
The more in cherete of hym holde.
The force of love makith hym do this:
Who wolde hym blame he dide amys?
He leseth more than ye may do;
His peyne is hard, ye may see, lo!
And Love in no wise wolde consente
That he have power to repente;
For though that quyk ye wolde hym sloo,
Fro love his herte may not goo.
Now, swete sir, is it youre ese
Hym for to angre or disese? . . .
Curtesie wol that ye socoure
Hem that ben meke undir youre cure.
His herte is hard that wole not meke,
Whanne men of mekenesse hym biseke.'
  'That is certeyn,' seide Pite;
'We se ofte that humilite
Bothe ire, and also felonye,
Venquyssheth, and also malencolye.
To stonde forth in such duresse,
This cruelte and wikkidnesse.
Wherfore I pray you, sir Daunger,
For to mayntene no lenger heer
Such cruel werre agayn youre man.   (3509–51)

So far from giving newly observed insights into the tortuous
workings of the human mind the allegorical method may be, rather,
a way of *evading* giving them. It is we, perhaps, who wish to see allegory
as a tool for the exploration of personality. Its creators may have conceived it as an attractive, undemanding framework on which to hang
their 'taffeta phrases, silken terms precise'. The later development of
courtly allegory in the work of Guillaume de Machaut (*c.* 1300–77) and
his contemporaries is linked with an intense interest in elegance of expression; and this does not seem to be accompanied by any noticeably
new insights of a psychological kind.[13]

Machaut's *Remede de Fortune* (before 1342) is not a deeply allegorical
poem; it simply has the trappings of allegory.[14]

---

cherete charity   *blame he dide amys* condemn him for acting wrongly
leseth loses   *quyk* i.e. even if you killed him alive   *is it youre ese* does it help
you?   *disese* make unhappy   *Hem that ben meke . . .* those who are patient
under treatment   *wole not meke* are not willing to be merciful
stonde forth . . . persist in such sternness   *This* this is

The narrator, referred to as *L'Amant*, The Lover, dare not approach his Lady directly for fear of a rebuff. Instead he sets himself to make verses and songs. She accidentally happens upon a *lai* he has written and without knowing that it is his asks him to recite it to her. When she enquires more closely about it, he is struck dumb with confusion and retires to a 'very beautiful garden' (784) to compose a *complainte* against Fortune. A handsome supernatural lady then appears to him. Her name is *Esperance* and she explains that these little setbacks are only superficial unkindnesses of Fortune. She goes off, singing a *baladelle*; the Lover, slightly revived, sings a *balade* himself. After this he makes his way homeward, finds his Lady in a gay company and is invited to join their pastimes. When it is his turn to perform, he sings a *virelai (chanson balladée)*. On the return of the company to the château, his Lady interrogates him about his bizarre and confused behaviour. He confesses his love and is accepted as her *ami*. After a day of courtly occupations—such as going to Mass, attending a banquet, games, dancing and music—they exchange rings and part, whilst *Esperance* looks on. Joy inspires him to sing a *rondelet*. On his next visit to the château the Lover is dismayed to find himself coldly received by his Lady. She explains, in due course, the necessity for discretion and dissimulation. The Lover reconciles himself to this, not without difficulty, and the poem ends with a speech of homage to *Loial Amour*.

In this poem Machaut has invented the lightest and slightest of allegorical actions in order, it seems, to have something on which to drape his fine speeches, his discourse of love. In this particular instance the discourse has an unusual interest, for it is more than once elevated into song—not the 'song' merely of high-style romance, like the *Canticus Troili* quoted above (p. 176), but real song with a musical setting. Machaut was not only a poet but the greatest French musician of his generation; and the *Remede de Fortune*, amongst other things, is a sort of *summa* of fourteenth-century lyric. It gives text, context and music for all the major types of song from the noble and stately *lai* down to the light and lively *virelai*. Song, as well as speech, is a symptom of the joyousness, the *joie* which characterizes courtly experience. The *musician*, the lover and the poet are 'of imagination all compact'.

One example of Machaut's heightened discourse must suffice to show the ever intensified concentration on verbal elegance and metrical virtuosity. It is the first stanza of the Lover's *complainte*:

> Tels rit au main qui au soir pleure
> Et tels cuide qu' Amours labeure
> Pour son bien, qu'elle li court seure
>   Et mal l'atourne;

Et tels cuide que joie aqueure
Pour li aidier, qu'elle demeure.
Car Fortune tout ce deveure,
    Quant elle tourne,
Qui n'atent mie qu'il adjourne
Pour tourner; qu'elle ne sejourne,
Eins tourne, retourne et bestourne,
    Tant qu'au desseure
Mest celui qui gist mas en l'ourne;
Le sormonté au bas retourne
Et le plus joieus mat et mourne
    Fait en po d'eure.

(The man who laughs in the morning weeps at night; and he thinks that Love is working some good thing for him, while she is attacking him and plotting against him. He thinks that he is acquiring Joy to aid him, when she is holding back. For Fortune consumes all this, when she turns, and she does not wait for day to break to turn [her wheel]; for she does not rest but turns, turns again and overturns until she brings up on top the man who lay downcast in the roadway; the man who is on high she brings down to earth again, and she makes the most happy creature miserable in a very short while.)

The third quatrain of this stanza shows, on a small scale, how Machaut enjoyed playing with word-sounds (sounds rather than meanings); but to do real justice to his virtuosity it would be necessary to quote the whole *complainte*, of 36 stanzas, since the main technical challenge of it for the poet is the invention of rhyme, for no rhyme may be repeated. (That is to say, no stanza may use rhymes previously used in another.) Thus any young versifier is able to write a short *complainte*; but it takes a great metrician to write a long one. Machaut's has 576 lines in all.

I have argued that growing, or continued, interest in psychological ethical debate, particularly in the ethics of love-debate, may have contributed to the increased popularity of love-allegory based on the personification of mental and moral qualities. But the allegorical method, we see, can easily relapse. In many instances the allegorist has nothing new to say about the mind's experiences; the encounter between the Lover and 'Esperance' in Machaut's *Remede* tells us only what we knew before (and not much even of that) about hope and despair. Allegory reverts with facility into being a vehicle on which 'discourse of love' can be carried. It is none the worse for that, if the discourse is worth hearing. 'Kan he wel speke of love?' is again the question we must answer before we discard allegorical romance as an unmitigated bore.

It will have become apparent that the concerns of this chapter overlap to some extent with those of Chapter 3, 'Man and Society', which described the social idealisms arising, paradoxically, from the analysis of the experience of love between two individuals. The Wife of Bath's discourse on 'gentilesse' is the centre-piece of her tale, and the success or failure of the tale stands upon our reaction to it. My last example in this chapter is from Chaucer's prolific and admired contemporary, John Gower. His *Confessio Amantis*, briefly described earlier (p. 41), is in deed as in name a Lover's Confession and perhaps the most massive piece of 'luf-talkyng' produced by a great 'luf-talkyng' century.[15] This huge but tidily constructed poem is itself only in an extended sense a romance. It serves, however, as the frame for many short romances as well as for much 'dalliance' and discourse of love and could never have been conceived without the long traditions of medieval romance behind it. The 'morality' of the *Confessio* is first and foremost a courtly morality; as he says in his first book:

> To hem that ben lovers aboute
> Fro point to point I wol declare
> And wryten of my woful care,
> Mi wofull day, my wofull chance,
> That men mowe take remembrance
> Of that thei schall hierafter rede:
> For in good feith this wolde I rede
> That every man ensample take
> Of wisdom which is him betake
> . . . and therefore I
> Woll wryte and schewe al openly
> How love and I togedre mette,
> Wherof the world ensample fette
> Mai after this, whan I am go,
> Of thilke unsely jolif wo,
> Whos reule stant out of the weie,
> Nou glad and nou gladnesse aweie.   (i.72–90)

The poem proper opens with all the expected features of a fourteenth-century courtly romance. The poet depicts himself as a Lover walking

---

rede (78) advise   *betake* entrusted   *ensample fette* have an example   *thilke unsely* . . . of that unhappy–happy misery   *Whos reule* . . . whose conduct is unpredictable   *aweie* away in a wood, listening to the bird-song, in the month of May; he is melancholy and prays to Venus to alleviate his pain ('yif me som part of thi grace'); he has a vision of the King of Love, who pierces him with a fiery dart, and his queen who introduces him to Genius her priest. As the Lover's confessor, Genius urges him to tell all:

> 'What thou er this for loves sake
> Hast felt, let nothing be forsake,
> Tell pleinliche as it is befalle.' (i.209-11)

The confessional, like Chaucer's pilgrimage, is to a large extent just an excuse for telling a huge number of good stories; within the ample scheme of analysis provided by the Seven Deadly Sins, there is room for narrative examples of every kind of virtue and vice. But the *ars amatoria* aspect of the *Confessio* is also prominent, especially in the way Amans, the lover, describes his moods, his sentiments and his experiences. Between the various stories there are lengthy passages of dialogue in which the Priest describes the vices and virtues of a life devoted to love and the Lover confesses how he has behaved in each case. In the following exchange of speeches the point at issue is 'Cheste', anger expressing itself in evil, unrestrained use of the tongue:

> So with his croked eloquence
> He spekth al that he wot withinne. (iii.440-1)

The Lover protests his innocence of 'wicke tunge':

> Bot I spak never yit be mowthe
> That unto Cheste mihte touche . . .,
> For so yit was I nevere above,
> For al this wyde world to winne
> That I dorste eny word beginne,
> Be which sche mihte have ben amoeved
> And I of Cheste also reproeved.
> Bot rathere, if it mihte hir like,
> The beste wordes wolde I pike
> Whiche I cowthe in myn herte chese . . . (484-501)

He goes on to claim at some length:

> . . . I withoute noise or cri
> Mi pleignte make al buxomly
> To puten alle wraththe away. (545-7)

---

be mowthe by mouth   *unto . . . touche* might border on   *For so yit . . .* for
I have never in my life been so disposed . . . that I dared [taking *above*
temporally]   *amoeved* distressed   *pike, chese* choose   *buxomly* agreeably
To puten . . . to forestall all her anger

His Confessor strengthens the Lover's resolution by saying that if he knew *all* the effects of 'Cheste' on love and on 'his well willinge':

> Thou woldest flen his knowlechinge
> And lerne to be debonaire.
> For who that most can speke faire
> Is most acordende unto love:
> Fair speche hath ofte brought above
> Ful many a man, as it is knowe,
> Which elles scholde have be riht lowe
> And failed mochel of his wille.   (600–7)

Like much other courtly literature, Gower's *Confessio* not only talks about but itself stands as a monument of 'curtesye'. The passage above goes one further: it is a passage of 'luf-talkyng' which has 'luf-talkyng' for its subject. The values it inculcates are the values it incorporates—'fair speche', easy, ingratiating (in the best sense), untroubled, elegant and *de-bon-air*. We may well feel as Gawain's hosts did when he arrived at Bertilak's castle,

> Wich spede is in speche unspurd may we lerne   (918)

and, finally, agree with Gower that

> . . . who that most can speke faire
> Is most acordende unto love.

---

flen his knowlechinge avoid recognizing its existence   *brought above* promoted to high position   *failed mochel* . . . failed largely to attain his desires *Wich spede* . . . 'now we can learn, without asking, what sort of thing success in conversation is' (Waldron)

1. I have used the edition by John Orr (1948). Since this chapter was written, a translation of the poem by Pauline Matarasso has been published (1971) by Penguin Classics, *Aucassin and Nicolette and other Tales*.

2. Trans. Matarasso.

3. ibid.

4. It is continued, for instance, in *La Belle Dame sans Merci*.

5. I adopt the old spelling of the word, following the suggestion of J. Lawlor, *Chaucer*, pp. 14–15, to distinguish it from the modern term and concept.

6. The definition is the OED's definition of ELOQUENCE, q.v.

7. Puttenham, *The Arte of English Poesie* (Ed. Willcock & Walker), p. 196.

8. These are the subject of Puttenham's Book III, 'Of Ornament'.

9. *The Lost Domain*, pp. 159–60 (see p. 34 above).

10. I have adopted, in line 544, the reading of B.N. 375; see Micha's edition, p. 208.

11. Trans. Comfort.

12. ibid.

13. It is noteworthy that even in the *Roman de la Rose* itself (Part I) some of the most moving and imaginative passages, psychologically speaking, work through unexplicated symbol and symbolic action and not through the discourse of personified mental qualities. See p. 158 above, the Well of Narcissus.

14. Ed. Hoepffner, vol. ii; pp. iff. introd.; pp. 1–157, text. The music of the songs is edited by L. Schrade, *Polyphonic Music of the Fourteenth Century*, vols. ii and iii (1956); the *complainte* is at ii.106.

15. Machaut's *Le Voir Dit* must be a close second: this romance pictures the relationship between the aging poet and an eighteen-year-old girl; it consists of 46 letters in prose, exchanged by the lovers, various lyrics and songs, and some 9000 lines of octosyllabic couplets. Not in Hoepffner's edition; but Ed. P. Paris (1875).

THE STORYTELLER AND THE POET

It has become a commonplace of recent criticism to insist on the importance of the narrator's role in medieval poetry and to distinguish it from the poet's. But, so strongly embedded are our assumptions about literature as the experience of the printed page, the unknown author and the silent reader, that the insistence is still necessary. Chaucer, living in a border-age between a predominantly oral culture and a predominantly written culture, made his poems public (published them, we would say) in the first instance, by performing them himself at court. Professor Lawlor has well distinguished the difference between Chaucer's position and that of a modern novelist. In so doing he has described the position of all medieval court poets in relation to their audiences:

The modern reader must see Chaucer standing in the circle of a small society, each known to him, and each his feudal superior, as the Corpus Christi MS 'frontispiece' shows him to us. His task is hazardous indeed: his first problem therefore to open the range, to gain some distance from his audience. In this he differs most markedly from the author of a printed book, who meets an unknown audience through the silent traffic of the printed page; and who can meet that audience only as an individual, a solitary reader, in every instance. The traditional problem of the novelist has therefore been to gain intimacy, to establish and sustain a one-to-one relationship between himself and his 'gentle reader'. The task of the oral narrator is exactly the opposite. He must win a certain detachment (and resourcefully vary it, in tune with the developing mode of the story) away from his small, well-known audience, who are unalterably a group, with a group's reactions.[1]

Chrétien de Troyes must have had the same kind of problem, though we know far less about him than about Chaucer. The prologues, which were evidently an expected part of twelfth-century, as of later, romance, are devised with care to 'win a certain detachment' from the audience the poet knows he will address. They serve also other purposes—some of them paradoxical: to establish the truth and authority of the story he is going to tell; to dissociate himself sometimes from anything in it that might offend (or, to put it another way, to dissociate *it* from his own experience); to ingratiate himself in the most pleasing possible way with his patron. So Chrétien, introducing his *Lancelot*:

> Puis que ma dame de Chanpaigne
> vialt que romans a feire anpraigne,
> je l'anprendrai molt volentiers
> come cil qui est suens antiers
> de quan qu'il puet el monde feir
> sanz rien de losange avant treire. (1-6)

(Since my lady of Champagne wishes me to undertake to write a romance, I shall very gladly do so, being so devoted to her service as to do anything in the world for her, without any intention of flattery.)[2]

He continues in the same vein of courtly compliment. If he were a flatterer he would say that his 'lady of Champagne' (Marie, daughter of Eleanor of Aquitaine and step-daughter of Henry II of England) was the most wonderful woman on earth. He would say that compared to other queens she was a diamond amongst lesser jewels. But, no, he will keep quiet—but it's true all the same! (*s'est il voirs maleoit gré mien*, 20). The prologue ends:

> Del CHEVALIER DE LA CHARRETE
> comance Crestïens son livre;
> matiere et san li done et livre
> la contesse, et il s'antremet
> de panser, qui gueres n'i met
> fors sa painne et s'antancïon. (24-9)

(Here Chrétien begins his book about the Knight of the Cart. The material and the < significance > of it are given and furnished to him by the Countess, and he is simply trying to carry out her concern and intention. Here he begins the story.)[3]

Some critics, reading *Lancelot* as an 'idealization of adultery' and finding it distasteful, have seen this prologue as evidence that Chrétien did, too, and that he wishes to shift the responsibility on to the shoulders of his beautiful patroness. It seems to me much more likely that Chrétien should gracefully attribute everything that really matters in the poem to her inspiration, merely reserving to himself the credit of having done some work at it. It is the kind of exaggerated compliment that everyone is pleased to receive and no one takes too seriously. It is Chrétien's lowest and most elegant bow.

He achieves the same ends, of compliment and detachment, in the prologue to *Perceval*, which is 'dedicated', as it were, to Count Philip of Flanders:

> le plus preudome
> Qui soit en l'empire de Rome. (11-12)

(the worthiest man in the empire of Rome.)

The tone in which Chrétien proves the hyperbolical proposition that the Count is a better man than the Emperor Alexander is both high-flown and serious; the note of whimsical, quasi-amorous and extravagant gallantry is, of course, here entirely absent, as between man and man. Count Philip never listens to evil talk (*vilain gap ne parole estoute*); he loves *justise/Et loiauté et sainte eglise*. What is more, he is a model of Christian generosity; he follows the Gospel commandment, 'Let not thy left hand know what thy right hand doeth'. But why, Chrétien asks (he was not a *clerc* for nothing), why does the Gospel say, *Les biens a ta senestre cele*? Because, according to *l'estoire*, the left hand signifies the vainglory that results from false hypocrisy whereas the right hand signifies

> Carité, qui sa bone oevre
> Pas ne se vante, ançois se coevre,
> Si que ne le set se cil non
> Qui Diex et caritez a non.
> Diex est caritez, et qui vit
> En carité selonc l'escrit
> Sainz Pols le dist et je le lui
> Il maint en Dieu, et Diex en lui. (43-50)

(Charity, which does not boast of its good works but rather covers them up so that no one knows of them save Him who is both God and charity. According to the text, God is charity and whoever lives in charity—St Paul says it and I have read it—abides in God and God in him.)[4]

The quotations from Matthew vi and I John iv help to make this an altogether weightier tribute than is customary; *Perceval* is, after all, to be a work of wider implications than *Lancelot*—though not on that account more solemn, for it is often extremely funny. Chrétien ends, however, as before, by transferring responsibility, and by implication credit, from himself to his patron. It is *par le comandement le conte* that Chrétien has undertaken

> A rimoier le meillor conte
> Qui soit contez a cort roial:
> Ce est li *Contes del Graal*, (64–6)

(To put into rhyme the best tale that may be told in a royal court. That is, the story of the Grail.)[5]

and it is the Count who gave him the book (*li bailla le livre*).

More often, perhaps, the author will appeal to a book, or *the* book, as distinct from a patron's commands, to enforce the lesson that he will teach:

> And out of olde bokes, in good feyth,
> Cometh al this newe science that men lere.

Chrétien got the story of *Cligés* out of a book in the library of *mon seignor saint Pere a Biauvez* (Chrétien apparently chose it for himself this time). And this testifies to its truth and gives it authority. We know what happened in days gone by (*del siegle que fu jadis*) through books. The medieval reverence for books could only be recaptured in the modern world if all books, papers and printing presses were totally destroyed, and only the contents of one or two large libraries survived, so that everything had to be written out and passed round again by hand. We can dimly glimpse it if we ponder on the fact that *auctor* (author) and *auctoritas* (authority) are cognate words.

Marie de France, and other writers of *lais*, cannot generally appeal to *la lettre e l'escriture* but, like Chrétien himself in *Erec et Enide*, are dependent on the tales told by travelling *conteors*—*cil qui de conter vivre vuelent*. Even so Marie, at least, insists on their authenticity (*les contes ke jo sai verrais*). In the case of stories taken from oral tradition there is perhaps a greater need for the author to establish a claim to be doing something worthwhile. Chrétien says that everyone ought to bend his mind (*panser et antandre*)

> a bien dire et a bien aprandre

—to speak and to teach well. He is going to make *une molt bele conjointure* (a beautiful structure?) out of the story which popular entertainers have mangled and mutilated.[6] Marie de France says that if God has given you *escience* (knowledge) and *de parler bon' eloquence* (eloquent utterance), it is your duty to speak out. The good needs to be heard; then it will flourish:

> Quant uns granz biens est mult oïz,
> Dunc a primes est il fluriz,
> E quant loëz est de plusurs,
> Dunc ad espandues ses flurs.   (*Prologue*, 5–8)

(When a < great good > is heard by the many, then for the first time does it blossom forth, and when it is praised by the multitude, then has it burst into full bloom.)[7]

There is one further way in which a medieval author can establish his detachment from his story, a way which became increasingly popular from the thirteenth century onward: he can become a Dreamer. The *Roman de la Rose* opens with an argument about dreams:

Some people say that dreams are false. But we can dream dreams that come true; this we have on the authority of Macrobius, who wrote about the *avision* that Scipio had. Whatever anyone else may think, I am sure

> que songes est senefiance
> des biens as genz et des anuiz,
> que li plusor songent de nuiz
> maintes choses covertement
> que l'en voit puis apertement.   (16–20)

> (That dremes signifiaunce be
> Of good and harm to many wightes,
> That dremen in her slep a-nyghtes
> Ful many thynges covertly,
> That fallen after al openly.)[8]

The importance of this opening argument becomes plain immediately afterwards. The poet says that in the twentieth year of his age, the time when 'Love taketh his cariage [his due toll] of yonge folk' (*qu'Amors prent le paage/des jones gens*), he took to his bed:

> et vi un songe en mon dormant
> qui mout fu biaus et mout me plot.   (26–7)

> (Me mette such a swevenyng
> That lyked me wonders wel.)[9]

The author can then go on to say, *la matire est et bone et nueve* ('the mater fayre is of to make') without being accused of inventing it. This is

clearly of the highest importance. All the openings of poems so far
quoted show how resolutely determined the medieval author was *not*
to claim to be writing out of his own experience. Few authors go as far
as Chaucer in *Troilus*:

> Forwhi to every lovere I me excuse,
> That of no sentement I this endite,
> But out of Latyn in my tonge it write.   (ii.12–14)

Nevertheless, it is unquestionably true that to claim an experience,
event or feeling as meaningful *because it happened to me* would have
struck a medieval audience as foolish and presumptuous. 'Experience'
may be 'ryght ynogh' for the comic and heretical Wife of Bath; it
certainly does not behove her creator or any medieval 'maker' to
claim it for himself.

The ordinary, everyday *conteor*, *disour*, 'segger' or minstrel, of course,
had no problem. He was there to tell a story, and the quicker he got
on with it the better. Sometimes, as in *Sir Orfeo* and *Sir Degaré*, the
narrator did without any kind of introduction at all:

> Knightus that werey sometime in lande
> Ferli fele wolde fonde,
> And sechen aventures bi night and dai
> Hou they mighte here strengthe asai;
> So dede a knyght, Sire Degarree.   (1–5)[10]

But, generally speaking, he followed the advice of the author (the very
word seems misapplied) of *Emaré*, who lays down in stanza 2:

> Menstrelles that walken fer and wyde,
> Her and ther in every a side,
>   In mony a dyverse londe,
> Sholde, at her begynnyng,
> Speke of that ryghtwes kyng
>   That made both see and sonde.
> Who so wylle a stounde dwelle,
> Of mykyll myrght Y may you telle,
>   And mornyng ther-amonge;
> Of a Lady fayr and fre,
> Her name was called Emare,
>   As I here synge in songe.   (13–24)

Forwhi therefore   *sentement* personal experience   *Ferli fele* . . . would try out
many marvels   *sonde* sand   *stounde* a while   *mykyll myrght* much joy
ther-amonge mixed with it

The English redactor of Chrétien's *Yvain* felt the propriety of a prayer strongly enough to add to *Ywain and Gawain* an initial six lines which are not in the French. Some narrators match the courtly appeal to *auctoritas* with an appeal to antiquity, coupling it with solid moral virtue:

> For they that were borne or wee
> Fayre adventuris hadden they;
> For evere they lovyd sothfastenesse,
> Faith with trewthe and stedfastnesse.
> Therefore schulde man with gladde chere
> Lerne goodnesse, undirstonde, and here. (*Guy of Warwick*, 11–16)

Their model is in this case to be that rumbustious crusader, Guy of Warwick:

> So mani Sarrazin he slough that day,
> That ich on other ded lay;
> So mani to ded ther he dede,
> That the hepe lay to his girdel stede. (3579–82)

The narrator of a 'popular' romance is little more than a mouthpiece for his story.[11] At least, if he was more, the evidence is not in the text, not in the *words* we have. However, we ought not to forget that a medieval storyteller could be an actor, too—probably a whole company of actors, playing the several parts of the story he was relating. The narrator of a courtly romance, on the other hand, has established a distance between himself and his tale. It remains to be seen what use he made of it.

In general terms, it can be said, the convention of an *auctoritas*, whether it is a patron's instructions, a dream, a traditional tale, or as most often, a book, helps to give the narrator a more natural role in romance than in the novel and one less hampered by naturalistic requirements. His role is more natural because, having an objective story to tell (or pretending that he has), the necessity for him to act as story-teller is unquestionable. It is less naturalistic, because he does not have to pretend to 'be there' or to invent excuses for knowing things that he could not possibly know, for he stands outside the tale. This distance can also be used to great artistic effect, as we shall see in the case of Chaucer's *Troilus*. Earlier romancers, including Chrétien de Troyes,

---

or wee before us   *here* hear   *to ded . . . dede* killed   *lay to . . .* came up to his waist

seem content with much simpler usages: the management of the story, commentary upon it, and the 'sentimental' or moral direction of the audience's feelings.

The simplest type of narrative device is used by Chrétien, as by every other poet, to shorten his tale (or claim to be doing so, at least) and avoid boring his audience—an alarming prospect if they are actually sitting around you:

> Ja parole n'an iert retreite;
> Que trop i avroit a conter   (*Yvain*, 5838–9)

(I won't tell you about that, for there would be too much to relate.)

Such common devices often merge imperceptibly and naturally into implied comment. So when Chrétien says, 'Even if it were to weary you, I mustn't omit to tell you something about the *vergier* [the Enchanted Garden]' (*Erec*, 5685–8), we know for sure that what is to come will be of unusual importance. And when he says, 'You'd think me a fool if I told you the truth [about Queen Guenevere's lock of hair]' (*Lancelot*, 1480–1), it puts us in the mood for hyperbole.

Another stock device of medieval narrative is direct address to the audience. But what in 'popular' romance is merely a call for silence and attention ('Herkneth to me, gode men!') is in Chrétien often an enlistment of sympathy, or its opposite. Of the maiden who was accompanying Lancelot when he almost fell off his horse in a swoon, he says, *s'ele ot peor/ne l'en blasmez* ('don't blame her if she was afraid'; *Lancelot*, 1431). Later, striking a more Chaucerian note, he addresses the lovers in his audience: 'You will understand the situation perfectly, you who have done as he did' (4550–1)—this is when Lancelot is pretending to be sleepy, so as to have an excuse for going to his bedchamber. Some of the narrator's interjections verge on coyness, as when he tells us about Yvain's expressed wish to peep secretly at the funeral procession of Laudine's husband, whom he has just killed:

> Mes il n'avoit antancion
> N'au cors n'a la procession;
> Qu'il vossist qu'il fussent tuit ars,
> Si li eüst costé mil mars.
> Mil mars? Voire, par foi, trois mile.
>   Mes por la dame de la vile,
> Que il voloit veoir, le dist.   (1275–81)

(Yet he had no interest in either the corpse or the procession, for he would gladly have seen them all burned, even had it cost him a thousand marks. A thousand marks? Three thousand, verily, upon my word. But he < made the request > because of the lady of that town, of whom he wished to catch a glimpse.)

There is a sort of knowingness here that gives the passage as a whole a faintly ironic air. The rhetorical question suggests that the hero's reactions, whilst wholly to be expected, and indeed admired, are at the same time slightly absurd.

More ambitiously still, in the same episode, the narrator states that Love with his sugar and honeycombs (*de son çucre et de ses bresches,* 1356) has sweetened Yvain again. Love has made a raid into his territory; and his enemy has taken his heart away prisoner. *S'aimme la rien/ qui plus le het*—he now loves the thing (Laudine) that hates him most. The Lady has truly revenged her husband's death and yet she does not know it. And so the paradoxical propositions roll on—a *tour de force* on the narrator's part. The narrator's general comments here are scarcely distinguishable from his way of presenting the situation as a whole. We are not clearly conscious either of the narrator as a personality or of the presence of the audience. The comments have merged into a general discourse on love and have become part of the rhetoric of romance.

I have carefully spoken of the 'narrator' in this discussion and not of Chrétien. But the precaution is surely less necessary than it is when we come to Chaucer's poetry. Even when the speaker of Chrétien's romances puts on the language of hyperbole to describe the way his lovers feel and behave and, by so doing, delicately 'hints a fault' in them, we never feel that he himself, the narrator, is being manipulated. Chrétien is wholly behind his narrator, even if the whole of Chrétien is not there (how could it be?) in any one poem.

A final passage, also from *Yvain,* shows Chrétien speaking, through his narrator, strongly on the side of 'curtesie'. After the union of Yvain and Laudine King Arthur is given a truly royal welcome to the castle of Laudine, and his whole court with him. Describing the ceremonial exchange of greetings between the king and Laudine, the narrator says he will not tell us how she made much of every one else, though he could have:

> De la joie assez vos contasse
> Se ma parole n'i gastasse.

He will simply remind us, he says, of the acquaintance between the Sun and the Moon.

          de l'acointance
Vuel feire une brief remanbrance,
Qui fu feite a privé consoil
Antre la lune et le soloil.

Do we know what he is referring to?

        Savez, de cui je vos vuel dire?
Cil, qui des chevaliers fu sire
Et qui sor toz fu renomez,
Doit bien estre solauz clamez . . .

He means Gawain:

        Que de lui est tot autressi
Chevalerie anluminee,
Con li solauz la matinee
Oevre ses rais et clarté rant
Par toz les leus, ou il s'espant.   (2393–408)

([I might tell you much of the joy should I not be wasting words, but] I wish to make brief mention of an acquaintance which was made in private between the moon and the sun. Do you know of whom I mean to speak? He who was lord of the knights, and who was renowned above them all, ought surely to be called The Sun. [I refer of course to my lord Gawain] for chivalry is enhanced by him just as when the morning sun sheds its rays abroad and lights all places where it shines.)[12]

The Moon, he goes on to explain, is Lunete (Laudine's lady-in-waiting), not just because of her *buen renon* but also because she is called *Lunete*. Gawain claims her as his *amie*. (The compliment is so magnificent that one cannot help reflecting whether Chrétien may have meant it to refer to some noble couple within the court circle.)

    Between Chrétien's conception of the narrator's part in the story and that of the authors of *Havelok* and *Guy of Warwick* there is a huge gulf. Yet another lies between Chrétien's conception and Chaucer's. Chaucer's presentation of 'Chaucer' in *The Canterbury Tales*, *The House of Fame* and in the Prologue to *The Legend of Good Women*, to name no others, would require a chapter in itself. But the height of his subtlety is undoubtedly displayed in *Troilus and Criseyde*.

    Chaucer's own role in the poem is not a simple one. It is, in fact, multiple. He appears as mere translator and storyteller; as courtier and would-be lover; as epic poet, 'tragedian'; and lastly as philosopher and Christian moralist. He has, then, many roles in the poem. Nor can we assume that any one of the three or four parts that he plays represents Chaucer as he really was. On the contrary he dramatises himself, makes a public personality for himself, in accordance with the needs of his story.

Anyone who believes that this is thinking too precisely upon the event should compare Chaucer's presentation of 'Chaucer' in *Troilus and Criseyde* with his rather different presentation in *The Canterbury Tales* and elsewhere.[13] The relationship of these fictional 'Chaucers' to the actual historical person (at any moment in his career) cannot be our concern. What interests us is the function of the fictional 'Chaucer' in any one poem. We are familiar with the 'first-personal' novel—the narrative told by a single speaker—*Moll Flanders*, *David Copperfield*, *Lord Jim*, *The White Peacock*. There the artistic problem is simpler (or at any rate can be more simply stated) because the story-teller is more often than not involved as a character in his own story. In Chaucer, as in the eighteenth-century novel (e.g. Sterne), the story-teller devises a stage-personality, a public role, for himself; he is more intimate with the audience than with his characters.

In his basic role as narrator or storyteller, 'Chaucer' comes forward at convenient moments, like other courtly romancers, to link one episode to the next, to introduce or end digressions, and to point climaxes in the story. For example, near the beginning of Book I, after addressing his courtly audience on Love the poet says:

> But for to tellen forth in special
> As of this kynges sone, of which I tolde,
> And leten other thing collateral,
> Of hym thenke I my tale forth to holde,
> Bothe of his joie and of his cares colde;
> And al his werk as touching this matere,
> For I it gan, I wol therto refere.   (i.260–6)

This is all straightforward narrative technique, or so it at first appears. Let us now see how Chaucer the poet exploits, uses for his own artistic purposes, the role of storyteller. He has two gambits. He stands, first, in a relationship to his audience; he must please not pain them, interest not bore them. And, secondly, in a relationship to his sources; he must appear to have *auctoritas* behind him and yet has at the same time something individual to say. The first stand is useful because if Chaucer wants to skip over something rather quickly (the rhetorical device of

---

leten . . . put adventitious matter aside   *For* (266) because   *refere* go back to

occupatio), the narrator says he is afraid it will bore his hearers. Sometimes, indeed, it might; but sometimes it is just a storyteller's trick. For
example, he draws a veil over Diomede's wooing of Criseyde:

> And shortly, lest that ye my tale breke,
> So wel he [Diomede] for hymselven spak and seyde,
> That alle hire sikes soore adowne he layde. (v.1032–4)

The real reason for this reticence is that the episode lies outside Chaucer's
main design and its inclusion might unbalance the poem. Diomede's
amorous techniques, and even Criseyde's psychological weakness, are
at this stage irrelevant.

Chaucer's exploitation of his sources is, to say the least, two-faced.
He is capable of the contradictory suggestions: (1) 'It's all in the book
—you're getting the facts on the highest authority'; and (2) 'This is
only what the book says. Believe it at your own risk'. So, on the one
hand, for instance, he invokes the authority of his apparently imaginary
auctor, 'Lollius', for saying that every word in Troilus's song (i.400) is
exactly as he sung it—'every word right thus'. The song is, in fact, as
noted earlier, a translation of a well-known sonnet by Petrarch. On
the other hand, in Book V, when telling of Criseyde's false-heartedness,
he uses phrases implying a faint scepticism towards the 'authority'
previously held to be impeccable:

> And after this *the storie telleth us*,
> That she hym yaf the fair baye stede,
> The which he ones wan of Troilus. (v.1037–9)

And again:

> I fynde ek *in the stories elleswhere*
> Whan thorugh the body hurt was Diomede
> Of Troilus, tho wepte she many a teere . . . (v.1044–6)

The 'stories elleswhere' is a most delicate underscoring of the narrator's
reluctance to pursue and to condemn Criseyde. These two main ploys
do not exhaust the possibilities Chaucer creates out of his relationship
to a source or sources. Sometimes the narrator makes the 'excellence'
of his author almost in itself an excuse for brevity.

> But soth is, though I kan nat tellen al,
> As kan myn auctour of his excellence . . . (iii.1324–5)

---

breke interrupt   *sikes soore* . . . alleviated her painful sighing

Or, contrariwise, the alleged deficiencies of his author, of the books he claims to be consulting, provide him with good reason for avoiding plain and full statement.

All this manœuvring on the narrator's part can be used to suggest either detachment from or the most delicate sympathy for the protagonists. Or, more positively, Chaucer can use the narrator's role to provide a commonsense standpoint in the everyday world from which the happenings of the story can be judged. Sometimes he is drily humorous:

> And therwithal Criseyde anon he kiste,
> Of which certein she felte no disese. (iii.1275–6)

Sometimes, sardonic and commonsensical, with the wisdom of the ages:

> But, Troilus, thow maist now, est or west,
> Pipe in an ivy lef, if that the lest!
> Thus goth the world. God shilde us fro meschaunce,
> And every wight that meneth trouthe avaunce. (v.1432–5)

The personality of the storyteller, the chronicler of 'old unhappy far-off things', shades gently into the person of the lover among lovers, the sympathetic expositor of 'plesaunce of love . . . In gentil hertes ay redy to repaire'. Chaucer introduces us to this facet of his public self in the third stanza of Book I:

> For I that God of Loves servauntz serve,
> Ne dar to Love, for my unliklynesse,
> Preyen for speed, al sholde I therfore sterve,
> So fer am I from his help in derknesse.
> But natheles, if this may don gladnesse
> Unto any lovere, and his cause availle,
> Have he my thonk, and myn be this travaille! (i.15–21)

Chaucer, with all the exquisite tact that he could command, puts himself forward very diffidently. He must have been properly conscious of being inferior in social status to many in the society of the court. So he describes himself as one who does not dare to pray to Love for personal success, because of his 'unliklynesse' (uncomeliness, or unsuitableness, perhaps an inability to please). The highest reaches of

---

disese discomfort   *Pipe in an ivy lef* i.e. engage in a futile activity   *meschaunce* mischance   *every wight . . .* and (may God) prosper everyone who has a loyal heart   *Ne dar . . .* and dare not, because of my uncomeliness, pray to love to give me success, even though it means my death   *thonk* thanks

romantic love were reserved for men and women of 'worship', for those who were of the court, courtly. The son of a family of successful wine-merchants with a modest record of court-service did not feel fully entitled to 'bathe' in the 'gladness' of love. But he is both able and willing to be their servant and delightfully pretends that it will be for his own final good to be their sympathetic minister.

The role of 'clerk' in the service of courteous love enables Chaucer to present from the inside, as it were, the love between Troilus and Criseyde. He makes much of this dramatic sympathy in the first half of the poem. In his capacity as 'clerk' he leads the courtly lovers of his audience in a 'bidding prayer' (i.29–51). He asks them to pray for those who fall in love, like Troilus; for himself who has this story to tell; for all lovers in despair or in ill repute; and for all lovers who are success-ful, that they may remain constant. The liturgical analogies are obvious; they are to pray 'for the whole estate of *Cupid's* church militant here on earth'. The climax of Chaucer's courtly sympathy comes in Book III. The Proem is a paean, a hymn to Love; and the narrator's discourse abounds in moments of poignant tenderness and the deepest imaginative sympathy:

> O blisful nyght, of hem so long isought,
> How blithe unto hem bothe two thou weere!
> Why nad I swich oon with my soule ybought,
> Ye, or the leeste joie that was theere?
> Awey, thow foule daunger and thow feere,
> And lat hem in this hevene blisse dwelle,
> That is so heigh that al ne kan I telle. (iii.1317–23)

At the same time, partly through the narrator's implied personal regret, Chaucer manages to suggest a certain detachment even in moments of the greatest exaltation. Like Pandarus, he is better, he says, at helping others than at furthering his own cause. Indeed, he goes farther, in the Proem to Book II. Whereas in the opening of the whole poem he has hinted lack of success in love (a natural 'unlyklinesse' con-demns him to 'derknesse'), now, in a passage already quoted, he seems to disclaim all experience of love at first hand:

> Forwhi to every lovere I me excuse,
> That of no sentement I this endite,
> But out of Latyn in my tonge it write. (ii.12–14)

---

daunger power of evil (?) *feere* fear *al ne kan* . . . I cannot describe it fully
sentement experience

A little later, he is again emphatic:

> Ek though I speeke of love unfelyngly,
> No wondre is, for it nothyng of newe is;
> A blynd man kan nat juggen wel in hewis. (ii.19-21)

(That is to say, 'I've always been like this; I lack the true experience of this kind of love'). So, in the first book the narrator is a positive advocate:

> Now sith it may nat goodly ben withstonde,
> And is a thing so vertuous in kynde,
> Refuseth nat to Love for to ben bonde,
> Syn, as hymselven liste, he may yow bynde. (i.253-6)

But in the second he is already preparing positions to withdraw to: 'You all understand love much better than I do. The ways of love differ from country to country, from man to man.'

> Myn auctor shal I folwen, if I konne. (ii.49)

Thus by oscillating between one position in which he is advising them and another in which he is ready to take advice *from* them, the narrator in his role as Courtly Lover manages both to suggest his solidarity with his courtier audience (and, of course, his sympathy with Troilus and Criseyde) and at the same time his detachment. He is an outsider as well as an 'insider'. This poise, an achieved balance, is one of the master-strokes of the poem; it is one of the things which make it so rich in meaning and indeed must distinguish a poem as such from a homily in verse. The net result of this dextrous sitting on the fence is, surprisingly enough, to create an impression neither of inconsistency, nor of unresolved contradiction, lack of commitment or indifference, but, in fact, of the most delicately critical sympathy.

The third facet of the public personality which meets us in the poem presents us with the epic poet and rhetorician. This is the character Chaucer displays for us when he is invoking the Muses, remembering his great predecessors, and dedicating his book to Gower and Strode. In the very first stanza of his poem the poet asks not a Muse but a Fury, appropriate to torment and suffering, to help him:

> Thesiphone, thow help me for t'endite
> Thise woful vers, that wepen as I write. (i.6-7)

---

juggen judge   *in kynde* in its essential nature   *vers, that wepen* verses which weep

There may be a borrowing here from late classical epic; but whether Chaucer has learnt this role from Virgil, Statius, Dante or Boccaccio, the invocations and the lofty Proems themselves set Chaucer's poem for the moment in a grander and more solemn world than that of medieval vernacular romance. The narrator turns back to Tisiphone and her sisters again at the beginning of Book IV and links them with Mars:

> O ye Herynes, Nyghtes doughtren thre,
> That endeles compleignen evere in pyne,
> Megera, Alete, and ek Thesiphone;
> Thow cruel Mars ek, fader to Quyryne,
> This ilke ferthe book me helpeth fyne . . .   (iv.22–6)

Elsewhere he invokes Clio, the muse of history, and Calliope, the muse of epic poetry. He could scarcely make his elevating and 'magnifying' intentions more clear.

Finally, we encounter in *Troilus* a narrator who speaks neither as a storyteller pure and simple, nor as a lover among lovers, nor as a mouthpiece of the Latin and Italian literary traditions, but as moralist and philosopher. Our first hint of this side of the narrator's presence (a better word than 'character' in the context) is in the course of Book I. The God of Love, angry with Troilus's aloof superiority to the 'lewed observaunces' of lovers (i.e. their stupid behaviour as he sees it), draws his bow and shoots the 'peacock' Troilus 'atte fulle'. Even before describing the effect on Troilus himself, the narrator bursts out with a solemn apostrophe:

> O blynde worlde, O blynde entencioun!
> How often falleth al the effect contraire
> Of surquidrie and foul presumpcioun;
> For kaught is proud, and kaught is debonaire.
> This Troilus is clomben on the staire,
> And litel weneth that he moot descenden;
> But alday faileth thing that fooles wenden.   (i.211–7)

The mind behind this authoritative and sombre pronouncement on the silly certitudes of 'man, proud man' is obviously capable of a deeper 'philosophy' of love than earlier avowals—about serving the servants of the God of Love—have led us to expect. Our new sense of his under-

---

Herynes Furies   *Quyryne* Romulus   *fyne* finish   *falleth . . . contraire* turns out contrary to expectation   *surquidrie* overweeningness   *litel weneth* little thinks   *alday* all the time   *wenden* supposed to be so

standing is fully borne out by a subsequent stanza, in which the
narrator explains his pronouncement, that pride comes before a fall,
by linking the inevitable falling in love of a young courtier with the
fundamental forces of creativity in the universe, symbolized by Nature
or 'Kynde'.

> Forthy ensample taketh of this man,
> Ye wise, proude and worthi folkes alle,
> To scornen Love, which that so soone kan
> The fredom of youre hertes to hym thralle;
> For evere it was, and evere it shal byfalle,
> That Love is he that alle thing may bynde,
> For may no man fordon the lawe of kynde.   (i.232–8)

As the poem progresses our sense of a weight of authority accumulat-
ing behind and around it (one can only speak metaphorically) is not,
of course, wholly due to such pronouncements as this, which come
somewhat rarely. A Boethian wisdom builds up as a result also of our
response to the irony of philosophical pronouncements made by the
characters themselves—Criseyde's disquisition, for instance, on the
happiness of this world, 'which clerkes callen fals felicitee' (iii.814).
But after the love-climax of the poem in Book III the narrator becomes
gradually a little more prominent in his role as moralist or, better,
philosophical commentator (he never passes direct moral judgment on
his characters). And, at the end, when the story is over, he emerges to
address in overtly Christian language the young courtiers in his
audience. The stanzas have deservedly become famous; their emotional
force cannot be doubted:

> O yonge, fresshe folkes, he or she,
> In which that love up groweth with youre age,
> Repeyreth hom fro worldly vanyte,
> And of youre hert up casteth the visage
> To thilke God that after his ymage
> Yow made, and thynketh al nys but a faire
> This world, that passeth soone as floures faire.
>
> And loveth hym, the which that right for love
> Upon a crois, oure soules for to beye,
> First starf, and roos, and sit in hevene above;

Forthy therefore   *To scornen* i.e. *not* to scorn love   *fordon* . . . undo the law
of Nature   *Repeyreth* return   *hom* i.e. to heaven and heavenly things
up casteth . . . turn the face of your heart upwards to God   *al nys but a
faire* . . . this world is only a fair   *beye* redeem   *starf* died

> For he nyl falsen no wight, dar I seye,
> That wol his herte al holly on hym leye.
> And syn he best to love is, and most meke,
> What nedeth feynede loves for to seke?   (v.1835–48)

The epilogue to *Troilus*, of which this address forms part, may serve
both to sum up these comments on the narrator's art, and to emphasize
the artificiality of categorizing them. In the course of a few stanzas all
his other roles come momentarily to the surface again—the storyteller:

> And if I hadde ytaken for to write
> The armes of this ilke worthi man,
> Than wolde ich of his batailles endite;   (v.1765–7)

—the would-be courtly lover, 'dallying' with the ladies:

> Bysechyng every lady bright of hewe,
> And every gentil womman, what she be,
> That al be that Criseyde was untrewe
> That for that gilt she be nat wroth with me;   (v.1772–5)

—and the selfconsciously literary, epic poet:

> Go, litel bok, go, litel myn tragedie . . .
> And kis the steppes, where as thow seest pace
> Virgile, Ovide, Omer, Lucan, and Stace.   (v.1786–92)

The narrator's art has developed a long way from the stage of
'Herkneth to me, gode men'; Chaucer is its supreme exponent.

---

nyl falsen will not betray anyone who is ready to trust him absolutely
al be that even though   *that* (1775) [redundant]   *pace* pass   *Stace* Statius [epic
poet]

1. Lawlor, *Chaucer*, pp. 19–20.

2. Trans. Comfort.

3. ibid.

4. Trans. Loomis.

5. ibid.

6. On the much-disputed term, *conjointure*, see p. 154 above, and note.

7. Marie de France, *Lais*, Ed. Ewert, p. 163.

8. Trans. Chaucer, Fragment A.

9. ibid.

   H

10. Ed. French and Hale, i.288 (I have slightly regularized the text).

11. He is a mouthpiece also in a different sense:
     At the beginning of ure tale
     Fil me a cuppe of ful god ale! (*Havelok*, 13–14)

12. Trans. Comfort.

13. B. H. Bronson, *In Search of Chaucer* (USA, 1960), has stimulating things to say about the 'current fashion, not to say fad' of discussing the '*persona* in works of fiction'. See especially pp. 29–32 on Chaucer's approach. It is important, I think, to see Chaucer adopting a role (as we all do to suit different circumstances) rather than devising a *separate* fictional self, i.e. becoming a character *within* the poem.

EPILOGUE:

THE PERVASIVENESS OF ROMANCE

This book started from the proposition that romance is permanent. As a genre, or rather a series of related genres, it is characterized by conventions, motifs, archetypes, which have grown up to express certain experiences in their essential nature. The experience *creates* the conventions, because it cannot be described so well in any other way. The same experience *re*-creates the same conventions. The central experiences of romance are idealistic, and in the Middle Ages they are, principally, idealized love, idealized social living, idealized valour or integrity, idealized religious aspiration. The creation, and continuous renewal, of stories which would express these idealisms, especially the stories of King Arthur, is one of the great imaginative achievements of the Middle Ages. There are good reasons, I think we can now see, why romance should be the principal type of medieval fiction, the major genre. It grew into being to express 'the claim of the ideal' in an age which needed to formulate a secular idealism, to fashion an image for *li roi del siècle*, the princes of this world, and, by doing so, to complement rather than (at first) to challenge the traditional religious idealisms.

In this brief epilogue I do not wish to go over the ground again, even in summary, nor to extend the time-range of the central arguments in the way that my introductory chapter suggests could be done.[1] Instead I shall draw the reader's attention to ways in which the themes and modes of romance were used during the Middle Ages outside the genre itself. As Geoffrey Shepherd has written, 'Romance invaded public life as well as private fancy'.[2]

In suggesting that romance was a strangely pervasive thing and crept into all sorts of corners where one would not have expected to find it, I am conscious of one particular difficulty. I may give the misleading impression that we are dealing with a purely literary problem. To disentangle the so-called 'literature' of the Middle Ages from its roots in social life, ceremony and entertainment is a difficult and delicate business. The major romances, certainly, stand on their own as arte-facts, self-sustaining, if not self-contained. Not so most courtly lyrics. To be brief, much of what we today call the 'literature' of medieval England is a symptom of a certain kind of social activity. Of no 'literature' is this more true than of the literature of courtly love. But the observation holds, equally, for the mass of devotional verse and prose. No one would now think of explaining the resemblances be-tween certain versified prayers, hymns, 'commandments', and so forth, as 'literary' resemblances. The verses are alike because they reflect the religious activity of a community. Once anachronistic ideas of 'litera-ture' have been discarded it is, of course, easy to see that devotional poetry is a symptom. This is because the religious activity which nourished it and gave it meaning expressed itself in many other ways —in the liturgy, in the religious drama, in the architecture of our cathedrals. The liturgy of the Church survives, but the ritual of courtly living has largely perished. It is this ritual which we have to reconstruct in imagination, if we are to understand the courtly lyric which it nourished and which adorned it.[3] Courtly romance provides one kind of document from which, with due circumspection, a reconstruction could be attempted.

The connection between courtly lyric and romance is clear and con-tinuous. In so far as romance is the major form, one is tempted to say that the lyric is largely parasitic, that the romance gave it imaginative life and created the conditions in which it could be understood. But, once again, this is to oversimplify—first, by isolating literature from life and assuming a closed system of cause and effect, which I have already argued is wrong; secondly, because one of the first symptoms of the twelfth century's 'cultural revolution' is an intense and vital activity in the field of song. The extraordinary phenomenon of Provençal lyric, surpassing the lyric of other vernaculars in variety and in excellence of achievement, had more to teach than to learn from the romancers; Jaufré Rudel (*c.* 1125-50) did not have to wait for the author of *Flamenca* (*c.* 1250) to tell him about *amor de lonh*, a love that spans continents and finds an object without a 'face or name':

Lanquan li jorn son lonc, en may,
M'es belhs dous chans d'auzelhs de lonh;
E quan mi suy partitz de lay,
Remembra·m d'un 'amor de lonh;
Vau de talan embroncx e clis
Si que chans ni flors d'albespis
No· m valon plus qu'iverns gelatz.

(When the days are long, in May,/I'm pleased by the sweet song of birds from afar: and when from that I've turned away,/I remember a love from afar./ I go, with longing sombre and bowed down,/so that neither song nor whitethorn blossom/avails me more than icy winter.)[4]

In later centuries the situation was somewhat reversed. Poets seem to be increasingly dependent on something outside the poem to give meaning to the pattern they have created, the commonplaces they have strung together:

Thus musyng in my mynd, gretly mervelyng
Houghevyr such dyversite in on person may be,
So goodly, so curtesly, so gentill in behavyng;
And so sodenly will chaunge in every degre;
As solen, as stately, as strange toward me,
As I of aquayntance had never byn afore;
Wherefore I hope to fynd a speciall remedy
To lett itt over pass, and thynk theron no more.[5]

The repetition of so threadbare a motif (the changeable, unpredictable sweetheart) in language so grey and inert does nothing. It is mere verbal wadding and waits for something to stiffen it and put some life into it —a social setting, a frame of living relationships real or imagined.

If romance fragmented into lyric, it was also diluted into history. This is not surprising, for two reasons. The first is that it was one way of satisfying a need, a need for a terminology. A terminology is a set of verbal categories; it provides tools for describing and explaining things. Whatever other ways were available for describing and interpreting past events, a writer had at least the choice, in French, of the language of the *chanson de geste* and the language of romance. A fascinating Anglo-Norman poem, which gives an account of the war between England and Scotland in 1173-4, is written in the idiom of the *chanson de geste*.[6] The poet, Fantosme, opens characteristically:

---

on one   *degre* respect   *solen* strange, unsociable

Oez veraie estoire (que Deu vus beneie!)
Del mieldre curuné ki unkes fust en vie.
Talent m'est pris de faire vers, dreiz est que jo's vus die.   (1–3)

(Hear a true account—God's blessing on you!—of the best monarch who ever
lived. I have a desire to make verses and it is right that I should relate them
to you.)

Professor Bezzola describes these lines as 'du pur cliché des chansons
de geste'.[7] The same could be said of lines 15–16; they are the commonplace of battle description:

Maint hume deschevalchié, mainte sele voidié,
Maint bon escu estroé, mainte bruine faillie.

(Many a man thrown off his horse, many a saddle emptied, many a good
shield pierced, many a breastplate broken.)

Fantosme's use of epic idiom is not mere poetic colouring; his *chronique*
shows that his whole conception of this historical episode is in keeping
with an epic and feudal point of view.

   Fantosme wrote hard upon the events he describes; not so the author
of the 'historical' romance of *Richard Cueur de Lyon* (early fourteenth
century). His presentation of King Richard is highly romantic, as in
this exploit:

Kynge Rycharde gan hym dysguyse
In a full stronge queyntyse.
He came out of a valaye
For to se of theyr playe,
As a knyght aventorous.
His atyre was orgulous:
Al togyder coleblacke
Was his horse, without lacke; . . .
He bare a shafte that was grete and stronge,
It was fourtene fote long;
And it was bothe grete and stoute,
One and twenty inches aboute.
The first knyght that he there mette,
Full egerly he hym grette
With a dente amyd the shelde;
His horse he bare downe in the felde:
And the knyght fell to the grounde,
Full nye deed in that stounde.   (267–94)

---

stronge queyntyse strange fashion   *orgulous* proud   *stounde* moment

King Richard follows this exploit by appearing, again anonymously, as a Red Knight, and then as a White Knight. His various emblems, the black raven, the red hound and the white dove, etc., all have a Christian significance in relation to the Crusade he is about to undertake —'in palmeres gyse/The Holy Lond for to devyse' (595–6).

So determined was this author not to let the prosaic complexities of every day cloud the enchanted mirror of his romance view of life that he abolished Richard's mother, Queen Eleanor (as if her personal legend were not romantic enough in all conscience!), and provided Henry II with an Eastern princess for queen who comes in a ship like Cleopatra's galley itself:[8]

> Swylk on ne seygh they never non;
> Al it was whyt off ruel-bon,
> And every nayl with gold begrave
> Off pure gold was the stave,
> Here mast was of yvory
> Off saymite the sayl wytterly . . .
> And in that schyp ther were idyght
> Knyghtes and ladyys off mekyll myght;
> And a lady therinne was,
> Bryght as the sunne thorw the glas.   (61–76)

Of a slightly later generation of French chroniclers, Huizinga has written:

The conception of chivalry constituted for these authors a sort of magic key, by the aid of which they explained to themselves the motives of politics and of history. The confused image of contemporaneous history being much too complicated for their comprehension, they simplified it, as it were, by the fiction of chivalry as a moving force (not consciously, of course). . . . History thus conceived becomes a summary of feats of arms and of ceremonies.[9]

It is a ticklish business to decide when and to what degree any particular romance-writer thought he was writing history.[10] Perhaps only the most sophisticated minds of the age were able to distinguish between fact and fiction in past events—or, rather, wished to be aware of criteria by means of which fact and fiction could be distinguished. Amongst the things which hampered them were their reverence for 'authority', their philosophical idealism, which sought 'vertical', heavenly, rather than 'horizontal', causal explanations, and their lack of any developed sense of period. Only an age of extraordinary naïveté

---

ruel-bon ivory

could have accepted as serious history, as apparently they did, the *History of the Kings of Britain* which served as our 'island story' for several centuries and also launched, in effect, the legend of King Arthur on its triumphal career.

Geoffrey of Monmouth's *Historia Regum Britanniae* was one of the most popular and influential books of the twelfth century; some two hundred medieval manuscripts of it survive and three early printed copies. Geoffrey's professed aim in writing was, as Professor Thorpe has said:

> to trace the history of the Britons through a long sweep of nineteen hundred years, stretching from the mythical Brutus, great-grandson of the Trojan Aeneas, whom he supposed to have given his name to the island after he had landed there in the twelfth century before Christ, down to his last British king, Cadwallader, who . . . finally abandoned Britain to the Saxons in the seventh century of our era.[11]

In Geoffrey's long account of British history, three personalities stand out: Brutus, the founder; Belinus, who 'is supposed to have captured and sacked Rome'; and Arthur 'with his beautiful wife Guinevere, Mordred who betrayed him, and his four brave knights, Cador of Cornwall, Gawain son of Loth, Bedevere the Cup-bearer and the Seneschal Kay'.[12] Already we have an Arthurian company in embryo, though it was not until Chrétien's time that the company was given a courtly meaning.

Within a few years rival chroniclers began to pick holes—one huge hole, in fact—in Geoffrey's history. They said, what later scholarship has confirmed, that most of it was made up. But this did nothing to decrease the work's popularity. Indeed, one can be reasonably sure, as I have said, that Geoffrey's original readers for the most part neither knew nor cared about the difference between fact and fiction. 'Story' and 'history' which for us have come to denote opposites, for them seem often to have merged into one.[13] Geoffrey's *historia*, amplified from Celtic legend, became the most famous and extended *matière* of European fiction, and even today its possibilities are not exhausted.[14]

Another area invaded by romance has already been under scrutiny to some extent (Chapter 6, 'Man and God: Religion and Romance'). I recounted there the well-known story from the *Ancrene Wisse* which tells how Christ, as a Knight, wooed and died for his sweetheart, man's soul. It could well be called a courtly *parable*. Most of the material of that discussion was chosen to illustrate the opposite state of affairs, the use by romance writers of religious experience, religious motifs. But, as the *Ancrene Wisse* story shows, romance invaded religion, as well as *vice versa*. There are many medieval curiosities of this kind, such as *Sacrum Commercium*, a 'romance' which describes the wooing of Lady Poverty by St Francis of Assisi; and amongst orders of chivalry there is one which assigns degrees of knightly rank to each of the twelve Apostles.[15] These conjunctions strike us now, perhaps, as slightly comic —though we should always be on our guard when we find ourselves laughing too easily at the past; the more imaginative blendings, in fiction, of religion and romance still retain their power to move us. Such a blending is to be found in the fourteenth-century poem, *Pearl*.

Pearl, of which the unique copy is in the same manuscript as *Sir Gawain and the Green Knight*, tells quite a simple story in poetry of the highest elaboration, alliterative, rhymed and stanzaic.

A man has lost a pearl in an 'erber grene'. He falls asleep and dreams he is in a marvellous forest, where he meets a maiden in courtly dress, his lost pearl, eventually to be identified with a two-year-old girl-child now dead (thought to be his daughter). In his delight at finding her he presumes he will now join her and live with her. His presumption is rebuked. To his enquiries she replies that she is married to the Lamb and is a queen. The Dreamer asserts that God has acted too generously to one so young and ignorant, at which she tells him the New Testament parable of the labourers in the vineyard, all of whom received a penny. The innocent and no others receive the joys of heaven as of right. The Maiden describes the shared but equal bliss of the 144,000 wives of the Lamb. The Dreamer, now much enlightened, is allowed a glimpse of the Holy City, the New Jerusalem, from outside. But when in a state of mad excitement he tries to cross the stream, to his dismay he wakes up. Men, he reflects, should and must accept the dispensations of God. The poem ends with a prayer in which he entrusts his pearl to Him:

> And sythen to God I hit bytaghte
> In Krystes dere blessyng and myn
> That in the forme of bred and wyn
> The preste vus schewes uch a daye.
> He gef vus to be his homly hyne
> Ande precious perles unto his pay.

> Amen. Amen. (1207–12)

The courtliness of *Pearl* is no superficial, laid-on thing. It is pervasive

---

bytaghte commended   *vus* us   *uch a* every   *He gef vus . . .* May he grant us to be his household servants   *unto his pay* for his pleasure

—in the setting, in the relationships, in the ideas and in the language. At the beginning of the poem, the poet's unique lost pearl is described in royal and exotic terms:

> Perle, pleusaunte to prynces paye
> To clanly clos in golde so clere,
> Out of oryent, I hardyly saye,
> Ne proved I never her precios pere.   (1–4)

(Pearl, pleasing to a prince's delight to set fairly in gold so bright, I say firmly, that I never found her precious equal among those of the orient.)[16]

It is essential that we should read this freshly and wonderingly and not anticipate meanings of 'perle' and 'prynce' which the rest of the poem exists to create. The atmosphere of this first scene is defined at least as much by the courtly associations of

> I dewyne, fordolked of luf-daungere
> Of that pryvy perle wythouten spot   (11–12)

(I pine, mortally wounded by the power of love, because of that special pearl of mine without flaw.)[17]

as by the Scriptural suggestions of

> For uch gresse mot grow of graynes dede;
> No whete were elles to wones wonne   (31–2)

In words like 'luf-daungere' we hear the language of love, as in the description of the pearl—'so smal, so smothe her sydes were'. It is some time, in fact, before we even know for sure that it is a religious and not a romance dream-vision that we are reading. And then, when we do know, the courtliness does not simply drop out of the poem. The early suspicion that the relationship between the Dreamer and the pearl is itself courtly, even a love-relationship, does not become irrelevant when we discover she was only two years old. On the contrary, our feeling that the relationship between father and baby-daughter (never made explicit by the poet) stands for more than it is is enhanced. The Dreamer's possessive attitude to the pearl-maiden, and his presumptuous belief that she somehow 'belongs' to him again, have to give way before the 'cortaysye' of Heaven. Heaven is a court (how else, unless as a garden, could civilized bliss be depicted?) presided over by Mary, 'the quene of cortaysye'. But, unlike in earthly courts, everyone is a

---

gresse grass, corn   *to wones wonne* brought home [harvested]

queen there: 'Of courtaysye, as sayth Saynt Poule,/Al arn we membres of Jesu Kryst' (457–8). Christ is no niggard; all spotless souls are his wives ('The mo the myryer, so God me blesse'), and all, including the pearl-maiden, can say:

> In compayny gret our luf con thryf
> In honour more and never the lesse.   (851–2)

It is 'cortaysye' that holds this court together and expresses the relationship between God and man which, in theological terms, is grace.

The poem culminates in a vision of the Holy City, based on the descriptions in *Revelation* but having through its language and context an unmistakable affinity with the marvellous castle of romance, the idealized medieval walled town:

> I syghe that cyty of gret renoun,
> Jerusalem so nwe and ryally dyght,
> As hit was lyght fro the heven adoun.
> The borgh watz al of brende golde bryght
> As glemande glas burnist broun,
> Wyth gentyl gemmes an-under pyght
> Wyth banteles twelve on basyng boun,
> The foundementes twelve of riche tenoun.   (986–93)

Romance, then, its themes, motifs and conventions, was an extraordinarily pervasive thing during the medieval centuries. The visual arts, including tapestries, illuminations and ivories constitute another realm of the creative imagination which for lack of expertise as well as space I have not been able to explore in these pages. But even the uninstructed gazer can experience the elegance and refinement, in a word, the courtliness, of such a magnificent tapestry as *La Dame à la Licorne*,[18] and can enjoy the 'Siege of the Castle of Love' as it is portrayed on the back of an ivory mirror-case: the ladies are energetically hurling down roses whilst the knights assault their stronghold from below.[19]

The musician's world, too, was pervaded by the ethos of the courtly romance. But, because of the nature of musical experience itself, and because of the highly abstract aesthetic which, in the Middle Ages, governed its composition, we can do little more than speculate.

---

con thryf does prosper *syghe* saw *As hit was* . . . as if it had descended from heaven *borgh* town *brende* refined *As glemande* . . . polished bright like gleaming glass *an-under pyght* supported underneath *Wyth banteles* . . . with twelve tiers fixed on their foundation *The foundementes* . . . the twelve layers [of the foundation] *of riche tenoun* 'having elaborately joined tenons' (Gordon)

However, the troubadours and the *trouvères* state, in innumerable instances, a connection in their poems between love and song, between
the joy of *fine amors* and *bien chanter*. And such a song as Giraut Riquier's
'Fis et verais e pus ferms que no suelh' seems to represent in musical
terms one of the central paradoxes of courtly experience, the combination of *mesure* (restraint, moderation) and *joie* (spontaneous life and
delight).[20]

But these are subjects for other books. I mention them here in the
conclusion because they show that the study of romance, in its medieval
shapes, need not, and indeed cannot properly, remain a purely literary
study. In the Middle Ages, romance—at least for the chosen few—was
part of a way of life.

1. Gillian Beer's short book, *Romance*, contains many stimulating suggestions
   covering the period from the Middle Ages to the present day.

2. In Bolton, *The Middle Ages*, p. 79.

3. See my *Music and Poetry*, p. 151, from which the sentences above are quoted.
   In ch. 9, 'The "Game of Love" ', and 10, 'The Courtly Makers', I attempted
   the reconstruction for late medieval England.

4. Trans. A. R. Press.

5. The poem is from *The Fayrfax Manuscript*, (*temp.* Henry VII) pr. in my *Music
   and Poetry*, appendix A, p. 359.

6. The episode which Jordan Fantosme chose for his poem was part of the
   larger struggle between Henry II and his sons, 'Henry the Young King',
   Richard Cœur de Lion and Geoffrey who were abetted in their rebellious-
   ness by their mother, Eleanor of Aquitaine. William the Lion, King of
   Scotland, seized the opportunity of this European family-quarrel to lay
   claim to Northumberland.

7. Bezzola writes in his account of the poem, 'All this shows yet once more that,
   when one turned from Latin to French, reality took on a different aspect,'
   (*Les Origines*, pt. 3, vol. i, pp. 200 fn. 1 and 204).

8. Amongst the romance motifs of the poem are, in addition to the two already
   quoted: Richard's disguising himself as a pilgrim; an 'exchange of blows'
   (cf. *Sir Gawain*, except that the stipulated interval is one day); a fight with
   a lion; and several others. They are listed by Brunner in the introduction
   to his edition, pp. 60–7. He also enumerates the true and the false historical
   facts of the romance.

9. Huizinga, 57.

10. Uncommonly interesting in this respect is a group of Anglo-Norman
    romances, described by Miss Legge as 'ancestral', which appear to celebrate,
    even if sometimes rather obliquely, the achievements of the great baronial

families of England (see *Historical Note*, p. 238 below). The 'truest' of the group is the prose romance, *Fouke Fitzwarin* (*c.* 1260) which romanticizes the life of Fulk III.

11. Geoffrey of Monmouth, *History*, translated by Lewis Thorpe; I am much indebted to his introduction, from which the quotation is taken (p. 9), and to his translation.

12. Thorpe, trans., introd., pp. 19–20.

13. 'It might be a salutary exercise to . . . ponder just what [Geoffrey] meant by the word *historia*, or indeed what medieval French writers meant by *histoire, historie* and *estoire*, all of them so close etymologically to our modern word "story" and so far away from the modern connotations of the word "history" ' (Thorpe, p. 28).

14. The first version in English is Layamon's *Brut* (see *Historical Note*, p. 238 below).

15. The legend, the treatise (*Sacrum Commercium Beati Francisci cum Domina Paupertate*) and Dante's treatment in *Paradiso*, canto xi, are discussed by Auerbach in his *Scenes from the Drama*, ch. 2, pp. 79 ff. (I thank Peter Dronke for this reference.)

16. Trans. Gordon, p. 45 note.

17. The precise meaning of *luf-daungere* is not clear; it would normally refer to the lady's power, through her aloofness; here it may mean loss of love.

18. Often reproduced; the original is in Musée Cluny, Paris; early sixteenth century.

19. The original (*c.* 1360) is in the Victoria & Albert Museum, London; reproduction in Joan Evans, *Life in Medieval France* (3rd edn. 1969), plate no. 64.

20. Paris, Bibliothèque Nationale MS 22543, f.107.

HISTORICAL NOTE ON ENGLISH AND
FRENCH ROMANCES

The history of romance in the European vernaculars begins with a group of anonymous 'classical' romances of the mid-twelfth century, *Le Roman de Thèbes, Le Roman d'Enéas, Le Roman de Troie*. The first major development after this is in the work of Chrétien de Troyes whose five romances, *Erec et Enide, Yvain, Cligés, Lancelot* and *Perceval* (to give them their modern titles) are traditionally dated between 1165 and 1181. Among Chrétien's patrons was Marie, Countess of Champagne, daughter of Eleanor of Aquitaine, queen to Henry II of England (1154–89); there is a firmly established connection between courtly romances and the Plantagenet dynasty.

Three factors, besides the success of the classical romances, contributed strongly: the development of refined and sophisticated attitudes towards heterosexual love in the poetry of the troubadours from Guillaume IX (1071–1127), Eleanor's grandfather, onwards; the wide dissemination of Celtic legends, especially by travelling Breton storytellers and minstrels; and the popularity of the Arthurian version of British history, originally concocted by Geoffrey of Monmouth (c. 1100–55), the *Historia Regum Britanniae*. Geoffrey's history, which traced the line of British kings back to Brutus, great-grandson of Aeneas, was soon translated (rewritten, rather, in true medieval style), first by the Norman chronicler, Wace (1155), in octosyllabics like the contemporary romances and then by an Englishman, Layamon (late twelfth-century), in alliterative verse derived from late Old English epic. Chrétien's work combined all three factors, together with sympathetic understanding of the equally important developments in Christian spirituality associated with the Cistercian monks and their leader, St Bernard of Clairvaux (? 1101–67).

Out of this creative upsurge in the second half of the twelfth century arose several romance traditions. One of the lightest was the tradition of the *lai*. The Anglo-Norman poetess Marie de France (*temp.* Henry II) could be called its foundress; her *lais* (short-story romances, as it were) are the best of what was evidently a flourishing and popular genre, closely related to the songs and tales of the Breton *conteurs*. Numerous *lais* in French and English survive: *Sir Orfeo* (early fourteenth-century) is perhaps the finest, until we come to Chaucer's *Franklin's Tale*, which if it is not an authentic *lai* certainly passes itself off as one.

The central French tradition of Chrétien which launched the knights of the Round Table on their successful careers eventually produced the voluminous and influential prose-romances of the thirteenth century known today as the Vulgate cycle, comprising principally: the *Lancelot*, the *Queste del Saint Graal*, and the *Mort Artu*. Malory's use of these, two centuries later (1469–70), for his *Morte Darthur* is generously documented in Vinaver's monumental edition of Malory's 'works'. In the history of romance the expansion (almost an explosion) of the Grail legend out of Chrétien's unfinished *Conte del Graal* (his Perceval romance) is a fascinating phenomenon. The principal documents are: four actual continuations of Chrétien's romance (early thirteenth-century); Wolfram von Eschenbach's *Parzival* (1200–12; one of the masterpieces of German literature); Robert de Boron's *Joseph d'Arimathie* (*c.* 1200; he is thought to be the first to have identified the *graal* with the sacramental vessel of the Last Supper), and the *Perlesvaus* (?1191–1212?).

Two other Arthurian developments are worth noting. The first centres on King Arthur himself. In the tradition just described Arthur had fallen into the background and his court had become, in terms of story at least, merely a point of departure and return. But Layamon in his *Brut* (i.e. 'story beginning with Brutus') made Arthur the central character, the hero in effect, of the relevant part of his massive verse-chronicle. The tradition with its epic undertones is taken up in the fourteenth century by the author of the alliterative *Morte Arthure*, one of the best poems of the alliterative movement, used closely by Malory in the early books of his *Morte Darthur*. These later writers treat movingly, though differently, the later part of Arthur's personal story—the change in his fortunes, the fall of the Round Table and his own death.

The second Arthurian development is in the Tristan (Tristram) story. Tristan and Isolde seem to have been drawn into the Arthurian orbit in the second half of the twelfth century. Marie de France wrote a *lai* (*Chevrefoil*) about them; another Anglo-Norman poet, Thomas, a long romance of which only fragments survive. From Thomas's romance derives the greatest Tristan poem, Gottfried von Strassburg's (*c.* 1210); and, incidentally, a Norse version, *Tristrams Saga* (1226). Another early Tristan poem is Beroul's (late twelfth-century, Norman).

One aspect of medieval romance which has been little studied and is therefore hard to fit into any pattern is the tradition (one can certainly call it that on the basis of known relations) of Anglo-Norman romance (*Horn, Havelok, Boeve de Haumtone, Waldef,* Hue de Roteland's *Ipomedon* and others). Perhaps they are best viewed as 'ancestral' romances (Miss Legge's term), 'written to lend prestige to a family which, for one reason or another, could be regarded as parvenu' (p. 174). They have little to say about *courtoisie*; one or two of them, indeed, are written in *laisse*-form and use some of the idioms of the *chanson de geste* (e.g. *Horn*).

It is natural to wish to see a meaningful connection between these romances and the surviving English romances, some of which tell the same stories. *King Horn* (*c.* 1250), *Floris and Blauncheflur* (*c.* 1250), *Havelok* (*c.* 1300), *Amys and Amiloun* (late thirteenth-century), *Ywain and Gawain* (early fifteenth-century MS; composed earlier?), *Sir Beves of Hamtoun* (*c.* 1330–40), *Guy of Warwick* (*c.* 1330–40), and many others, have French analogues. Such a connection is not easy to establish; the English poems are usually regarded as, in some sense, popularizations. (A few are translations; many are more or less crude adaptations.) Many of the manuscripts are significantly worn; some lack heads or tails; they cannot preserve more than a portion of the stories of adventure and sentiment which were in circulation.

A significant point of new departure in French literature was the *Roman de la Rose*. Not that allegory was new; allegory is perhaps co-terminous with conscious mental experience. But its extended and systematic use by a court-poet to convey the courtly experience of love *was* new. The first part (*c.* 1225) by Guillaume de Lorris, a comparatively straight 'allegory of love', was followed fifty years later by Jean de Meun's lengthy continuation and completion. Jean de Meun's contribution is encyclopedic, powerful and often deeply sceptical; whatever it is, it is not romance. From de Lorris's poem developed a tradition of love-allegory (Machaut, Froissart, Deschamps) something of which was to filter into English through Chaucer's early poems. Chaucer's greatness is to have combined what the French poetic traditions could teach him with the Latin and Italian and to have made English a natural vehicle for it all. *Troilus and Criseyde* (*c.* 1385), one of the greatest narrative poems in English, could not have come into being without the long traditions of French, as well as of English, romance.

The finest poems contemporary with Chaucer are the result of a new wave of creativity in alliterative poetry. (A 'revival', perhaps, though with such a low and chancy rate of survival, it is hard to be sure.) Some of it flowed into the form of romance. There is every reason to think that alliterative poetry was, in no derogatory sense, provincial, and that its patrons were chiefly 'aristocratic households and families of some substance' (D. J. Williams, in Bolton, *Middle Ages*, p. 111). Not only the *Gawain*-poet but others show a familiarity with French romance (*Chevalere Assigne*, *William of Palerne*, etc.); what is more, the thundering alliterative style, so evidently apt for the description of battles and ceremonies, proves itself equally apt for the pathos of sorrow and the refinements of courtesy.

Finally—Malory, writing over two hundred years later than most of his sources, 'the Frenche book' to which he frequently refers. As has already been implied, Malory is responsive not only to the traditions of French prose romance (which, however, he only imperfectly understood) but to the 'English' Arthur of the alliterative *Morte*. Malory's *Morte Darthur* is not a work of individual genius like *Troilus* but in its own, perhaps more 'medieval', way sums up and has transmitted to posterity 'the romance tradition'.

Among the books which are most useful for information are: R. S. Loomis's huge scholarly compendium on Arthurian literature, M. D. Legge's *Anglo-Norman Literature* (i.e. the French literature of medieval England), Dieter Mehl's book on English romances, Jessie Crosland's introductory account of medieval French literature in general; Renwick and Orton's bibliographical students' guide (in the revised edition by Wakelin) to Old and Middle English literature. D. Pearsall's article, 'The Development of Middle English Romance', lists and sifts fifty romances of the thirteenth and fourteenth centuries; and D. S. Brewer's essay in his *Chaucer and the Chaucerians* stresses the importance to Chaucer of the English tradition.

BOOKLIST

BOOKLIST

This list is primarily intended as a guide to the texts and studies I have referred to by author or short title in the course of the book. I have, however, included a number of anthologies and translations that may be of use.

The following abbreviations are used:

CFMA   Classiques Français du Moyen Age
EETS OS/ES   Early English Text Society Old Series/Extra Series
SATF   Société des Anciens Textes Français

A. TEXTS, ANTHOLOGIES, TRANSLATIONS

ALANUS DE INSULIS [Alain de Lille], *De Planctu Naturae*: Latin text in Migne, *Patrologia Latina 210* (1855). Trans. D. M. MOFFAT, *The Complaint of Nature*, Yale Studies in English *36* (1908).

ALEXANDER, M., Trans. *The Earliest English Poems*, Penguin Classics (1966).

Amys and Amiloun, Ed. MacE. Leach, EETS OS *203* (1937).

Aucassin et Nicolette, Ed. M. Roques, CFMA, 2nd ed. rev. (1954). Trans. MATA-RASSO, *q.v.*

Battle of Maldon, in WYATT, *Anglo-Saxon Reader*, *q.v.*; separate ed. E. V. Gordon (1937).

BENNETT, J. A. W., see GOWER.

BEROUL, *The Romance of Tristran*, Ed. A. Ewert, vol. i (1956). Trans. A. S. FEDRICK [with *Folie Tristan*], Penguin Classics (1970).

BOETHIUS, *De Consolatione Philosophiae*, parallel text ed. Trans. H. F. STEWART, Loeb Classical Library (repr. 1953). Trans. Chaucer, in F. N. Robinson's ed.

BROWN, Carleton, *Religious Lyrics of the Fourteenth Century*, 2nd ed. rev. G. V. Smithers (1952).

CAPELLANUS, Andreas, *De Arte Honeste Amandi*. Trans. J. J. PARRY, *The Art of Courtly Love* (1941).

Chançun de Willame, Ed. Nancy V. Iseley (USA 1961).

Chanson de Roland, Ed. F. Whitehead, Blackwell's French Texts (1957).

CHAUCER. *The Works of Geoffrey Chaucer*, Ed. F. N. Robinson (2nd ed. 1957); see also ROOT and DONALDSON.

CHILD, F. J., *English and Scottish Popular Ballads*, one-volume ed., G. L. K[ittredge] (USA 1904).

CHRÉTIEN DE TROYES. *Erec et Enide*, Ed. M. Roques, CFMA (1955). *Cligés*, Ed. A. Micha, CFMA (1957). *Le Chevalier de la Charrete* [Lancelot], Ed. M. Roques, CFMA (1958). *Le Roman de Perceval ou le Conte du Graal*, Ed. W. Roach, Textes Littéraires Français (1959). *Yvain* (*Le Chevalier au Lion*), Ed. T. B. W. Reid, French Classics (Manchester, 1942, repr. 1952).

COMFORT, W. W., Trans. *Arthurian Romances* (1914) [Chrétien].

Les Deus Amanz, see MARIE DE FRANCE.

DONALDSON, E. T., Ed., *Chaucer's Poetry* (USA 1958).

The Dream of the Rood, in WYATT, *Anglo-Saxon Reader*, *q.v.*; separate ed. B. Dickins and C. Ross (4th ed. 1963).

FANTOSME, Jordan, *Chronique de la Guerre entre les Anglois et les Ecossois en 1173 et 1174*, Ed. F. Michel, Surtees Soc. (1834).

FEDRICK, A. S., see BEROUL.

Flamenca, Ed. R. Lavand and R. Nelli in *Les Troubadours*, Bibliothèque Européenne (1960) [with modern French translation]. Trans. [English] H. F. M. PRES-COTT (1930).

Floire et Blancheflor, Ed. Wilhelmine Wirtz, Frankfurter Quellen und Forschungen Heft 15 (Frankfurt 1937).

Floris and Blauncheflur, Ed. J. R. Lumby, re-Ed. G. H. McKnight, EETS OS*14* (1901).

FRENCH, W. H. and HALE, C. B., Eds., *Middle English Metrical Romances* (USA 1930).

Gamelyn, Tale of, in FRENCH and HALE, and in SANDS, *q.v.*

GEOFFREY OF MONMOUTH, *Historia Regum Britanniae*, Ed. Acton Griscom (1929). Trans. L. THORPE, *The History of the Kings of Britain*, Penguin Classics (1966).

GIBBS, A. C., *Middle English Romances*, York Medieval Texts (1966).

GORDON, E. V., see *Pearl*.

GORDON, R. K., Ed., *The Story of Troilus* (1964).

GOTTFRIED VON STRASSBURG, *Tristan and Isolt*, Ed. [slightly abridged] A. Closs, Blackwell's German Texts (1947). Trans. A. T. HATTO [with the *Tristan* of Thomas], Penguin Classics (1960).

GOWER, John, *Confessio Amantis*, Ed. G. C. Macaulay, EETS ES *81–82* (1900; repr. 1957). *Selections from John Gower*, Ed. J. A. W. Bennett, Clarendon Medieval and Tudor Series (1968).

Guigemar, see MARIE DE FRANCE.

Guingamor, Ed. G. Paris, in *Romania* viii (1879) 50ff. [anonymous *lai*].

Guy of Warwick, Ed. J. Zupitza, EETS ES *42, 49, 59* (1883–91).

Havelok the Dane, Ed. W. W. Skeat, 2nd ed. rev. Sisam (1915); also in FRENCH and HALE, and in SANDS, *q.v.*

JOHNSTON, R. C. and OWEN, D. D. R., Eds., *Fabliaux*, Blackwell's French Texts (1957).

KENNEDY, C. W., Trans. *An Anthology of Old English Poetry* (New York 1960).

King Horn, Ed. J. R. Lumby, re-Ed. G. H. McKnight, EETS OS *14* (1901); separate ed. J. Hall (1901).

Le Lai de l'Ombre, see RENART.

Lanval, see MARIE DE FRANCE.

LOOMIS, R. S. and L. H., *Medieval Romances* (USA 1957) [contains translations of Chrétien's *Perceval*, Gottfried's *Tristan* and other romances].

MACHAUT, Guillaume de, *Remede de Fortune* in *Oeuvres*, Ed. E. Hoepffner, SATF (Paris 1908).

MALORY, Sir Thomas. *Works*, Ed. Eugène Vinaver, 3 vols., 2nd ed. (1967). *The Morte Darthur*. Ed. D. S. Brewer, York Medieval Texts (1968).

MAP, Walter, *De Nugis Curialium*, Ed. M. R. James (1914). Trans. F. TUPPER and M. B. OGLE, *Courtier's Trifles* (1924).

MARIE DE FRANCE, *Lais*, Ed. A. Ewert, Blackwell's French Texts (1960).

MATARASSO, P., Trans., *Aucassin and Nicolette and other Tales*, Penguin Classics (1971) [includes *Le Lai de l'Ombre*].

Morte Arthure, Ed. E. Brock, EETS OS *8* (rev. ed. 1871); abridged ed. J. Finlayson, York Medieval Texts (1967) [the alliterative *Morte*].

PARRY, see CAPELLANUS.

Pearl, Ed. E. V. Gordon (1953).

PRESS, A. H., Ed. and Trans., *Anthology of Troubadour Lyric Poetry*, Edinburgh Bilingual Library (1971) [texts and translations].

La Queste del Saint Graal, Ed. A. Pauphilet, CFMA (Paris 1959). Trans. P. MATARASSO, *The Quest of the Holy Grail* (1969).

RENART, Jehan, *Le Lai de l'Ombre*, Ed. J. Orr (1948). Trans. MATARASSO, *q.v.*

Richard Cueur de Lyon, Ed. K. Brunner, Wiener Beiträge zur englischen Philologie, *42* (Vienna 1913).

Roman de la Rose, Ed. Félix Lecoy, CFMA, 3 vols. (1965–70). Trans. H. W. ROBBINS (New York 1962).

ROOT, R. K., Ed., *Troilus* (1926).

SANDS, D. B., *Middle English Verse Romances* (USA 1966).

Sir Beves of Hamtoun, Ed. E. Kölbing, EETS ES *46, 48, 65* (1885–94).

Sir Gawain and the Green Knight, Ed. Tolkien and Gordon, 2nd ed. rev. N. Davis (1967); Ed. R. A. Waldron, York Medieval Texts (1970).

Sir Launfal by Thomas Chestre, Ed. A. J. Bliss (1960).

Sir Orfeo, Ed. A. J. Bliss (1954).

THOMAS, *Les Fragments du Roman de Tristan*, Ed. Bartina H. Wind, Textes Littéraires Français (1960).

WALDRON, see *Sir Gawain*.

WOLFRAM VON ESCHENBACH, *Parzival*. Trans. Helen M. Mustard and Charles E. Passage (New York 1961).

WYATT, A. J., *An Anglo-Saxon Reader* (1919; often repr.).

Yonec, see MARIE DE FRANCE.

Ywain and Gawain, Ed. A. B. Friedman and N. T. Harrington, EETS 254 (1964).

B. SECONDARY MATERIAL

Arthurian Literature, see LOOMIS.

AUERBACH, E., *Literary Language and its Public* (1958, trans. 1965).

AUERBACH, E., *Scenes from the Drama of European Literature* (USA 1959).

BAYRAV, S. *Symbolisme Médiéval* (1957).

BEER, Gillian, *Romance*. The Critical Idiom (1970).

BEZZOLA, R. R., *Le sens de l'aventure et de l'amour* (Paris 1947).

BEZZOLA, R. R., *Les Origines et la Formation de la Littérature Courtoise en Occident 500–1200*, pt. 3, vol. i. (1963), 'La Cour d'Angleterre comme centre littéraire. . . .'

BOLTON, W. F., Ed., *The Middle Ages*, Sphere History of Literature vol. 1 (1970).

BREWER, D. S., Ed. *Chaucer and the Chaucerians* (1966).

CHAYTOR, H. J., *From Script to Print* (1945).

CONRAD, Joseph, *The Shadow-Line*, collected ed. (1950).

CROSLAND, Jessie, *Medieval French Literature* (1956).

CURTIUS, E. R., *European Literature of the Latin Middle Ages*, English trans. (1953).

DRONKE, P., *Medieval Latin and the Rise of the European Love-Lyric*, 2 vols. (1965–6).

DRONKE, P., *Poetic Individuality in the Middle Ages* (Oxford 1970).

FRAPPIER, Jean, *Chrétien de Troyes, l'homme et l'oeuvre*. (Paris 1957); see also in LOOMIS, *Arthurian Literature*, ch. 15.

FRYE, Northrop, *Anatomy of Criticism* (1957).

HOUGH, Graham, 'The Allegorical Circle', *Critical Quarterly* iii (1961).

HUIZINGA, J., *The Waning of the Middle Ages*, English ed. (1924, repr. 1950).

JAMES, Henry, *The American*, 2 vols. (1883); preface first published in New York ed. (1907–17), vol. 2.

LAWLOR, J., *Chaucer*, Hutchinson University Library (1968).

LAWLOR, J., Ed., *Patterns of Love and Courtesy: Essays in Memory of C. S. Lewis* (1966).

LEGGE, M. D., *Anglo-Norman Literature and its Background* (1963).

LEWIS, C. S., *The Allegory of Love* (1936).

LEWIS, C. S., *Studies in Medieval and Renaissance Literature* (1966).

LEWIS, C. S., *Studies in Words*, 2nd ed. (1967).

LOOMIS, R. S., *Arthurian Tradition and Chrétien de Troyes* (1949).

LOOMIS, R. S., Ed., *Arthurian Literature in the Middle Ages: a Collaborative History* (1959).

LOOMIS, R. S., *The Development of Arthurian Romance* (1963).

MÂLE, Emil, *The Gothic Image*, trans. from 3rd ed. (1961).

MEHL, Dieter, *The Middle English Romances of the thirteenth and fourteenth centuries* English trans. (1968).

MUSCATINE, C., *Chaucer and the French Tradition* (1957).

OWEN, D. D. R., Ed., *Arthurian Romance: seven essays* (1970).

PEARSALL, Derek, 'The Development of Middle English Romance', *Medieval Studies 27* (1965).

RABY, F. J. E., *Christian-Latin Poetry*, 2nd ed. (1953).

RENWICK, L., and ORTON, H., *The Beginnings of English Literature to Skelton*, 3rd ed. rev. M. F. Wakelyn (1966).

ROBERTSON, D. W., *Preface to Chaucer* (USA 1963).

ROUGEMONT, Denis de, *Passion and Society*, English ed. rev. and augmented (1962).

SOUTHERN, R. W., *The Making of the Middle Ages* (1953).

SPEARING, A. C., *Criticism and Medieval Poetry*, 2nd ed. (1972).

STEVENS, John, *Music and Poetry in the Early Tudor Court* (1961).

VINAVER, E., *The Rise of Romance* (1971).

WATT, Ian, *The Rise of the Novel* (1957).

INDEX

INDEX